MW00721093

GEMSTONES

Properties, identification and use

First published in 2008 by New Holland Publishers (UK) Ltd
London • Cape Town • Sydney • Auckland

10 9 8 7 6 5 4 3 2 1

www.newhollandpublishers.com

Garfield House, 86–88 Edgware Road, London W2 2EA, UK
80 McKenzie Street, Cape Town 8001, South Africa
Unit 1, 66 Gibbes Street, Chatswood, NSW 2067, Australia
218 Lake Road, Northcote, Auckland, New Zealand

ISBN: 978-1-84537-602-4

Editorial direction: Rosemary Wilkinson
Editors: Gareth Jones, Charlotte Judet and Kate Parker
Design and cover design: Namrita Price-Goodfellow, D&N Publishing
Illustrator: William Smuts
Production: Melanie Dowland

Reproduction by Pica Digital PTE Ltd
Printed and bound by Star Standard Industries, Singapore

Note: The author and publishers have made every effort to ensure that the
information given in this book is safe and accurate, but they cannot accept liability
for any resulting injury or loss or damage to either property or person, whether
direct or consequential and howsoever arising.

GEMSTONES

Properties, identification and use

Arthur Thomas

Contents

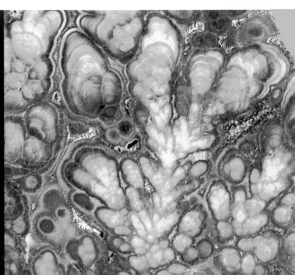

Part 3: The Art of the Gem 208

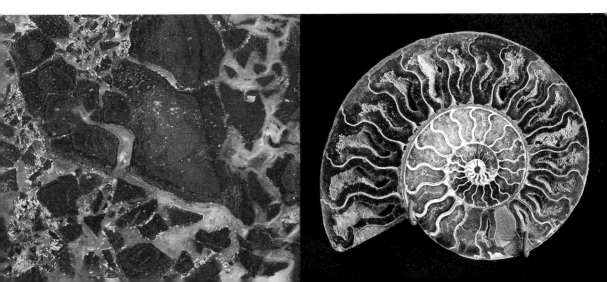

HOW TO USE THIS BOOK

Part Two of this book consists of a guide to a wide range of gemstones including many that are very rare. For ease of use, each entry is organised as follows:

Gem name(s)

Specific gem names have varied with time. The most widely used current name(s) is given here and many alternatives or misnomers are mentioned in the text.

Chemical composition

Where possible this is the currently accepted version of the chemistry of a gem mineral. In cases where this is not given it is because rocks and many aggregates do not have a constant chemistry.

Properties table

The table that accompanies each gem lists its optical and physical properties, sources and mineral class. Where a property is inapplicable e.g. Bi-refingence, Optic Sign or Pleochroism in the case of stones belonging to the singly-refractive cubic system, this is indicated by the abbreviation N/a. Where data is unavailable, as in the case of some of the rarest stones, this is indicated by a dash (–). Where two figures are given under Refractive Indices they indicate the full range of the species. The hardness quoted is based on the Mohs' scale. The entries under sources are not meant to be exhaustive but they do serve to give a good indication of the distribution of each gem.

Gem image(s)

The entry for each gem variety is illustrated with at least one close-up image of the best available crystal, cut or rough stone. Some of the more popular jewellery stones are also shown in settings.

Main text

The pronunciation and in most instances the derivation of the name is given, followed by details of deposits and associated minerals, varieties, production, cuts and the use of the gem.

Diagrams

(Diagrams A and B do not apply to amorphous minerals, ornamental rocks or organic gems since they lack crystal form.)

Diagram A illustates the crystallographic axes of a gem mineral (*see* Chapter 3, Crystallography).

Diagram B shows one of the most prevalent crystal habits (*see* Chapter 3, Crystallography).

Diagram C shows one of the popular cuts used for the gemstone (*see* Chapter 9, Lapidary).

Bullet point(s)

Bullet points highlight any interesting or unusual facts about the gemstone.

Chemical composition — $Na(Li,Al)_3Al_6Si_6O_{18}(BO_3)_3(OH)_4$

TOURMALINE

Gem name(s)

Gem image(s)

Properties table

Refractive Indices	1.622- 1.643
Birefringence	0.018 –0.020
Optic Char./Sign	Uniaxial/–
Hardness	7–7.5
Specific Gravity	2.98–3.20
Crystal System	Trigonal
Habit	Longitudinal striae, hemimorphic
Lustre	Vitreous
Colour Range	Blue, brown, colourless, green, pink, red, violet, yellow, black
Pleochroism	Strongly dichroic
Cleavage	Nil
Fracture	Sub-conchoidal
Dispersion	0.017
Sources	Afghanistan, Australia, Brazil, Democratic Republic of Congo, Italy, Kenya, Madagascar, Mozambique, Myanmar, Namibia, Nigeria, Pakistan, Russia, Sri Lanka, Tanzania, USA, Zambia, Zimbabwe
Transparency	Transparent–opaque
Class	Silicates

Main text

Tourmaline (*TOUR-mah-leen*) occurs in granitic pegmatites, granites, gneiss and contact metamorphic zones. It occurs in the form of inclusions in beryl, feldspar, quartz and zircon. It is found in association with albite, apatite, beryl, cassiterite, feldspar, garnet, lepidolite, scapolite, spodumene and topaz. The chemical composition and physical properties of tourmaline vary to some extent with colour. The pink and red varieties from lithium-rich pegmatites have a lower density, usually around 3.03, than the dark green and blue varieties that generally average about 3.10. Varietal names that are still widely used include achroite (colourless), dravite (brown), indicolite (blue), liddicoatite (polychromatic), rubellite (red), siberite (violet), schorl (black), tsilaisite (yellow/brown) and verdelite (green). Brazil is the source of Paraiba tourmaline. This material is usually heat-treated to produce the famous electric blue and fluorescent green hues. Tourmaline frequently exhibits two or more colours in a single crystal. In bi-colour or parti-colour tourmalines the crystal changes colour along its length. Crystals may also exhibit concentric zones of colour when viewed parallel to their 'C' axis. Crystals with a red centre, a white or colourless inner and a green outer are called watermelon tourmaline. Liddicoatite, named in honour of Richard Liddicoat the renowned American gemologist, is a fascinating polychromatic variety of calcium-rich lithium tourmaline discovered in Madagascar. An emerald-green variety of tourmaline that occurs in Tanzania is marketed as chrome tourmaline regardless of the fact that in a large proportion of the specimens tested the dominant chromophore has proved to be vanadium. Some of these vanadian tourmalines exhibit a marked colour change, appearing deep emerald-green in daylight and intense red under incandescent light. Tourmaline exhibits pyro-electricity (it acquires an electric charge when heated) and piezo-electricity (it builds up an electric charge when it is rubbed). Tourmaline can be cut as attractive cat's-eye cabochons when it contains oriented fine needle-like inclusions or hollow tubes.

TOP LEFT: *Tourmaline on feldspar*
TOP RIGHT: *Pink tourmaline and lepidolite crystals*
ABOVE: *Green tourmaline from Zambia*

■ Paraiba tourmaline is characterized by the presence of a trace of copper in its composition.

Bullet point(s)

Diagram A
Diagram B
Diagram C

a1 a2 a3

MINERAL GEMS 91

The World of Gemstones

Chapter 1
Basics

Designed as a reference guide for gem and crystal collectors, gemmologists, gem dealers, jewellers, gem-setters, goldsmiths, lapidaries and rock-hounds, this amply illustrated book will have appeal for anyone who can appreciate the incredible variety of hue and form to be found in the gem and mineral kingdom.

A brief summary deals with the structure of the Earth and the nature of the rocks and minerals comprising the lithosphere (crust) and the upper mantle. The crystal systems and the effects that structure and composition have on the properties of the various gem materials are described. Gem identification both in the field and in the laboratory, the cutting and polishing of gems and methods of gem enhancement and gem grading are summarized. A section is devoted to the methods employed in the synthesis of gem materials and the manufacture of gem simulants. The various organic gems such as amber, ivory, jet, natural and cultured pearls are described, then the collection and housing of gem crystals from micro-mounts to cabinet specimens and of cut gems is reviewed.

Minerals may be the stars of this show but the world of gemstones is far from being inanimate. Vibrant, dynamic and multi-faceted it is populated with a human cast of incredible diversity.

LEFT: *A diamond brillianteer checking a facet*

LEFT: *An East African gem dealer inspects tanzanite*

The mining and marketing of gems assumes particular importance in the poorer countries of the developing world where it creates many jobs and brings in much needed hard currency. Working accessible gem deposits or 'noodling' the dumps of established mines provides a living for the garimperos of Angola, Mozambique and Brazil, the 'pork-knockers' of Venezuela, the

diggers of South-East Asia, India, Sri Lanka, Madagascar, Central, East and West Africa and countless others. The rough they produce is then sorted, graded, marketed and processed. The gem-cutting industry is labour-intensive, currently employing more than a million people in India alone, a figure that is growing by 15 per cent per annum. Other important gem-cutting centres are Thailand, Sri Lanka, China, Korea and Taiwan. As well as providing employment on such a large scale, the products of the industry bring pleasure to countless millions.

LEFT: *Buyers at a trade fair examine strands of pearls and discuss their merits*

Chapter 2

The Geology of Gem Occurrences

A stone must possess the attributes of beauty, durability and rarity to a marked degree in order to merit the appellation *gemstone*. Beauty in a gem may take many forms from the richly saturated violet-blue of a fine lapis lazuli cabochon to the shifting, hypnotic play of spectral colour in an opal, or the dazzling display of brilliance and dispersion from a diamond wakened by a ray of sunlight.

Fashioned gemstones are created to be seen and often worn and therein lies the importance of durability. Mounted and displayed in items of jewellery, they are inevitably subjected to a great deal of wear and tear and it is essential that they are both hard and tough. Put in the simplest of terms, hardness can be described as the ability to resist scratches and toughness as resistance to damage from impact.

While rarity is a significant part of a gem's appeal, it is ironic that a stone may be too rare to achieve recognition. The economic reality is that there must be sufficient established reserves of rough material available to justify the high cost involved in developing awareness and creating markets for a new gemstone. Extremely rare gems such as benitoite (a gem that combines the colour of a sapphire and the life of a diamond), painite (red) and taaffeite (pink & lilac) are therefore destined to remain relatively unknown unless some significant new find makes them viable.

Deposits of gem-quality zoisite were discovered in Merelani, Northern Tanzania in January 1967. The industry that has grown up around this resource exemplifies what can be achieved through the power of modern marketing. Launched by Tiffany & Co. under the trade name *Tanzanite*, the stone enjoyed unprecedented success. This despite the fact that the material is neither particularly tough or hard and the original colour of the majority of the production coming from the mines is yellow, khaki or brown. Stones of an intense natural violet-blue are relatively rare. In most cases the superb hue seen in the finished stones is the result of heat treatment.

For the purpose of this text the term *collectors' stone* is used with reference to those stones, often somewhat lacking in durability, that are much sought after by specialist collectors for their beauty and rarity.

The term *ornamental stone* is employed for materials that are beautiful but too plentiful to be regarded as gems. Agate, jasper, malachite and travertine are examples of stones that would fall into this category.

Traditionally, diamond, ruby, sapphire and emerald were known as *precious stones* and other gemstones were then grouped together under the meaningless expression *semi-precious*. These terms are archaic and their use should be discouraged.

Not all gems are minerals; some, for example pearl and coral, are built by animals while others such as amber and jet are of vegetable origin. These and other varieties are dealt with in Chapter 6, which discusses gems of organic origin.

Nevertheless, the vast majority of natural gemstones occur in the form of colourful and durable minerals that originate from the rocks of the Earth's crust. Therefore, some knowledge of these rocks and minerals will greatly assist the development of a better understanding and appreciation of gems.

Below the Earth's surface

Knowledge of the surface of planet Earth has improved vastly as a result of man's tentative ventures into space, but we still know relatively little about that which lies beneath our feet.

Just how deeply has man penetrated the Earth's crust? The Witwatersrand Gold Fields of South Africa boast the world's deepest mines. Western Deep Levels, in the West Rand area of Witwatersrand, hold the record with a depth currently in excess of 4km. The ultra-deep levels are targeted to reach a depth of 5km.

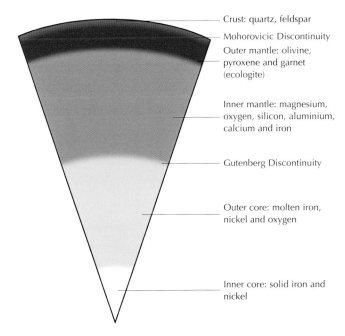

Crust: quartz, feldspar

Mohorovicic Discontinuity

Outer mantle: olivine, pyroxene and garnet (ecologite)

Inner mantle: magnesium, oxygen, silicon, aluminium, calcium and iron

Gutenberg Discontinuity

Outer core: molten iron, nickel and oxygen

Inner core: solid iron and nickel

LEFT: *Cross-section of the Earth, showing the prevalent mineralization of each zone*

The deepest exploratory diamond drill hole to date is situated on the Kola Peninsula, where a Russian team succeeded in drilling to a depth of 12.26km. Although the crust of the Earth is relatively thin overall, with an average depth of 20km, the continental crusts average 35km in thickness. Evidently man must look elsewhere for data relating to the inner structure of the Earth since he clearly has a long way to go before he develops a technology that can successfully take samples directly from the upper mantle.

Seismology, a branch of science that employs sensitive seismographs to measure and study vibrations within the Earth, is able to offer some clues.

Seismic movements can be classified into four types of waves, two of them being relatively unimportant in studies of the Earth's structure since they are confined to surface effects. However, primary or compression waves 'P' and secondary or shear waves 'S' penetrate deep into the interior of the Earth. Primary 'P' waves can travel through both solids and liquids moving at double the speed of 'S' waves while compressing and dilating the matter they travel through. Secondary waves move through rock but cannot travel through liquids. Both 'P' and 'S' waves are subject to reflection or refraction when they encounter the junction of layers that exhibit different physical properties. Both types of wave move more slowly when travelling through hotter materials. These changes in speed and direction enable the seismologist to map out a broad outline and determine the presence of discontinuities within the Earth's structure.

The central core of the Earth is believed to be a solid pressure-frozen sphere of iron and nickel, suspended within a molten outer core of similar composition. A major discontinuity, positioned at the junction of the outer core and the lower mantle, is known as the 'D' layer or Gutenberg Discontinuity. About 240km thick, it constitutes approximately three per cent of the Earth's total mass.

The constituents of the lower mantle are believed to be mainly silicon, magnesium and oxygen, with smaller amounts of aluminium, calcium and iron. Volcanic material can be a fruitful source of data on the upper mantle, especially when it is obtained from kimberlites or lamproite pipes and fissures. In addition to transporting diamond crystals from the depths, some kimberlites host actual fragments of the upper mantle, termed eclogites. Eclogites largely consist of olivine, pyroxene and garnet. They may also contain pyrite and/or diamond crystals. Diamonds found embedded in eclogite are usually very well formed with flat faces, sharp crystal junctions and none of the evidence of etching or dissolution typical of diamonds that have been transported in the magma.

Minerals and Rocks

Mineral
In geological terms, a mineral can be defined as a naturally occurring, inorganic element or compound that has an orderly internal structure and is relatively constant in its crystal form, chemical composition and physical properties.

Rock
In geological terms, a rock is an aggregate of mineral particles and the Earth's crust is mainly made of rocks. Therefore a geologist would consider beds of sand or gravel to be rocks. While most rocks are mineral aggregates it is possible for a rock to consist of a single mineral provided it forms a large enough mass, for example limestone and marble are massive forms of the mineral calcite.

Rocks may be defined as belonging to one of three great classes namely *igneous:* rocks formed from molten magma, *sedimentary:* rocks resulting from the compaction of sedimentary deposits and *metamorphic:* rocks formed by the alteration of existing rocks by heat, pressure or a combination of both.

Igneous Rocks

The entire crust of the Earth was originally igneous in nature. However, these rocks have undergone the attacks of environmental forces for billions of years. It is now estimated that more than 70 per cent of exposed surface rock is sedimentary. This said, igneous rocks do still comprise a significant proportion of the Earth's surface. Igneous rocks that have the potential to host gem deposits can be broadly divided into two groups, intrusive and extrusive, based on the method of their formation:

Intrusive
Plutonic rocks occur at depth, where the magma cools slowly, forming individual crystals that are clearly visible to the naked eye. Granite, the most frequently encountered plutonic rock, is composed of quartz, feldspar and mica. Syenite, another plutonic rock, is granite-like in appearance but it lacks quartz and often carries sodalite and cancrinite. Anorthosite, another coarse-grained plutonic rock, appears spectacular in sunlight since it is largely composed of the attractive labradorite variety of feldspar.

ABOVE*: Syenite*

Pegmatitic dykes are narrow bodies of rock that seldom exceed 20m in width. Similar to granite in composition, they typically exhibit crystals of a very large grain size. The dykes exploit points of weakness in country rock, cutting discordantly across pre-existing structures. Pegmatites seldom occur in isolation; if one is found there are almost certain to be other members of the family close by. They form parallel outcrops, dip at the same angle and tend to have similar mineralization. Miners proceed with caution when they recognize a rather specialized form of granite that may indicate proximity to a gem pocket. Known as graphic granite, it exhibits an angular intergrowth of feldspar and quartz that bears a resemblance to ancient cuneiform writing. Pegmatitic magma is typified by its high water content and as it cools and contracts cavities, filled with gas and mineral-rich aqueous solutions, are created. Such conditions promote the formation of the well-developed *euhedral* crystals (regular well formed crystals with good faces) that frequently line the walls of 'pockets' in the pegmatite.

Pegmatites are an important source of such gem minerals as apatite, beryl, cassiterite, chrysoberyl, feldspar, petalite, phenakite, pollucite, quartz, spessartite, spodumene, topaz and tourmaline.

Ultramafic rocks, such as kimberlite or lamproite, occur in volcanic pipes, dykes, fissures and sills. Dark in hue, fine-grained and olivine-, serpentine- or mica-rich kimberlites may contain both *xenoliths*, fragments of eclogite and peridotite rock from the upper mantle, and *xenocrysts,* comprising foreign minerals such as chrome diopside, spinel and diamond.

Gems recovered from these rocks include chrome diopside, diamond, garnet, spinel and zircon.

LEFT: *Graphic granite*

Lamproites originate from depths in excess of 150km. Silica-deficient mantle-derived minerals are predominant in their composition. They may carry xenocrysts of diamond. The Argyle lamproite of Western Australia has a remarkably high diamond content, unlike the Crater of Diamonds lamproite in Arkansas, USA, where diamonds are very scarce.

Extrusive

Extrusive rocks are formed when liquid magma flows out of breaks in the Earth's crust then undergoes a rapid drop in temperature on exposure to the atmosphere. These rocks range in texture from extremely fine-grained e.g. basalt and rhyolite to glassy in the case of obsidian. Gas trapped by the rapidly cooling lava creates innumerable cavities variously described depending on their shape as geodes, vugs and vesicles. Mineral rich solutions frequently fill these cavities with secondary minerals (*see* hydrothermal metamorphism, p18).

Pyroclastic rocks, e.g. tuff, are formed through the compaction of fragments, ash and dust that have accumulated during a period of volcanic activity.

Sedimentary Rocks

There are two main groupings of sedimentary rocks: clastic and non-clastic.

Clastic rocks are formed by the compression of accumulated detritus that has resulted from the erosion of pre-existing rocks by wind and water, in the form of rain, hail, frost, snow, glaciers, streams, rivers, and the constant movement of the seas. Rock debris transported by streams and rivers is often deposited as gravel beds along the watercourse. Medium-sized fragments may be carried considerable distances, becoming increasingly water-worn and rounded. Small particles are sometimes carried far out to sea before they settle to the bottom where they are soon covered by millions of similar particles in addition to the skeletal remains of marine organisms.

Typical clastic rocks include:

Breccia	Embodying coarse angular rock fragments
Conglomerate	Rounded pebbles embedded in finer-grained rock
Sandstone	Compacted sand sized particles of quartz
Shale	Composed of fine clay particles
Siltstone	Compacted silt particles
Mudstone	A mixture of clay and silt particles

Non-clastic rocks are formed in place as a result of chemical precipitation, crystallization, evaporation or the lithification of organic matter.

Typical non-clastic rocks include:

Limestone	Calcium carbonate
Dolomite	Calcium magnesium carbonate
Silcretes	Silica
Chalk	Skeletal remains of marine micro-organisms
Coal	Lithified remains of plants

Metamorphic Rocks

Metamorphic rocks are formed from pre-existing igneous, sedimentary or metamorphic rocks that have undergone significant alteration in their nature while retaining their solid state, through the influence of heat, pressure and/or the intrusion of gases and liquids. There are three main groups of metamorphic rocks that have the potential to host significant gem deposits. They are: contact, hydrothermal, and regional.

Contact metamorphism
This the term used to describe the marked change that takes place in rock lying within the immediate periphery of an intrusive body of molten magma. In addition to being subjected to high temperature and pressure, the surrounding rock may also be permeated by hot fluids carrying new elements. In this case the process is termed *metasomatism* and it may result in the formation of such gem minerals as corundum; diopside; emerald; epidot; various garnets including andradite, grossular and hydro-grossular; lapis lazuli; lazurite; spinel; vesuvianite and wollastonite.

Hydrothermal metamorphism
This term refers to the altered state of rocks that have been impregnated by hydrothermal fluids* at high temperatures and under moderate pressures. Basaltic and rhyolitic rocks are frequently subjected to this form of metamorphism. Gemstones such as agate, amethyst, chalcedony, opal, turquoise and variscite may occur as secondary fillings in the numerous cavities present in this environment. The term *drusy* is used to describe a geode or vug that is lined with small bright crystals of amethyst, rock crystal or calcite.

   Hydrothermal vein deposits may be a result of hot solutions emanating from bodies of magma and moving up through the crust. Vein deposits of the metallic ores of copper, gold, lead, silver, tin and zinc form in this way. Other gem minerals occurring in hydrothermal veins include anatase, albite, barite, brookite, calcite, chrysocolla, dioptase, emerald, fluorite, pyrite, quartz, rhodonite and sphene. Minerals may also be emplaced through the action of chemical weathering or cool solutions. Copper-rich aqueous solutions form azurite or malachite in the presence of carbonates, zinc solutions form smithsonite and manganese solutions form rhodochrosite.

* The properties of water are transformed when, trapped under pressure, it attains relatively high temperatures and is known as super-heated water. Super-heated water will readily dissolve silicates such as quartz.

Regional metamorphism
This term is employed to describe the overall changes that take place in a vast mass of rock, situated deep in the Earth's crust, when it is subjected to increased temperatures and pressures. These are the forces that convert sandstone into quartzite and limestone into marble. In cases where impurities are present in the original rock these may be converted into new minerals. Minor impurities in the form of traces of alumina in the limestone deposits of Myanmar became the basis of the world's finest rubies and spinels.

Chapter 3
Crystallography

The vast majority of gemstones are cut from crystals or from the various forms of crystalline material. The orientation of a gem in relation to the structure of the original crystal will govern the way it handles in cutting and polishing and the life and colour it may achieve as a finished gem. Tourmaline rough provides a good example of the effect of orientation on colour. Light travelling through tourmaline exhibits a different wavelength depending on the direction of its movement within the crystal structure. The eye perceives these different wavelengths as different colours. Green material often shows a dark blackish or dull olive hue when viewed down the length of the crystal; therefore the majority of green tourmaline yields the best results when cut with the table parallel to the 'c' axis of the crystal. Pink stones on the other hand are often pale and lack intensity, exhibiting their strongest colour saturation down the length of the crystal. Pink material of this type will produce finer hues if stones are oriented with their table perpendicular to the 'c' axis. Clearly a basic knowledge of crystallography is essential for gemmologists, lapidaries and serious rock-hounds and is an essential key to the development of an understanding of the physical and the optical properties of gems.

CRYSTAL SYSTEMS

Celestite

Often referred to as the flowers of the mineral kingdom, well-formed mineral crystals enjoy a universal attraction. Homogenous bodies bounded by plane faces, the symmetry they display is an external expression of their regimented internal structure. The finest specimens are generally those that have crystallized out of aqueous solutions. Crystals that have grown from molten solids are seldom so perfect in external form and frequently carry numerous inclusions of associated materials.

Granite

Granite affords excellent examples of crystals formed from the molten state. When you next visit a shopping mall or bank take some time to have a closer look at the durable and attractive slabs of polished granite that are frequently used for flooring and wall-cladding. The blocky, white and/or pink crystals are feldspar, the glimmering dark flakes are mica and the grey crystalline material is quartz.

The Structure and Symmetry of Crystals

Crystal axes

These imaginary lines link the opposed faces of an ideal crystal intersecting at its centre. They form the basis for structural descriptions of each of the seven crystal systems.

Elements of crystal symmetry

The symmetry of crystals is described in terms of three elements namely, axes, planes and centres of symmetry.

Axes of symmetry

When rotated about an axis of symmetry, a crystal will occupy the same position in space two or more times in a revolution. If this occurs twice the axis is *digonal;* three times, *trigonal;* four times, *tetragonal* or six times, *hexagonal.*

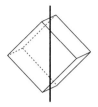 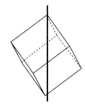 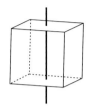

Digonal Axis   *Trigonal Axis*   *Tetragonal Axis*

Planes of symmetry

A crystal that is divided in half through a plane of symmetry will appear whole when that plane is placed against a mirror.

Centres of symmetry

A crystal possesses a centre of symmetry if like faces and edges occupy corresponding positions on opposite sides of a central point.

Cubic System

The cubic system has three crystallographic axes, intersecting at 90° and of equal length.

Symmetry

Crystals belonging to this system exhibit symmetry in the highest degree. They have nine planes of symmetry, 13 axes of symmetry (three tetragonal, four trigonal, and six digonal) and a centre of symmetry.

Hints for recognizing cubic crystals

Within the cubic system the cube, octahedron and dodecahedron are fixed forms meaning that the shape of the faces and the angles between those faces remain constant. Field characteristics of cubic minerals are their chunky cube-like to ball-like development and their predominantly square, triangular or diamond shape of faces.

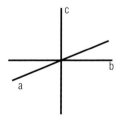

ABOVE: *Cubic crystal axes*

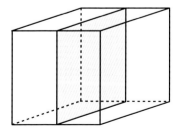

ABOVE: *Plane of symmetry in cube*

Cube

Octahedron

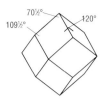
Dodecahedron

LEFT: *Spessartite garnet on quartz*
ABOVE: *Fluorite cubes*
RIGHT: *Pyrite, interpenetrant twinning*

Cubic mineral habits

In this context the term *habit* refers to crystal forms that are sufficiently prevalent to be considered characteristic of a particular gem or mineral.

Cube	diamond, fluorite, galena, halite, pollucite, pyrite.
Octahedron	chromite, diamond, fluorite, gahnite, magnetite, pyrite, spinel.
Dodecahedron	cuprite, diamond, garnet, magnetite, rhodizite, sodalite.
Tetrahedron	analcime, garnet, leucite.
Hexoctahedron	diamond.

Cubic gems

Analcime	Cobaltite	Cuprite
Diamond	Fluorite	Gahnite
Garnet	Haüyne	Lazurite
Leucite	Microlite	Periclase
Pollucite	Pyrite	Rhodizite
Smaltite	Sodalite	Sphalerite
		Spinel

Tetragonal System

Tetragonal crystals have two crystallographic axes of equal length that intersect at 90° and a third axis of unequal length that is perpendicular to their plane.

Symmetry
Ideal crystals exhibit five planes of symmetry, one tetragonal and four digonal axes of symmetry and a centre of symmetry.

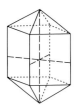 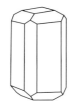 

Zircon   *Idocrase*   *Rutile*

ABOVE: *Tetragonal crystal axes*

Hints for recognizing tetragonal crystals
Crystals tend to have a typically square or octagonal cross-section with pyramidal terminations and to be longer along the 'C' axis.

Tetragonal mineral habits

Square prisms	idocrase, apophyllite.
Square prisms with pyramidal terminations	rutile, scapolite, zircon.
Dipyramids with short or no prisms	anatase, scheelite, cassiterite.
Flattened square prisms	wulfenite, torbernite.

Tetragonal gems

Anatase	Apophyllite	Cassiterite
Ekanite	Idocrase	Melinophane
Rutile	Scapolite	Scheelite
Wardite	Wulfenite	Zircon

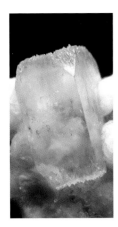

LEFT: *Apophyllite*
ABOVE: *Scapolite*
RIGHT: *Zircon*

Orthorhombic System

This system has three crystallographic axes of different lengths that intersect at 90°.

Symmetry
Ideal crystals have three planes of symmetry, three digonal axes and a centre of symmetry.

Hints for recognizing orthorhombic crystals
Prismatic crystals such as andalusite, danburite and topaz usually have rather ovoid or diamond shaped cross-sections. Varieties with a more flattened tabular habit tend to be boxy and rectangular in shape with lozenge-shaped cross-sections. Faces on rhombic crystals frequently exhibit variations in lustre, striations and etch marks with opposing faces revealing similar irregularities.

Rhombic mineral habits
Prismatic	andalusite, chrysoberyl, danburite, staurolite, topaz.
Prismatic, long	natrolite.
Prismatic, tabular	autunite, barite, celestite.
Prismatic, stubby	anglesite, chrysoberyl, peridot, topaz.

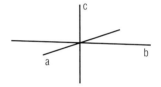

ABOVE: *Orthorhombic crystal axes*

Topaz

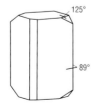

Andalusite

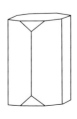

Staurolite

Barite   *Danburite*   *Topaz*

Orthorhombic Gems

Andalusite	Anglesite	Aragonite
Barite	Boracite	Bronzite
Brookite	Celestite	Cerussite
Chrysoberyl	Chrysocolla	Danburite
Dumortierite	Enstatite	Fibrolite
Hambergite	Iolite	Kornerupine
Marcasite	Natrolite	Peridot
Prehnite	Pyrophyllite	Sinhalite
Staurolite	Stibiotantalite	Thomsonite
Topaz	Varsicite	Witherite
Zoisite		

Hexagonal System

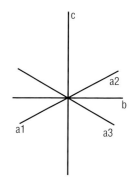

ABOVE: *Hexagonal crystal axes*

The hexagonal system has three crystallographic axes of equal length intersecting at 60° and a fourth of unequal length that is perpendicular to their plane.

Hexagonal symmetry
Euhedral crystals have seven planes of symmetry, one hexagonal and six digonal axes of symmetry and a centre of symmetry.

Hints for recognizing hexagonal gems
In prismatic crystals the six fold symmetry and length along the 'C' axis is usually unmistakable. Terminations are often flat but may be modified by pyramidal faces. Sometimes etch marks and pits or growth hillocks on basal planes may afford clues.

Beryl   *Apatite*   *Zincite*

Hexagonal crystal habits

Prismatic, long	beryl
Prismatic, short	apatite, beryl, vanadinite, pyromorphite
Prismatic, tabular	apatite, beryl *variety* morganite.

Apatite　　　　　*Emerald*　　　　*Zincite*

Hexagonal gemstones

Apatite	Beryl	Cancrinite
Niccolite	Painite	Taaffeite
Zincite		

Trigonal System

While the crystal axes are similar to those of the hexagonal system, the position of the centre is not equidistant along the horizontal axes. This results in a reduced degree of symmetry. N.B. *In the USA, earth scientists recognise six crystal systems and classify trigonal gems as modified versions of the hexagonal model.*

Trigonal symmetry
Trigonal crystals exhibit three planes of symmetry, one trigonal and three digonal axes of symmetry, and a centre of symmetry.

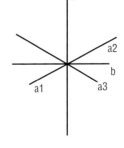

ABOVE: *Trigonal crystal axes*

Hints for recognizing trigonal crystals
A cross-section of a trigonal crystal will often exhibit three-fold symmetry. Etch marks, triangular pits or growth hillocks frequently occur on basal planes. Terminations may be pointed or wedge-shaped and striations run parallel to the 'C' axis in tourmaline or perpendicular to the 'C' axis in quartz.

　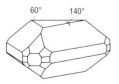　

Quartz　　　　　*Benitoite*　　　　　*Tourmaline*

Trigonal crystal habits.

Prismatic, long   calcite, quartz, tourmaline, willemite.
Prismatic, short   calcite, corundum, quartz, tourmaline.
Prismatic, tabular corundum *variety* ruby, hematite.
Rhombohedrons   calcite, rhodochrosite, siderite.

Tourmaline   *Rhodochrosite*   *Smoky quartz*

Trigonal gemstones

Benitoite	Calcite	Corundum
Dioptase	Friedelite	Hematite
Magnesite	Phenakite	Proustite
Quartz	Rhodochrosite	Smithsonite
Stichtite	Tourmaline	Willemite

Monoclinic System

The monoclinic system has three axes of unequal length, two of which intersect at an oblique angle and a third that is perpendicular to their plane.

Monoclinic Symmetry.

Monoclinic crystals exhibit one plane of symmetry and one digonal axis of symmetry.

Hints for recognizing monoclinic gemstones

Monoclinic crystals are often prismatic with rectangular or lozenge-shaped cross-sections and pointed or wedge shaped terminations. They resemble orthorhombic crystals but a closer examination will reveal the presence of faces that are out-of-square as a result of the influence of the single tilted axis. Radiating sprays of acicular prisms are characteristic of this system.

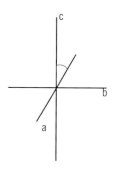

ABOVE: *Monoclinic crystal axes*

Datolite   *Epidote*   *Sphene*

Monoclinic crystal habits

Prismatic, long   spodumene, epidote.
Prismatic, short   amphiboles, orthoclase.
Blocky   azurite, datolite, orthoclase.
Platey   micas.

LEFT: *Spodumene*
ABOVE: *Sphene*
RIGHT: *Azurite*

Monoclinic gemstones

Augelite	Azurite	Bayldonite
Beryllonite	Brazilianite	Chondrodite
Colemanite	Crocoite	Datolite
Diopside	Durangite	Epidote
Euclase	Gypsum	Herderite
Howlite	Jadeite	Lazulite
Lepidolite	Malachite	Meerschaum
Mesolite	Nephrite	Orthoclase
Pectolite	Petalite	Serpentine
Shattuckite	Sphene	Spodumene
Tremolite	Ulexite	Whewellite
Wollastonite		

Triclinic System

The triclinic system has three axes all inclined to one another and of unequal length.

Symmetry

This system exhibits the lowest degree of symmetry with no planes or axes of symmetry, only a centre of symmetry.

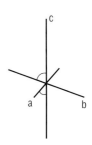

ABOVE: *Triclinic crystal axes*

Hints for recognizing triclinic gemstones

Crystals exhibit great variety of shape and proportion, in fact the best clue is probably their lack of any of the elements of symmetry that one normally finds in specimens of the other systems.

Axinite   *Albite*   *Rhodonite*

Triclinic crystal habits

Tabular	albite, axinite, kyanite.
Blocky	microcline, rhodonite.
Lath-like	kyanite.

Axinite   *Amazonite*

Kyanite

Triclinic gemstones

Amblygonite	Axinite	Labradorite
Kyanite	Microcline	Oligoclase
Rhodonite	Turquoise	

Twinning of crystals

The intergrowth of two or more crystals of the same species is governed by definite laws. Twinned crystals can usually be recognised by the presence of re-entrant angles (meaning angular recesses that cut back into the body of the specimen), which they frequently exhibit. There are three main types of twins:

Contact twins where two halves of a crystal are rotated through 180° about a joining plane, e.g. *macles* in diamond.

Interpenetrant twins where two crystals grow so that they penetrate one another often producing a cross, e.g. staurolite.

Polysynthetic or lamellar twins where a repeated series of contact twins form very thin plates with each crystal in reverse order to its neighbour, e.g. frequently encountered in corundum.

Glass

Opal

Obsidian

Amorphous Gems

Amorphous gems have no directional structure or properties and lack form.

Amorphous gemstones

Billitonite	Moldavite	Obsidian
Opal		

Chapter 4

Physical and Optical Properties of Gemstones

PHYSICAL PROPERTIES

Cleavage

Cleavage is the tendency of a crystal to split along a clearly defined plane dictated by the molecular structure of the mineral. This property is present to varying degrees in most gems. Cleavage planes always run parallel to a potential crystal face of the mineral involved. For example, diamond cleaves parallel to its octahedral faces and topaz parallel to the basal pinacoid even though these faces may not be present in the specimen that is to be cleaved.

Cleavage	Examples	Illustration
Basal	Emerald Topaz	
Octahedral	Diamond Fluorite	
Rhombic	Calcite	

Parting

This is a direction of weakness present in some crystals as a result of lamellar twinning (*see* p31). Corundum from some sources may exhibit well-developed parting parallel to the basal plane.

LEFT: *Parting in sapphire*

Fracture

Random chips or breaks in gemstones are termed fractures. When examining a stone to establish its identity it is important to note the nature of the exposed surface of any fractures. The most prevalent types of fracture are:

Nature	Appearance	Example
Conchoidal	Shell-like fracture as seen in chipped glass. Example is smoky quartz (Zambia).	
Uneven	A somewhat irregular surface. Example is sodalite (Namibia).	
Splintery	Seen in hematite, tiger's-eye and jades. Example is nephrite (Zimbabwe).	
Granular	Granular aggregates and some chalcedony. Example is blue chalcedony (Namibia).	
Sugary	Fine-grained 'icing sugar' appearance. Example is blue-lace agate (N.W. Cape)	
Earthy	Seen in fine metamorphosed sediments. This term also implies a lack of lustre. Example is jaspilite (N.W. Cape).	

Hardness

The measurement of hardness, or the ability to resist scratching, is of considerable value in identifying rough gem materials but it is to be avoided when working with finished stones. Friedrich

Mohs, a 19th-century German mineralogist, devised the most widely used scale of hardness. He proposed a series of minerals arranged on a scale of one to ten with each mineral scratching the one below it and being scratched by the one above. While it is far from precise in obtaining a measurement of hardness, Mohs' Scale is still in use today because of its practicality and convenience.

MOHS' SCALE

1. Talc	6. Orthoclase
2. Gypsum	7. Quartz
3. Calcite	8. Topaz
4. Fluorite	9. Corundum
5. Apatite	10. Diamond

A useful set of hardness pencils can be made employing slender metal tubes to house the appropriate mineral fragments bedded in dopping wax. The following will serve to give an indication of the lower values.

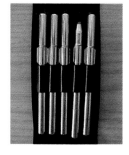

Fingernail	about 2.5
Copper	about 3.0
Window glass	about 5.5
Knife blade	about 6.0
Steel file	about 6.5

LEFT: *A set of hardness pencils*

Select the area to be tested carefully: it should be a smooth, fresh surface of the mineral free of oxidation or matrix. The hardness point must be sharp and it should be applied with a light firm touch. This is an important test in the field and it requires practice. An experienced hand will detect the 'bite' of the point and leave a scratch so fine that it can only be detected under magnification. (*See* appendix for hardness table.)

Specific Gravity

The specific gravity (SG) of a substance is its weight compared with the weight of an equal volume of pure water at a temperature of 4.0°C. For most purposes ordinary tap water at room temperature will give satisfactory results. Allow the tap water to stand for some time or boil it and leave it to cool. This is necessary since it removes air bubbles that might otherwise form on the stone or the basket and falsify results.

Hydrostatic method

$$\frac{\text{weight in air}}{\text{weight in air} - \text{weight in water}} = \text{Specific Gravity (SG)}$$

ABOVE: *Hydrostatic weighing*

Heavy liquid method

The heavy liquid method (whereby a stone will sink in a liquid of lesser, or float in a liquid of greater, relative density, giving an approximation of its SG) can be messy but comes into its own when testing very small individual specimens, sorting mixed parcels of small stones by density, or trying to establish very slight differences in SG (e.g. natural versus synthetic emerald).

Three basic heavy liquids serve to make up an effective test set for specific gravity determination in the range of 2.2 to 4.2. They are bromoform[1], methylene iodide and Clerici solution. Be aware that these heavy liquids are relatively expensive, light sensitive[2] and hazardous to work with. Small gem fragments can be used as indicators. A basic hydrocarbon such as benzene or toluene will also be required to dilute the bromoform or methylene iodide to the required levels of specific gravity. Toluene is preferable since it is not so volatile as benzene. Always be aware that Clerici solution is highly toxic. It must be diluted with distilled water. Store all heavy liquids securely in a light-proof box, which should be kept in a cool, dark place.

ABOVE: *A set of heavy liquids must be stored in cool, dark conditions.*

[1] If available acetylene tetrabromide (tetrabromoethane) SG 2.96 is an effective and often preferred substitute for bromoform.
[2] Keep a small piece of pure copper in the liquid; it will help to prevent it discolouring.

Magnetism

It is simple to distinguish natural hematite from the simulant *hematine* with the use of a conventional magnet. Hematine is strongly attracted to a magnet but there will be no reaction from genuine hematite.

The majority of synthetic diamonds carry distinct metallic traces and they will be attracted to a rare-earth magnet. These magnets are constructed from a neodymium boron iron alloy and they are very strong (NB they pose a risk to anyone with a pacemaker). Place the diamond pavilion side down on a piece of glass and see if it is attracted when the rare-earth magnet is brought close to it. If the diamond is mounted then place the piece of jewellery on a small Styrofoam raft floating on a basin of water. Bring the rare-earth magnet close and see if the raft is drawn towards it. If the diamond is drawn to the magnet it is either synthetic or a very heavily included industrial diamond. However, if the diamond is not drawn to the magnet it cannot be inferred that it is natural since some of the more recent synthetic gem diamonds do not react to magnetism.

Thermal Conductivity

Thermal Conductivity is the ability of a substance to transmit heat. Diamond is an extremely efficient heat conductor and while zircon and sapphire are good conductors they cannot rival diamond in this respect.

There are numerous electronic diamond testers on the market. The better units (e.g. Eikhorst Thermolyser or DiaThermo) can be calibrated using a known stone that approximates the sizes that are to be tested. The majority of inexpensive pre-set units can be relied on to give fairly accurate negative results but a positive reading should always be double checked with other tests. These instruments are quite likely to obtain positive readings from natural zircon, synthetic sapphire or moissanite and identify them as diamonds.

Ensure that stones are clean and cool before testing them. When testing mounted stones especially in close-set pavé do not test the adjacent stones immediately since the heat from the pointer will have been transmitted to them. Ensure that the pointer does not make contact with the metal of the setting (many instruments have a metal alert to warn you of this problem). If it is necessary to re-test a stone, wait until it has reached room temperature. Check frequently to ensure that the batteries are well charged.

Dual Testers
These electronic diamond testers check both thermal and electro-conductivity. They prove extremely useful for testing very small moissanites in settings.

SSEF Blue Diamond Tester
This is used to confirm the presence of electro-conductivity in natural blue diamonds.

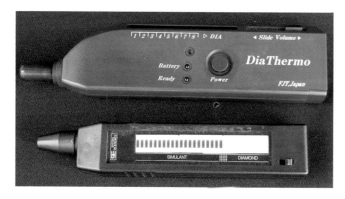

LEFT: *DiaThermo, Eikhorst Thermolyser*

OPTICAL PROPERTIES

Dispersion

Dispersion, often referred to as 'fire' in gemstones, is the power of a transparent medium to separate and release the colours of the spectrum when a ray of white light passes across two inclined faces of a prism.

ABOVE: *Dispersion in the following gems (from left to right): synthetic rutile, strontium titanate, moissanite, cubic zirconia, diamond*

Double Refraction

A crystal that splits a ray of light entering it into two rays, each travelling at a different velocity, is doubly refractive. All crystals have this ability with the exception of those belonging to the cubic system.

ABOVE: *Doubling as seen through calcite rhomb*

Polariscope & Conoscopes

The polariscope is a simple instrument consisting of two polaroid lenses mounted one above the other and a light that is housed below them in a sub-stage. The lower *polarizing lens* is fixed and the upper lens or *analyzer* is free to rotate. Some instruments like the GIA model illustrated have a glass-bottomed pan to hold the specimens while they are examined between the polars (lenses).

To use the polariscope, switch the light on and rotate the analyser until the light is extinguished. A singly refractive gem rotated between these crossed polars will either remain dark or exhibit the stress patterns shown in the illustrations overleaf. Crystalline aggregates such as chalcedony will remain light throughout. Doubly refractive stones will alternate between light and dark four times in a rotation. When a doubly refractive stone exhibits spectral colours between crossed polars it is oriented on its *optic axis* (the direction of single refraction in a doubly refractive stone). This can be resolved by the use of a glass sphere or *conoscope*. By holding a conoscope over the stone while it is in this position and bringing it down slowly until it makes contact it is possible to resolve an interference figure as illustrated. Gems belonging to the tetragonal, hexagonal and trigonal systems are *uniaxial* meaning they have a single optic axis and they will reveal concentric coloured circles overlaid with four dark brushes forming a cross. Orthorhombic, monoclinic and triclinic gems are *biaxial* and generally show a partial figure consisting of arcs of colour with two dark brushes.

With practise the polariscope will enable a quick determination between crystalline aggregates, singly and doubly refractive, uniaxial and biaxial gems and even determination of the optic sign and dichroism.

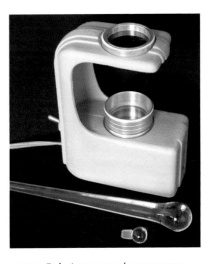

ABOVE: *Polariscope and conoscopes*

quartz bright position   *quartz dark position*   *quartz interference*

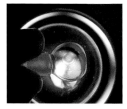

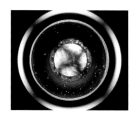

Uniaxial interference figure   *Biaxial interference figure*   *synthetic spinel stress*

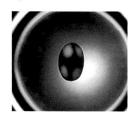

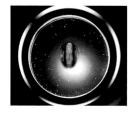

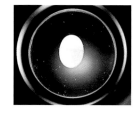

paste stressed   *paste stressed*   *aggregate reaction*

Hue

Idiochromatic gemstones, for example azurite or malachite, are stones that owe their colour to essential elements in their chemical composition (*idio* meaning 'inherent'). However, gemstones that are inherently colourless are still to be found in many different hues. These allochromatic gems (*allo* meaning 'other') often owe their various shades to colour inducing ions or chromophores. It requires remarkably few ions of one or more of the transition elements ranging from titanium, atomic number 22, to copper, atomic number 29 to fill a gemstone with colour. The richness of a gem's hue is graded in terms of its intensity, with vivid colours being the most desirable. However, it is possible for a gem to have too great a degree of colour saturation, so that it appears black in low light conditions.

Spectroscopes
These instruments are employed to analyse the light transmitted through or reflected from a gemstone. Their primary function is

to permit the observer to locate the presence and strength of absorption bands within the visible spectrum. These usually take the form of dark bands but in some cases, e.g. chromium in ruby, bright line spectra will be observed. There are two forms of hand or direct vision spectroscopes in general use:

Prism spectroscopes give a clear bright image but the spectrum is somewhat cramped at the red end of the spectrum.
Diffraction spectroscopes afford a more uniform spectrum but the field is duller and the absorption bands are more diffused.

TOP: *Almadine spectrum, prism spectroscope*

BOTTOM: *Almadine spectrum, diffracting grating spectroscope*

Colour filters

The perception of colour is a complex phenomenon. When an aquamarine and a synthetic spinel that have the same hue are viewed through an Aqua Filter, the aquamarine will retain its colour but the spinel will appear pink. Filters are designed to transmit a specific range of hues whilst absorbing others. One of the oldest, yet still most effective, colour filters is the Chelsea or emerald filter. Through this filter stones will appear red, green or a dull brown mixture of the two. Viewed under tungsten light fine Colombian emerald exhibits a striking red. Clean bright Sandawana emeralds from Zimbabwe usually show a deeper and somewhat duller red. Iron absorbs some of the red emission from chrome and the iron rich Kafubu emeralds from Zambia generally tend to blacken under the filter, rarely showing dark red. Prior to the advent of synthetic emerald the Chelsea filter was a powerful aid to gem identification, since genuine emerald showed red under it while the prevalent glass simulants remained a dull green. Most synthetic emeralds show a vibrant red under the emerald filter, exceptions to be aware of being Gibson 'N' type, Biron, Russian Hydrothermal and Lechleitner-coated beryl.

The gem enthusiast can now choose from many types of filter, the Hanneman/Hodgkinson Aquamarine, Emerald and Ruby Filters being the most useful of the range.

Transparency

Degrees of transparency:
Transparent: objects can be seen clearly through material.
Semi-transparent: objects are seen but appear somewhat blurred and indistinct.
Translucent: objects seen as silhouettes.
Semi-translucent: some transmission of light through thin edges.
Opaque: no light passes through material.

Lustre

Lustre is the measure of the reflection of light from fresh surfaces. Observation of the lustre will usually serve as a valuable indication of the refractive index of the material in hand.
Metallic: the highly reflective lustre of metals, pyrite
Adamantine: diamond like lustre, diamond
Vitreous: glass-like, quartz
Waxy: minerals that reflect only a little, chalcedony
Earthy: dull, non-reflective, limonite

Pleochroism

The differential selective absorption of the ordinary and extraordinary rays in uniaxial stones, *dichroism*, or of the three principal rays in biaxial stones, *trichroism*, is collectively referred to as pleochroism. In effect light will travel at different speeds and the eye will perceive different colours depending on direction within the stone.

Dichroscope
This small instrument is designed to facilitate the comparison of pleochroic colours in gems. It consists of a rhomb of optical

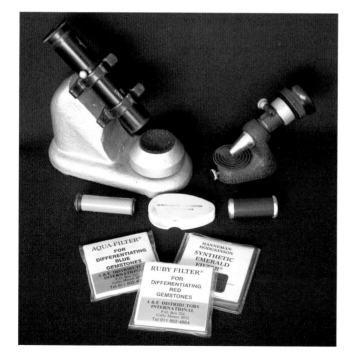

LEFT: *Spectroscopes* (LEFT), *dichroscopes* (RIGHT),*Chelsea colour filter* (CENTRE) *and colour filters* (BOTTOM)

calcite mounted in a metal tube with a lens at one end and a square window at the other. Seen through the eyepiece the window appears double. When a pleochroic stone is rotated in front of the window it is possible to compare the dichroic or pleochroic colours.

NB In dichroscopes of American manufacture, the calcite rhomb is frequently replaced with two pieces of polaroid film that are oriented at 90° to one another.

Reflection and Refraction

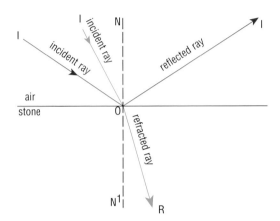

The Laws of Reflection
When a ray of light strikes a polished surface it is reflected at an equal but opposite angle.

The incident ray IO, the normal NO and the reflected ray OI are all in the same plane.

Reflectometer
Reflectometers were developed with a view to obtaining readings for the angle of the critical reflective ray in the case of stones with refractive indices that are too high to permit refractometer readings. They employ an infra-red light source and in most instances give a numeric digital readout, which must then be referred to a scale. If the instrument is checked against known samples before use it may serve to give an indication of identity. However the readings from models in use to date are too inaccurate to be considered definitive data.

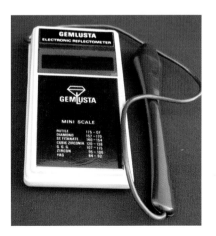

ABOVE: *Gemlusta reflectometer*

The Laws of Refraction
The sine of the angle of incidence <ION bears to the sine of the angle of refraction <N^{1}OR a definite ratio that depends on the media in contact and the nature of the light.

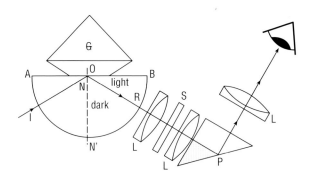

The incident ray, the normal at the point of incidence (O) and the refracted ray are all in the same plane.

The above laws of refraction establish that:

$$\frac{\text{Sine angle of incidence}}{\text{Sine angle of refraction}} = \text{a constant}$$

Refractometer

The angle at which a ray of light that strikes the surface of a stone is refracted into it and not reflected is termed the critical angle. The measurement of this angle serves to determine the refractive index of a gemstone. This is a major step towards establishing its identity. Refractometers are designed to measure this angle by throwing a shadow with its edge on the appropriate refractive index reading. Monochromatic sodium light will give the best results. If white light is employed, a thin fringe of spectral colour will be seen at the shadow edge.

ABOVE: *Rayner and GIA refractometers*

OPTICAL PHENOMENA

Physical and optical properties are always present and relatively constant. Phenomena, however, are brought about by random factors such as inclusions, and are therefore very inconsistent.

Sheen

A shimmering phenomenon from within the stone as opposed to lustre which is purely a surface effect. Sheen, also known as schiller, can usually be attributed to the presence of twinning planes or numerous microscopic inclusions.

LEFT: *Long-wave portable UV lamp* (TOP) *and short wave UV lamp* (BOTTOM)
ABOVE: *Rubies showing moderate to strong fluorescence under long-wave ultraviolet*

Fluorescence

Certain gemstones produce visible light when irradiated by ultra-violet, cathode, X-ray or gamma rays. If the stone continues to glow after the source of radiation is removed this effect is termed *phosphorescence*. The two UV lamps that are most useful in gem testing are the long-wave or near ultra-violet lamp that produces wavelengths from 4000 - 3150Å and a short wave or far ultra-violet lamp with dark light extending from 2800 - 2000Å.

ABOVE: *Synthetic spinel exhibiting intense fluorescence under long-wave ultraviolet*

Asterism

In star stones the mobile four- or six-rayed stars are the result of reflection of light from intersecting sets of fine oriented fibres.

Chatoyancy

More popularly known as cat's-eye, the mobile bright line running across a cabochon is the result of the reflection of light from numerous fine parallel fibres or fibrous cavities within the stone.

Opalescence

A shifting milky or pearly light that emanates from within the stone as the result of microscopic inclusions.

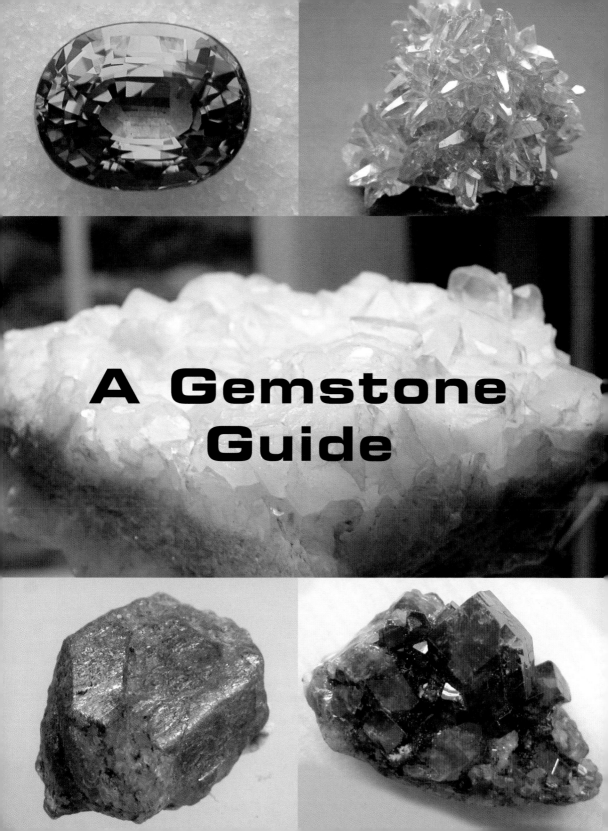

A Gemstone Guide

MINERAL GEMS

Early man's survival depended on his skilful use of minerals. Materials such as flint, agate and obsidan were worked to create sharp and durable points and edges for weapons and tools. Many stone age tools were expertly crafted from carefully chosen material; pick one up today and it still nestles perfectly in the hand. Nowadays, mineral gems have an even wider range of practical and decorative applications, and modern man is still as fascinated as ever with the search for useful and beautiful minerals.

This section, Mineral Gems, does not profess to deal with every conceivable aspect of the major gem varieties: diamond, emerald, ruby and sapphire. Instead, it attempts to present a more balanced approach, devoting space to a great many of the lesser-known gems and ornamental stones.

The gem entries have been ordered by crystal system and then within that system in descending order of hardness.

DIAMOND

C

Diamond (*DYE-ah-mond*) is a name derived from the Greek adamas implying extreme hardness. It is the hardest natural material and the most efficient conductor of heat.

For centuries diamond was known as 'the Indian stone' since India was believed to be the sole source. The discovery of diamonds in Brazil in 1725 was greeted with disbelief and years later Portuguese traders were still marketing Brazilian diamond production from their base in Goa.

In both India and Brazil the diamonds were recovered from alluvial deposits. The origin of the stones was to remain a mystery until the discovery of the first diamond-bearing kimberlite pipe in 1870 at Koffiefontein, in the Orange Free State, South Africa. Subsequent research established that the diamond crystals brought to the surface in volcanic pipes were formed in the upper mantle region 150km or more below the Earth's surface.

■ The ancients believed that the bearer of a sword with a diamond set in its handle was unconquerable.

Refractive Indices	2.417
Birefringence	N/a
Optic Char./Sign	Isometric
Hardness	10
Specific Gravity	3.52
Crystal System	Cubic
Habit	Octahedral, dodecahedral
Lustre	Adamantine
Colour Range	Colourless, brown, grey, yellow, black. Rarely – blue, green, pink, red, purplish
Pleochroism	N/a
Cleavage	Perfect octahedral
Fracture	Conchoidal
Dispersion	0.044
Sources	Angola, Australia, Botswana, Brazil, Canada, Central African Republic, People's Republic of China, Democratic Republic of Congo, Ghana, India, Indonesia, Ivory Coast, Lesotho, Liberia, Namibia, Russia, South Africa, Sierra Leone, Tanzania, USA, Venezuela, Zaire, Zimbabwe
Transparency	Transparent–opaque
Class	Elements

Kimberlites are bodies of ultramafic rock that occur in the form of volcanic pipes, dykes or sills. The composition of kimberlite is complex, with olivine, serpentine, diopside, phlogopite and apatite making up a large proportion of its composition. Other minerals that are present include garnet, spinel and zircon. Diamonds occur as rare xenocrysts in kimberlites, but many kimberlite bodies are either completely devoid of diamonds or have such a limited diamond content that they cannot be worked economically.

Some kimberlite pipes also carry xenoliths of eclogite to the surface. Eclogite is a rare coarse-grained metamorphic rock that, like diamond, is formed under temperatures and pressures that exist in the upper mantle or the lowest regions of thick continental crust. Freshly broken eclogite has a striking appearance, being largely composed of pink to red almandine-pyrope garnets in green pyroxene. Very rarely, eclogite may also enclose tiny diamonds.

Lamproite, the third type of rock that may act as a host for diamond, is closely related to kimberlite. Lamproites are mafic rocks composed mainly of olivine, diopside and richterite. Like kimberlite, lamproite is not a primary source of diamonds but simply transports them upwards from their origin in the region of the upper mantle. The typical lamproite is mushroom-shaped with the wide exposure at surface rapidly closing down to a narrow feeder pipe. Kimberlite pipes are more carrot-shaped and taper very gradually with depth.

Studies of eclogitic diamonds have revealed that they may be composed of organic carbon recycled from the ocean floor by plate tectonics.

A 1934 study revealed distinct variations in the properties of natural diamonds and proposed that they should be split into two categories, Type I and Type II. As the result of further research these two broad categories were subdivided and the existence of a Type III form of diamond was established.

Diamond Types Type Ia Diamonds contain platelets of nitrogen to a significant degree. Most natural diamonds are of this type. Type Ib Diamonds contain finely dispersed molecules of nitrogen. While they are seldom found as natural stones virtually all synthetic diamonds are of this type. Type IIa Diamonds have no significant nitrogen content. Rare in nature, these diamonds are above average in transparency and thermal conductivity. Type IIb Diamonds carry a trace of boron as an impurity. These diamonds are generally blue in colour and they act as semi-conductors passing an electrical current. Type III Diamonds have a hexagonal crystal structure. They occur in meteorites and they have also been synthesized.

TOP: *Fancy brown, trilliant cut diamond (4.10ct)*

■ Diamonds are often compared with ice. This is not merely a reference to their appearance. They are also very cold to touch because of their excellent heat transmission.

BELOW: *(From top to bottom): 18ct yellow and white gold and diamond ring; platinum and diamond ring; platinum, 18ct yellow gold and diamond ring.*

PREVIOUS PAGE
LEFT: *Octahedral diamond in ecologite, North Cape, South Africa*
RIGHT: *Light yellow, modified diamond octahedron (90.0ct), alluvial*

RHODIZITE

$(K,Cs)Be_4Al_4(B,Be)_{12}O_{28}$

Refractive Indices	1.69
Birefringence	N/a
Optic Char./Sign	Isometric
Hardness	8
Specific Gravity	3.3–3.4
Crystal System	Cubic
Habit	Dodecahedral
Lustre	Vitreous–adamantine
Colour Range	Colourless, grey, white, yellow
Pleochroism	N/a
Cleavage	Distinct
Fracture	Conchoidal
Dispersion	Nil
Sources	Madagascar, Russia
Transparency	Transparent–translucent
Class	Borates

■ Madagascar, the sole source of gem-quality rhodizite, has a ban on its export.

Rhodizite (*Rho-DEEZ-ite*) is a very rare borate mineral that is found in association with red elbaite tourmaline in pegmatitic environments. Crystals occur in Madagascar at Antandrokomby, Manjakandriana and near Antsirabe but the export of rhodizite specimens is forbidden. There are also occurrences at Sarapulsk and Schaitansk in the Ural Mountains of Russia. Rhodizite has such a high lustre and hardness that it would be used in jewellery but for its rarity and the small size of the available crystals. Faceted stones seldom exceed one carat in weight.

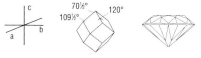

SPINEL

$MgAl_2O_4$

Spinel (*spin-ELL*) occurs in such metamorphic rocks as gneiss, marble and serpentinite in addition to some mafic igneous rocks. Typical associated minerals are calcite, corundum, dolomite and garnets. However, the vast majority of gem spinel rough is recovered from alluvial deposits, most notably the gem gravels of upper Myanmar and Sri Lanka and more recently the highly productive gem-rich alluvial gravels of Songea and Tunduru in southern Tanzania. Spinels are found in every shade of red from full-blooded carmine to orangey scarlet. The 'ruby red' of spinel is so convincing that two of the world's most famous and historic rubies – The Black Prince's Ruby and

ABOVE: *Rough alluvial spinel, Tanzania*

Refractive Indices	1.71–1.73
Birefringence	N/a
Optic Char./Sign	Isometric
Hardness	8
Specific Gravity	3.58–3.61
Crystal System	Cubic
Habit	Octahedral
Lustre	Vitreous
Colour Range	Black, blue, brown, green, orange, purple, red, violet
Pleochroism	N/a
Cleavage	Nil
Fracture	Conchoidal
Dispersion	0.020
Sources	Afghanistan, Brazil, Myanmar, Sri Lanka, Tanzania, Thailand, USA
Transparency	Transparent–opaque
Class	Oxides

■ The historic Black Prince's Ruby, a magnificent red spinel the size of a hen's egg, was given to Prince Edward by Pedro the Cruel, king of Castille.

■ A scientific study of spinels has afforded new evidence of the asteroid impact that killed the dinosaurs.

■ The name spinel probably derived from the Latin spina meaning a thorn.

LEFT: *A range of Spinel*

■ Perfect octahedra of gahnite, up to 3.0cm in diameter, occur at Falun, Sweden.

the Timur Ruby – are both spinels. Spinel also occurs in a wide range of blues, through violet and purple to lilac and various delicate shades of pink. Some of the stones cut from the Tunduru material that appear sapphire-blue by day will show an intense amethyst hue when viewed in incandescent light. Asterism is a rare phenomenon in spinel but occasionally a correctly oriented cabochon that is heavily included with rutile needles will produce a four or six-rayed star.

Gahnite, a rare zinc-rich spinel variety, forms in granitic pegmatites and zinc ore bodies. It is green in colour and has a significantly higher density (4.55–4.60).

Gahnospinel is another zinc-rich spinel variety that is light to dark blue in hue with a density range of 3.58–4.06 and a refractive index of 1.753.

GARNET GROUP

The garnets are a large group of silicates that form under conditions of high temperature and/or pressure. The members of this group share a common crystal form and a degree of similarity in their chemical composition. The majority of garnet varieties conform to the basic formula $X_3Y_2(SiO_4)_3$. X represents divalent elements such as iron, magnesium, manganese or calcium; Y represents trivalent elements, for example aluminium, chromium or vanadium. The garnet group provides classic examples of isomorphous replacement, meaning that metals of similar ionic radii are interchangeable and can form an isomorphous series. There are two such series in the garnet group. The pyralspite series includes pyrope, almandine and spessartite garnets; uvarovite, grossularite and andradite form the ugrandite series.

ABOVE: *Garnet brooch*

ALMANDINE

$Fe_3Al_2(SiO_4)_3$

Almandine (*AL-man-dine*) is the most frequently encountered variety of garnet. It typically occurs in mica schists and is often found in association with feldspar, quartz and staurolite. Isomorphous replacement is so prevalent within the garnet group that identification may be challenging. Theoretically, almandine is the iron-rich end member of a series, but in practice pure end member garnets are virtually non-existent. The iron component in almandine is readily replaced by magnesium and there is a continuous series between almandine and the magnesium-rich pyrope garnet. Red or purplish garnets that exhibit a distinct iron spectrum, a specific gravity above 3.95 and a refractive index greater than 1.78 are generally classed as almandine. Of the various names that have been proposed for the intermediate stones, 'rhodolite' is the most widely accepted within the gem and jewellery trades for those pyrope/almandine garnets that have a density of +/- 3.84, a refractive index of approximately 1.76 and most importantly an attractive violet-red to rhododendron-red hue. The most typical inclusions in almandine are numerous fine hornblende needles that intersect at 110° and 70°. If these inclusions are particularly dense, a correctly oriented cabochon will reveal a weak four-rayed star.

Refractive Indices	1.79–1.82
Birefringence	N/a
Optic Char./Sign	Isotropic
Hardness	7–7.5
Specific Gravity	3.95–4.25
Crystal System	Cubic
Habit	Trapezohedral, dodecahedral
Lustre	Vitreous
Colour Range	Deep red, purplish-red
Pleochroism	N/a
Cleavage	Nil
Fracture	Conchoidal
Dispersion	0.027
Sources	India, Madagascar, Sri Lanka, Tanzania, USA, Zambia, Zimbabwe
Transparency	Transparent–translucent
Class	Silicates

■ Garnet crystals were used as bullets both in Asia and the southwest of the USA.

PYROPE

$Mg_3Al_2(SiO_4)_3$

Pyrope (*PIE-rope*) – from the Greek words for 'fire' and 'I see' – is the only garnet that occurs more frequently in igneous than in metamorphic rocks. It is the prevalent garnet in eclogite and other ultramafic igneous rocks that contain olivine and/or diamond; in fact, chrome pyrope is a key indicator mineral for diamond prospectors. Pyrope is the magnesium-rich end member of the pyrandine series. In theory it should be colourless, but in practice it is always coloured either by traces of iron or, in the case of the finest crimson stones, by chromium. The prolific use of fine pyrope garnet peaked during the 19th century and it is sad to note that this richly coloured stone is not widely used in modern jewellery.

Refractive Indices	1.73–1.75
Birefringence	N/a
Optic Char./Sign	Isotropic
Hardness	7.25
Specific Gravity	3.65–3.80
Crystal System	Cubic
Habit	Rare in crystal form
Lustre	Vitreous
Colour Range	Reddish-brown, crimson red
Pleochroism	N/a
Cleavage	Nil
Fracture	Conchoidal
Dispersion	0.022
Sources	Australia, Brazil, Czech Republic, Myanmar, South Africa, Tanzania, USA
Transparency	Transparent–translucent
Class	Silicates

■ A belief that garnets will purify the blood when in contact with the skin, is still widespread in Italy.

SPESSARTITE (SPESSARTINE)

$Mn_3Al_2(SiO_4)_3$

Spessartite (*SPESS-are-tite*) is a rather rare garnet that occurs in manganese-rich metamorphic environments. It is also encountered in some granitic pegmatites and the finest facet grade material originates from this source. Associated minerals include feldspar, quartz, tourmaline, topaz, beryl and rhodonite. 'Mandarin garnet' is the trade name for a superb orange-hued spessartite that is mined near the Marienfluss River in the remote Kaokoveld of northern Namibia. The crystals are generally fragmented and finished stones in excess of five carats are very rare. Nigeria is an important source and there is some production from East and Central Africa but none of these deposits produces a spessartite with the pure vibrant orange of the Kaokoveld material.

Refractive Indices	1.79–1.81
Birefringence	N/a
Optic Char./Sign	Isotropic
Hardness	7.25
Specific Gravity	4.0–4.2
Crystal System	Cubic
Habit	Dodecahedral, trapezohedral
Lustre	Vitreous
Colour Range	Brown, golden, orange, red, yellow
Pleochroism	N/a
Cleavage	Nil
Fracture	Conchoidal
Dispersion	0.027
Sources	Brazil, Madagascar, Namibia, Nigeria, Pakistan, Sri Lanka, USA, Zambia
Transparency	Transparent–translucent
Class	Silicates

A continuous replacement series exists between almandine and spessartite. Even the purest spessartite inevitably contains some ferrous iron replacing manganese in its composition. Research on the widely varied range of East African garnets has revealed the presence of a solid solution series between spessartite and pyrope, an example being the attractive orange-coloured 'Malaia' garnets (Ki-Swahili – 'out of the family') of Tanzania. Another replacement pattern was detected between spessartite and grossular, the calcium aluminium garnet.

PREVIOUS PAGE: *Spessartite crystal, Namibia*
LEFT: *Antique cushion-cut spessartite, Zambia*

■ Spessartite was first discovered at Spessart, north-western Bavaria, Germany.

GROSSULAR (GROSSULARITE)
$Ca_3Al_2(SiO_4)_3$

Grossular (*GROSS-you-lar*), the calcium aluminium garnet, forms in contact or regional metamorphic environments. Like andradite, grossular is thought to originate from the metamorphism of impure siliceous limestones. Associated minerals include calcite, chlorite, diopside, idocrase, micas and serpentine. Grossular is allochromatic and the purest available specimens of this garnet are virtually colourless. However, such specimens are rare and the prevalence of trace elements is sufficient to ensure that grossular occurs in a wide range of colourful sub-varieties. Hessonite or 'cinnamon stone' is a yellow-brown, orange or orange-red grossular. Cut stones reveal a swirling syrupy interior when examined through the loupe. The name grossular is derived from the Latin for gooseberry and grossular occurs in many shades of green. In commercial terms tsavorite, a fine emerald-green

Refractive Indices	1.742–1.748
Birefringence	N/a
Optic Char./Sign	Isotropic
Hardness	6.5–7
Specific Gravity	3.55–3.67
Crystal System	Cubic
Habit	Dodecahedral, trapezohedral
Lustre	Vitreous
Colour Range	Brown, green, colourless, orange, pink, purple, red, yellow
Pleochroism	N/a
Cleavage	Nil
Fracture	Conchoidal
Dispersion	0.027
Sources	Canada, Kenya, Madagascar, Mexico, Russia, Sri Lanka, Tanzania
Transparency	Transparent–opaque
Class	Silicates

ABOVE LEFT: *Grossular garnet crystals, Canada*
ABOVE RIGHT: *Tsavorite*

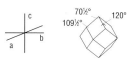

garnet coloured by vanadium, is the most important sub-variety of grossular. Unfortunately the crystals are invariably shattered in situ, so cut stones tend to be small and specimens above five carats in weight are rare. 'Merelani mint' is a bright, remarkably transparent green grossular that occurs in association with zoisite at the Merelani mines near Arushya, Tanzania. It has a refractive index of 1.75, is cut into very attractive faceted gems and its typical euhedral crystals make fine mineral specimens. A brown, olive-green or yellow garnet from Mali has been marketed as grossular/andradite. Generally referred to in the gem trade as 'Mali garnet', the relatively high refractive index of 1.77 may indicate the presence of some iron-rich andradite molecules in its composition.

ABOVE: 'Merelani mint' crystal, Tanzania

■ The ancient name for Hessonite, *lyncurium*, came from a belief that it was formed from Lynx urine and earth.

ANDRADITE

$Ca_3Fe_2(SiO_4)_3$

Andradite (*AND-rad-ite*), the calcium iron garnet, forms in contact or regional metamorphic environments, probably as a result of the alteration of impure siliceous limestones. Associated minerals are micas, chlorite, diopside and serpentine. Demantoid is the most important form of andradite garnet, the name being derived from its adamantine lustre. A radiating pattern of acicular byssolite fibres, referred to as 'horse tails', is the characteristic internal feature of this garnet. Demantoid has remarkable brilliance, a much higher dispersion than diamond and at its best a fine grass-green hue that approaches that of emerald. On the down side it is somewhat soft for use in rings, and cut stones are small – usually below one carat and rarely exceeding two carats in weight. Supply of fine demantoid seldom meets demand. There is a limited amount of very fine intense green demantoid reaching the market from new finds in the Ural Mountains of Russia and there is also some production from Namibia. These stones are lively and full of fire, but their body colours are generally rather subdued, tending towards sage or olive greens.

Topazolite is a misleading name originally applied to small yellow andradite crystals found in the Ala Valley of Italy and near Zermatt, Switzerland. Melanite is a jet-black form of andradite that has found use in mourning jewellery. It was especially popular in Victorian times.

Refractive Indices	1.82–1.89
Birefringence	N/a
Optic Char./Sign	Isotropic
Hardness	6.5–7
Specific Gravity	3.83–3.85
Crystal System	Cubic
Habit	Dodecahedral, trapezohedral
Lustre	Vitreous–sub-adamantine
Colour Range	Black, colourless, green, yellow-green, yellow
Pleochroism	N/a
Cleavage	Nil
Fracture	Conchoidal
Dispersion	0.057
Sources	Democratic Republic of Congo, Italy, Korea, Mali, Namibia, Russia, USA
Transparency	Transparent–translucent
Class	Silicates

HYDRO-GROSSULAR

$Ca_3Al_2(SiO_4)_3$

Refractive Indices	1.70–1.73
Birefringence	N/a
Optic Char./Sign	Nil
Hardness	6–7
Specific Gravity	3.36–3.55
Crystal System	Massive
Habit	Massive
Lustre	Waxy
Colour Range	Green, grey, pink, purple, red
Pleochroism	N/a
Cleavage	Nil
Fracture	Uneven
Dispersion	Nil
Sources	Canada, New Zealand, South Africa, USA
Transparency	Translucent–opaque
Class	Silicates

South African hydro-grossular is probably better known by its misnomer 'Transvaal Jade'. It occurs as an interaction product, occasionally forming thin crusts on the calc-silicate xenoliths that are randomly distributed in the Bushveld Igneous Complex. It is associated with other jade-like minerals including clinozoisite, idocrase, prehnite, saussurite and serpentine. At its best it exhibits a marked degree of translucency and intense emerald-green or pure red hues. Compact and extremely tough, it is a magnificent carving material. It is a massive variety that has no crystal form or symmetry, therefore there are no diagrams for these features.

LEFT: *Hydro-grossular in green and pink varieties*

UVAROVITE

$Ca_3Cr_2(SiO_4)_3$

Uvarovite is the only consistently green garnet and has a beautiful emerald-green colour. As with the other calcium garnets (andradite and grossular), uvarovite is formed from the metamorphism of impure siliceous limestones and some other rocks that contain chromium. It is often associated with serpentine. Mineral specimens of uvarovite are much sought after by collectors for their outstanding brilliance and colour.

Refractive Indices	1.84–1.85
Birefringence	N/a
Optic Char./Sign	Isotropic
Hardness	7
Specific Gravity	3.41–3.52
Crystal System	Cubic
Habit	Trapezohedral, dodecahedral
Lustre	Vitreous
Colour Range	Green
Pleochroism	N/a
Cleavage	Nil
Fracture	Conchoidal
Dispersion	Nil
Sources	Finland, Russia, South Africa, USA
Transparency	Transparent–translucent
Class	Silicates

POLLUCITE

(Cs,Na)$_2$Al$_2$Si$_4$O$_{12}$(H$_2$O)

Refractive Indices	1.525
Birefringence	N/a
Optic Char./Sign	Isotropic
Hardness	6.5
Specific Gravity	2.85–2.94
Crystal System	Cubic
Habit	Massive
Lustre	Vitreous
Colour Range	Blue, colourless, grey, pink, white, yellowish
Pleochroism	N/a
Cleavage	Nil
Fracture	Conchoidal, brittle
Dispersion	0.014
Sources	Italy, Mozambique, Pakistan, Zimbabwe
Transparency	Transparent
Class	Silicates

Pollucite (*pol-YOU-site*) occurs in lithium-rich granitic pegmatites, often in association with petalite. Usually contains white sphere-like inclusions. A rare gem material.

■ The metal caesium is an essential constituent of Pollucite.

PYRITE

FeS$_2$

Refractive Indices	Nil
Birefringence	N/a
Optic Char./Sign	Isometric
Hardness	6–6.5
Specific Gravity	4.95–5.10
Crystal System	Cubic
Habit	Pyritohedron
Lustre	Metallic
Colour Range	Brassy-yellow
Pleochroism	N/a
Cleavage	Indistinct
Fracture	Conchoidal
Dispersion	Nil
Sources	Germany, Peru, Russia, South Africa, Spain, USA
Transparency	Opaque
Class	Sulphides

Pyrite (*PIE-rite*) and marcasite are polymorphs. Associated minerals include calcite, fluorite, galena, gold, quartz and sphalerite. Brilliant cabochons and faceted gems can be cut from this common mineral.

■ The lustrous yellow crystals of pyrites are sometimes referred to as 'fool's gold'.

ABOVE LEFT: *Pyrite on calcite*
ABOVE RIGHT: *Twinned pyrite*

HAÜYNE

$3NaAlSiO_4.CaSO_4$

Refractive Indices	1.496–1.505
Birefringence	N/a
Optic Char./Sign	Isotropic
Hardness	5.5–6
Specific Gravity	2.44–2.50
Crystal System	Cubic
Habit	Dodecahedral
Lustre	Vitreous
Colour Range	Blue, colourless, green, grey, pink, red, white, yellow
Pleochroism	N/a
Cleavage	Dodecahedral (x6)
Fracture	Conchoidal, brittle
Dispersion	Nil
Sources	Afghanistan, Australia, Austria, Canada, China, France, Germany, Italy, Russia, Tajikstan, USA
Transparency	Transparent to translucent
Class	Silicates

Haüyne (*HOW-ne*), or in USA Haüynite, is one of the constituent minerals of lapis lazuli.

Named in honour of Abbé René Just Haüy (1743–1822), French crystallographer and mineralogist, it occurs in igneous rocks that are low in silica, particularly the extrusive types. Associated minerals include leucite and nephelite.

■ Haüyne belongs to the sodalite group. Fine crystal specimens originate from the Eifel Mountains in Germany.

ANALCIME (ANALCITE)

$NaAlSi_2O_6H_2O$

Analcime (*an-AL-seem*) occurs as a low temperature mineral in vesicular cavities in basalt, diabase and other igneous rocks together with calcite, prehnite, etc. Crystals may form as isometric trapezohedra or as modified cubes. Its name, which is sometimes rendered as analcite, is derived from the Greek for 'weak' and refers to the electric charge the mineral develops when heated or rubbed. It occasionally exhibits a white

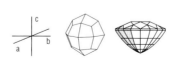

Refractive Indices	1.479–1.494
Birefringence	N/a
Optic Char./Sign	Isotropic
Hardness	5–5.5
Specific Gravity	2.22–2.29
Crystal System	Cubic
Habit	Trapezohedral
Lustre	Vitreous
Colour Range	Colourless, grey, greenish, pink, yellowish, white
Pleochroism	N/a
Cleavage	Indistinct
Fracture	Sub-conchoidal
Dispersion	Weak
Sources	Canada, Italy, Scotland, Switzerland, USA
Transparency	Transparent–translucent
Class	Silicates
Comments	Rarely fluorescent under ultraviolet

fluorescence under long-wave ultraviolet light; it has a low heat sensitivity and is brittle. Clean, colourless material is sometimes faceted as a collectors' stone.

SODALITE

$Na_4Al_3(SiO_4)_3Cl$

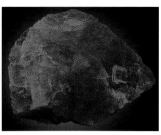

Sodalite (*SODA-lite*) is a rock-forming feldspathoid mineral that occurs in association with calcite, nepheline, cancrinite and other feldspathoids. Originally known as a component of lapis lazuli, it came into its own as an ornamental stone with the discovery of significant deposits of magnificent princess blue material in Canada. Substantial quantities of a very rich blue, highly crystallized sodalite are mined in northern Namibia. The rarely encountered euhedral crystals tend to be dodecahedral in habit but it is the massive material that is widely employed in the manufacture of cabochons, beads, slabs for inlay work, spheres and other ornamental objects.

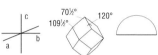

Refractive Indices	1.482
Birefringence	N/a
Optic Char./Sign	Isotropic
Hardness	5.5–6
Specific Gravity	2.15–2.35
Crystal System	Cubic
Habit	Massive, dodecahedral
Lustre	Vitreous–greasy
Colour Range	Blue, greenish, grey, red, white, yellowish
Pleochroism	N/a
Cleavage	Poor
Fracture	Uneven
Dispersion	Nil
Sources	Brazil, Canada, Greenland, India, Italy, Namibia, Norway, USA
Transparency	Transparent–opaque
Class	Silicates

■ Sodalite from Greenland deposits exhibits a very strong fluorescence under ultraviolet light.

ABOVE LEFT: *Sodalite*
ABOVE RIGHT: *Sodalite from Greenland fluorescing under long-wave ultra-violet light*

COBALTITE

CoAsS

Cobaltite (*co-BALL-tite*) is frequently found in metasomatic contact deposits or quartz rich gneiss. It is usually associated with other cobalt and nickel minerals, copper and silver ores. Crystal habits include cubes, octahedrons, pyritohedrons and combinations of these isometric forms. Cobaltite is also found in massive and granular forms. Since cobalt is a very strong chromophore the associated secondary minerals such as erythrite are vividly coloured and provide miners with useful indications of the presence of cobalt ores, such as cobaltite. Good crystals are usually available when new cobaltite deposits are found, much to the delight of collectors. Massive material is cut into cabochons.

Refractive Indices	Nil
Birefringence	N/a
Optic Char./Sign	Nil
Hardness	5.5
Specific Gravity	6–6.3
Crystal System	Cubic
Habit	Cube, pyritohedron
Lustre	Metallic
Colour Range	Silvery-white to reddish
Pleochroism	N/a
Cleavage	Distinct cubic
Fracture	Uneven
Dispersion	Nil
Sources	Canada, England, Germany, Norway, Sweden, USA, Zaire
Transparency	Opaque
Class	Arsenides

LAZURITE

$(Na,Ca)_8Al_6Si_6O_{24}(S,SO_4)$

Refractive Indices	1.5
Birefringence	N/a
Optic Char./Sign	Isotropic
Hardness	5–5.5
Specific Gravity	2.3–2.4
Crystal System	Cubic
Habit	Dodecahedral
Lustre	Vitreous
Colour Range	Blue
Pleochroism	N/a
Cleavage	Poor
Fracture	Uneven
Dispersion	Nil
Sources	Afghanistan, Chile, Italy, Russia, USA
Transparency	Translucent–opaque
Class	Silicates

■ The name Lazurite is derived from *lazhward*, the Persian word for 'blue'.

Lazurite (*LAZE-your-ite*): well-formed crystals of this deep blue mineral are rare and highly collectable. Lazurite is most frequently encountered in its massive form as the principal component of lapis lazuli. Lazurite belongs to the feldspathoid group. The feldspathoids are closely related and very similar to the alkali feldspars but have a lower silica content.

ABOVE LEFT: *Lazurite crystals*
LEFT: *Lapis lazuli carving*

MICROLITE

$Ca_2Ta_2O_7$

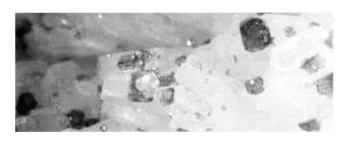

■ Microlite is rarely cut except for collectors.

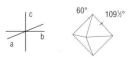

Microlite (*MY-crow-lite*): the name is based on the tiny size of the crystals at the site of its original discovery. Subsequent finds have produced larger crystals, some up to 2 cms (0.78 inches) in diameter from granitic pegmatite dykes and more rarely from carbonatites. Generally minerals of the tantalum/ niobium oxide group can be difficult to distinguish but microlite crystals are quite distinctive with their fine, slightly modified octahedral form. Microlite specimens are often slightly radioactive due to the presence of traces of rare earth elements in their composition. This is a rare mineral in any form and facet rough is seldom available. Excellent gems have been cut from orange-red material.

Refractive Indices	1.93
Birefringence	N/a
Optic Char./Sign	Isotropic
Hardness	5–5.5
Specific Gravity	4.3–5.7
Crystal System	Cubic
Habit	Octahedral
Lustre	Vitreous–resinous
Colour Range	green, olive, red, russet, pale yellow
Pleochroism	N/a
Cleavage	Octahedral, indistinct
Fracture	Subconchoidal
Dispersion	Nil
Sources	Australia, Brazil, Greenland, Madagascar, Norway, Sweden, USA
Transparency	Transparent–opaque
Class	Tantalates

PERICLASE

MgO

Refractive Indices	1.73–1.74
Birefringence	N/a
Optic Char./Sign	Isotropic
Hardness	5–6
Specific Gravity	3.6–3.90
Crystal System	Cubic
Habit	Cube, octahedron
Lustre	Vitreous–adamantine
Colour Range	Colourless, black, brown, grey, white, yellow
Pleochroism	N/a
Cleavage	Cubic
Fracture	Nil
Dispersion	Nil
Sources	Italy (Mount Vesuvius); Sweden (Nordmark); USA (California)
Transparency	Transparent–translucent
Class	Oxides

Periclase (*PERI-clase*) is occasionally cut as a gemstone although it is not particularly hard and is limited in colour range. It is a relatively scarce mineral that occurs in marbles formed through the dissolution of dolomites. Associated minerals include brucite, chondrodite, dolomite, forsterite and magnesite. Crystal specimens of periclase can be attractive. Produced synthetically the material is marketed as Lavernite.

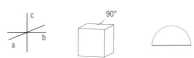

CUPRITE

Cu_2O

Refractive Indices	2.85
Birefringence	N/a
Optic Char./Sign	Isotropic
Hardness	3.5–4
Specific Gravity	5.85–6.15
Crystal System	Cubic
Habit	Octahedral
Lustre	Nil
Colour Range	Deep red–red-black
Pleochroism	N/a
Cleavage	Fair
Fracture	Uneven
Dispersion	Nil
Sources	Australia, Chile, Namibia, USA, Zaire, Zambia
Transparency	Transparent–translucent
Class	Oxides

■ Cuprite also occurs in a hair-like form called chalcotrichite.

LEFT: *Cuprite crystals on matrix*
BELOW LEFT: *Large oxidized cuprite crystal*

Cuprite (*KEW-prite*) is a major ore of copper mined in many places worldwide. Of all the copper ores except for native copper, cuprite gives the greatest yield of copper per molecule since there is only one oxygen atom to every two copper atoms. As a mineral specimen, cuprite shows fine examples of well-developed cubic crystal forms. Cuprite's dark crystals show internal reflections of the true deep red inside the almost black crystal. Very brittle and difficult to cut, it produces fine cabochons and dark faceted stones. The surface of cut stones darkens after a year or two but wiping with a soft tissue will usually clear this.

FLUORITE (FLUORSPAR)

CaF_2

Fluorite (*FLU-or-ite*) is a name derived from the mineral's ready fusibility. Hence it is used as a flux in the steel and aluminium industries. Its crystal habit is typically to form cubes and to a much lesser extent octahedra. In some deposits the

mineral is found as crusts or in botryoidal forms but these are less common. Among the numerous associated minerals are apatite, barite, calcite, chalcopyrite, galena, pyrite, quartz, sphalerite, willemite and witherite. Most fluorite exhibits a strong light-blue or violet fluorescence under long-wave ultraviolet light. Under short-wave light there is a similar but much weaker effect. There are numerous fluorite deposits in Britain, and the veins of massive material in Derbyshire were extensively worked during the Roman occupation. It is known locally as 'Blue John' and a wide range of ornaments are still manufactured from this colourful material. Fluorite's easy cleavage makes it a relatively simple matter to create artificial octahedra from blocky transparent fragments. Many of the fluorite specimens offered for sale at shows have been 'doctored' in this way. Faceted fluorites are often available in a wide colour range and tyro collectors can soon build up an attractive suite of stones at relatively low cost.

Refractive Indices	1.43
Birefringence	N/a
Optic Char./Sign	Isotropic
Hardness	4
Specific Gravity	3.17–3.19
Crystal System	Cubic
Habit	Cubic, massive
Lustre	Vitreous
Colour Range	Colourless, blue, brown, green, orange, pink, violet, yellow
Pleochroism	N/a
Cleavage	Octahedral
Fracture	Irregular, brittle
Dispersion	0.006
Sources	England, Brazil, Canada, China, Mexico, Namibia, USA, Zimbabwe
Transparency	Transparent–translucent
Class	Halides

TOP LEFT: *A cluster of cubic fluorite*
BELOW: *'Blue John' fluorite*

SPHALERITE

(Zn,Fe)S

Refractive Indices	2.37–2.42
Birefringence	N/a
Optic Char./Sign	Isotropic
Hardness	3.5–4
Specific Gravity	4
Crystal System	Cubic
Habit	Tetrahedral, massive
Lustre	Adamantine
Colour Range	Black, brown, colourless, green, reddish, yellow, white
Pleochroism	N/a
Cleavage	Perfect (x6)
Fracture	Conchoidal
Dispersion	0.156
Sources	Australia, England, Germany, Italy, Morocco, Peru, Spain, USA, Zambia
Transparency	Transparent–translucent
Class	Sulphides

Sphalerite (*SFAL-er-ite*) is an important ore of zinc that can make attractive cabinet specimens. It can have excellent lustre and it is usually associated with calcite, chalcopyrite, fluorite, galena, pyrite, pyrrhotite and quartz. Sphalerite has six directions of cleavage. If all of them were to be perfectly cleaved on a single specimen it would form a rhombic dodecahedron. Identifying all six directions in a single cleaved crystal is quite difficult due to multiple twinning. Transparent sphalerite has been cut for gemstones but its cleavage and softness limit its use as a gemstone to collectors only.

■ Sphalerite, also known as zinc-blende, is the principal ore of zinc.

TENNANTITE

$Cu_{12}As_4S1_3$

Tennantite (*TEN-an-tite*) forms in copper ore bodies associated with arsenopyrite, chalcopyrite, pyrite and quartz. It sometimes occurs with veins of chrysocolla, a combination that makes very striking cabochon material. The rare crystals are often dodecahedral.

Refractive Indices	Nil
Birefringence	N/a
Optic Char./Sign	Isometric
Hardness	3–4
Specific Gravity	4.37–4.49
Crystal System	Cubic
Habit	Massive
Lustre	Metallic
Colour Range	Black–steel grey
Pleochroism	N/a
Cleavage	Nil
Fracture	Uneven
Dispersion	Nil
Sources	Germany, Namibia, Switzerland, USA
Transparency	Opaque
Class	Sulphides

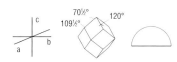

DOMEYKITE

Cu_3As

Domeykite (*DOE-me-kite*) is a semi-metallic alloy of copper and arsenic that is found in a number of Chilean copper deposits. It was named for 19th-century Chilean mineralogist Ignacio Domeyko. Domeykite can be used for ornamental purposes. Cut and polished it makes attractive cabochons or it is used for clock faces, bookends and carvings. Associated minerals include calcite, nickeline and various copper ore minerals. Field identification may be assisted by its garlicky odour.

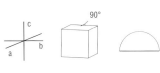

Refractive Indices	Nil
Birefringence	N/a
Optic Char./Sign	Nil
Hardness	3–3.5
Specific Gravity	7.2–8.1
Crystal System	Cubic
Habit	Botryoidal. Massive, reniform
Lustre	Metallic
Colour Range	White, copper-brown, yellow-brown, steel-grey
Pleochroism	N/a
Cleavage	Nil
Fracture	Hackly
Dispersion	Nil
Sources	Canada, Chile, USA
Transparency	Opaque
Class	Arsenates

BORNITE

Cu_5FeS_4

Bornite (*BORN-ite*), a copper iron sulphide, is an important ore of copper. It is closely associated with chalcocite, chalcopyrite and covellite. Weathered specimens have a distinctive iridescence. The rare crystals are cubic but often distorted with rough or curved faces or as interpenetrant twins. Massive copper sulphide ore including chalcopyrite and bornite is readily available and is usually sold at gem and mineral shows as 'peacock ore'. Compact pieces of this material can be used to cut attractive cabochons.

Refractive Indices	Nil
Birefringence	N/a
Optic Char./Sign	Nil
Hardness	3
Specific Gravity	4.9–5.4
Crystal System	Cubic
Habit	Massive
Lustre	Metallic
Colour Range	Iridescent peacock ore
Pleochroism	N/a
Cleavage	Poor
Fracture	Conchoidal
Dispersion	Nil
Sources	Chile, England, Germany, Morocco, Namibia, Peru, South Africa, USA, Zambia
Transparency	Opaque
Class	Sulphides

■ Bornite is known as peacock ore because of the vivid colours it shows when tarnished.

ZIRCON

ZrSiO$_4$

LEFT: *Zircon crystals on matrix*
ABOVE: *Zircon colour suite*

Refractive Indices	1.923–2.015
Birefringence	0.06
Optic Char./Sign	Uniaxial/+
Hardness	7.5
Specific Gravity	4.6–4.7
Crystal System	Tetragonal
Habit	Prismatic
Lustre	Adamantine
Colour Range	Blue, black, brown, colourless, gold, green, red, yellow
Pleochroism	Low
Cleavage	Imperfect
Fracture	Conchoidal
Dispersion	0.038
Sources	Australia, Canada, Malawi, Myanmar, Sri Lanka, Tanzania, Thailand, USA
Transparency	Transparent–translucent
Class	Silicates

Zircon (*ZIR-con*) commonly occurs in granite, syenite and diorite. In a pegmatitic environment it often forms good-sized euhedral crystals. It occurs with less frequency in granular limestone, chloritic schists and gneiss. It is found in two forms: the high type or normal zircon and low or metamict zircon, which represents a decomposed state of normal zircon with lower physical and optical properties. This breakdown is attributed to a degree of radioactivity in rare trace elements present in the material. Metamict zircon is always green in colour with a density of approximately 4.0, a refractive index of +/- 1.80 and it is virtually isotropic. Minerals occurring in association with zircon include albite, biotite, garnet, monazite and xenotime. Zircon is found in a wide range of natural colours. However, the most popular colours to be used in items of jewellery are colourless (such specimens were once widely used as a diamond substitute), blue and golden, all colours that result from the heat-treatment of reddish-brown zircon. Heating the stones in an oxidizing atmosphere will produce golden-yellow and colourless stones. A reducing atmosphere will yield blue and colourless stones. The properties of the green low-type zircon can be largely if not totally restored to those of normal high-type zircon by judicious heating.

■ The name zircon may originate from the Persian zargoon meaning 'gold-coloured'.

■ Heat-treated colourless zircon was widely marketed as Matara diamond.

IDOCRASE (VESUVIANITE)

Ca$_{10}$(MgFe)$_2$Al$_4$(SiO$_4$)$_5$(Si$_2$O$_7$)$_2$(OH)$_4$

Idocrase (*EYE-doe-crase*) is marketed under a range of names: cyprine is light blue; californite is mottled green; xanthite is a massive, opaque, yellow-green variety. The name idocrase is derived from the Greek for 'mixed form' and alludes to the fact that its crystals tend to combine the forms of other minerals. It is also called vesuvianite with reference to the recovery of material from Mount Vesuvius. In common with hydro-grossular garnet, with which it is often confused, idocrase forms as a result of the contact metamorphism of impure limestone. Rarely found in facet quality, this material is best known when employed in its massive form as a substitute for jade.

Refractive Indices	1.712–1.721
Birefringence	0.005
Optic Char./Sign	Uniaxial/–
Hardness	6.5
Specific Gravity	3.3–3.5
Crystal System	Tetragonal
Habit	Prismatic, massive
Lustre	Vitreous–greasy
Colour Range	Blue, brown, green, purple, yellow
Pleochroism	N/a
Cleavage	Poor
Fracture	Conchoidal–uneven
Dispersion	0.019
Sources	Canada, Italy, Russia, Switzerland, USA
Transparency	Transparent–opaque
Class	Silicates

■ Idocrase was first discovered on Mount Somma, Italy in 1795.

SCAPOLITE

$Na_4(Al,Si)_{12}O_{24}Cl$ to $Ca_4(Si,Al)_{12}O_{24}(CO_3,SO_4)$

Scapolite (*SKA-pol-ite*) is a collective name for a group of aluminium silicates that includes meionite, wernerite, mizzonite and marialite. The word is derived from the Greek word for 'shaft' and refers to the typical square-section prismatic shape of the crystals. Individual members of this series are identifiable by the proportion of calcium in their composition. Scapolite often exhibits fluorescence, yellow, yellow-green or more rarely red under long-wave, and orange or red under short-wave ultraviolet light. Gem scapolite is substantially composed of wernerite, the mid-member of the series.

Refractive Indices	1.55–1.57
Birefringence	0.022
Optic Char./Sign	Uniaxial/–
Hardness	5–6
Specific Gravity	2.7
Crystal System	Tetragonal
Habit	Prismatic, massive
Lustre	Vitreous
Colour Range	Colourless, greenish, pink, violet, yellow
Pleochroism	Distinct
Cleavage	Distinct (x2)
Fracture	Sub-conchoidal
Dispersion	0.017
Sources	Brazil, Madagascar, Mozambique, Myanmar, Tanzania, USA, Zimbabwe
Transparency	Transparent–translucent
Class	Silicates

LEFT: *Scapolite crystals*

CASSITERITE

SnO_2

The hardy Phoenician seafarers, who traded in commodities throughout the ancient world, obtained tin from the Iron Age people of a group of islands they called the Cassiterides, meaning 'tin isles'. These islands, situated off the west coast of Europe, are now known as the British Isles. Cassiterite (cah-SIT-er-ite) is found in association with magmatic intrusions. It is believed to crystallize directly from volatile elements emitted by the molten magma. It occurs in a variety of forms: acicular, blocky, botryoidal, fibrous, granular, and massive. Typical habits are octagonal prisms and stubby crystals terminated by four-sided or more complex pyramids. Twinning is common, especially the 'elbow twins' that are typical of this mineral. Bolivia, where the mineral is mined from hydrothermal veins, is now the main producer of primary cassiterite but the greater part of world production is sourced from secondary alluvial deposits. Facet rough is hard to find but very rewarding to cut since it yields lustrous gems of exceptional fire. Fine cut specimens in excess of two carats attract fairly high prices.

Refractive Indices	1.997–2.093
Birefringence	0.098
Optic Char./Sign	Uniaxial/+
Hardness	6–7
Specific Gravity	6.6–7.1
Crystal System	Tetragonal
Habit	Eight sided prisms
Lustre	Adamantine, greasy
Colour Range	Black, colourless, reddish brown, yellow
Pleochroism	Definite
Cleavage	Distinct x2
Fracture	Conchoidal, tough
Dispersion	0.071
Sources	Australia, Bolivia, England, Malaysia, Mexico, Nigeria
Transparency	Transparent–opaque
Class	Oxides

■ Cassiterite is the principal ore of tin.

NARSARSUKITE

$Na_2(Ti,Fe)Si_4(O,F)_{11}$

Narsarsukite was named for the mineral-rich locality of Narsarsuk in Greenland. The agpaitic pegmatites of this locality are high in sodium and other alkaline metals and also contain unusual elements such as fluorine, titanium and rare earth metals. Associated minerals include aegirine, albite, amphiboles, calcite, carletonite, microcline and natrolite.

Refractive Indices	1.601–1.647
Birefringence	0.031
Optic Char./Sign	Uniaxial
Hardness	6–7
Specific Gravity	2.6–2.8
Crystal System	Tetragonal
Habit	Tabular, prismatic
Lustre	Adamantine–greasy
Colour Range	Brown, colourless, green, pink, yellow
Pleochroism	–
Cleavage	Perfect (x2)
Fracture	Uneven–sub-conchoidal
Dispersion	–
Sources	Canada, Greenland, USA
Transparency	Transparent–translucent
Class	Silicates

Narsarsukite is also found at Mont St. Hilaire in Quebec, Canada, and to date the best specimens have originated from this source. The Canadian pegmatites also yield a limited amount of gem rough that can be faceted into small attractive gems.

RUTILE

TiO$_2$

Refractive Indices	2.62–2.90
Birefringence	0.285–0.305
Optic Char./Sign	Uniaxial/+
Hardness	6–6.5
Specific Gravity	4.2–4.3
Crystal System	Tetragonal
Habit	Prismatic
Lustre	Adamantine
Colour Range	Black, blue, brown, red, violet, yellow
Pleochroism	Strong
Cleavage	Distinct (x2)
Fracture	Subconchoidal
Dispersion	0.30 very strong
Sources	Brazil, France, Italy, Madagascar, Russia, Scandanavia, Switzerland, USA
Transparency	Transparent–opaque
Class	Oxides

■ Rutile crystals frequently form as geniculate (elbow) twins.

Rutile (*RUE-tile*) is probably best known in the form of the very fine hair-like inclusions that occur in quartz crystals. Golden-coloured crystals typically exhibit a slender acicular form. Red crystals are blockier and frequently of such a dark tone that they are virtually black since the colour can only be seen in very thin sections. Rutile forms twins very readily, either as 'elbow twins' that meet at 60° angles or as cyclic twins.

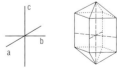

LEFT: *Rutilated quartz bracelet*

TUGTUPITE

$Na_8Al_2Be_2Si_8O_{24}$

Refractive Indices	1.496–1.502
Birefringence	0.006–0.008
Optic Char./Sign	Uniaxial/+
Hardness	4
Specific Gravity	2.33–2.57
Crystal System	Tetragonal
Habit	Massive, fine-grained aggregates
Lustre	Vitreous
Colour Range	White, pink, cyclamen–red
Pleochroism	Moderate
Cleavage	Distinct
Fracture	Conchoidal, uneven
Dispersion	N/a
Sources	Canada, Greenland, Russia
Transparency	Transparent - semi-opaque
Class	Silicates
Comments:	Piezo-electric

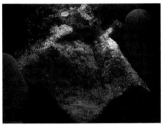

Tugtupite (*TUG-tup-ite*) is named after the promontory in Greenland where it was first discovered by geologists in 1957. Of course the Inuit had known all about the rock that changed colour for centuries, Literally translated, *tugtup* means reindeer. Cabochon-quality material appears cyclamen-red under normal light but fluoresces bright orange under long-wave ultraviolet light and deep salmon-red under short-wave. Tugtupite is tenebrescent: when it is newly mined it is a pale pink but warmth and exposure to ultraviolet light from the Sun or a lamp causes the cyclamen red hue to intensify. Tugtupite cabochons often carry traces of associated minerals such as aegirine, analcime, chkalovite and lujavrite.

■ Seldom seen, Tugtupite crystals are pseudo-cubic in form (meaning they belong to a different crystal system but assume forms with a strong resemblance to cubic crystals).

TOP: *Tugtupite cabochon*
LEFT: *Tugtupite fluorescence*

ANATASE

TiO_2

Refractive Indices	2.493–2.554
Birefringence	0.06
Optic Char./Sign	Uniaxial/–
Hardness	5.5–6
Specific Gravity	3.82–3.95
Crystal System	Tetragonal
Habit	Tetragonal dipyramid
Lustre	Adamantine
Colour Range	Blue, brown, black
Pleochroism	N/a
Cleavage	Perfect (x 2)
Fracture	Sub-conchoidal
Dispersion	Ord – 0.213, Ext – 0.259
Sources	Brazil, England, France, Switzerland, USA
Transparency	Transparent–translucent
Class	Oxides

Anatase (*ANA-tase*) occurs in granites, gneisses and mica schists, often in association with apatite, brookite, hematite, quartz, rutile and sphene. Together with rutile and brookite it forms a polymorphic group. When exposed to high temperatures anatase reverts to the rutile structure. Anatase is the rarest mineral of this group. It is very similar to rutile in lustre, hardness and density but differs in its crystal habit and especially in its cleavage. It has a low heat sensitivity and is brittle. Crystals of anatase frequently form tetragonal dipyramids with elongated points. The mistaken assumption that these crystals exhibit octahedral form has resulted in anatase being inaccurately referred to as 'octahedrite'. The good lustre and interesting shape ensure that anatase specimens are always in demand with collectors.

Fine crystal specimens come from the Bourg d'Oisans district of France. Brazil is the most likely source of facet rough. In its rare transparent form, anatase facets into brilliant gems.

■ Anatase takes its name from the Greek *anatasis* meaning 'elongation'.

LEUCITE

KAlSi$_2$O$_6$,

Leucite (*LEW-site*) is a name derived from the Greek word for 'white'. The symmetry of crystals is stated to be the external expression of their orderly internal structure. Leucite is the exception to this rule. At temperatures in excess of 625°C leucite crystals have an isometric structure. At lower temperatures they assume a tetragonal internal structure without modifying their typical trapezohedral external shape. Crystals are usually twinned and transparent facet grade rough is very rare. In common with other feldspathoid minerals, leucite is found in rocks that have a low silica content. Associated minerals include augite, biotite, labradorite, nepheline and olivine.

Refractive Indices	1.508–1.509
Birefringence	0.001
Optic Char./Sign	Uniaxial +
Hardness	5.5–6
Specific Gravity	2.45–2.50
Crystal System	Tetragonal
Habit	Pseudo-trapezohedral
Lustre	Vitreous
Colour Range	Colourless, greyish, reddish, yellowish
Pleochroism	–
Cleavage	Poor
Fracture	Conchoidal
Dispersion	0.010
Sources	Brazil, Canada, Germany, Italy, USA
Transparency	Transparent–opaque
Class	Silicates

■ Leucite is a rare mineral, the principal source being the volcanic lava of Mount Vesuvius, Italy.

MELINOPHANE

(Ca,Na)$_2$Be[(Si,Al)$_2$O$_6$(F,OH)]

Melinophane (*mel-IN-oh-fane*) or meliphanite, is a name derived from the Greek for 'honey' and 'to appear', and refers to the mineral's golden yellow colouring. The sole source of gemmy rough is the deposit in the Langesundfjord district of southern Norway. This unusual mineral is cut into cabochons for specialist collectors.

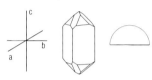

Refractive Indices	1.592–1.672
Birefringence	0.008–0.019
Optic Char./Sign	Uniaxial/–
Hardness	5–5.5
Specific Gravity	3.01–3.03
Crystal System	Tetragonal
Habit	Prismatic, slender or tabular
Lustre	Vitreous
Colour Range	Colourless, yellow, yellowish-red, red
Pleochroism	yellow/dark yellow
Cleavage	Perfect
Fracture	Uneven, brittle
Dispersion	–
Sources	Italy, Norway, Russia, USA
Transparency	Transparent–translucent
Class	Silicates

WARDITE

NaAl$_3$(PO$_4$)$_2$(OH)$_4$·2H$_2$O

Wardite (*WARD-ite*), a blue-green mineral resembling turquoise, is found filling cavities in nodular variscite, another hydrous aluminium phosphate. It is formed as an alteration product and its physical properties differ from those of variscite. Associated minerals are amblygonite, crandallite, feldspar, lazulite, quartz and variscite. Wardite can be cut into attractive cabochons and the rare crystals make interesting specimens.

Refractive Indices	1.597–1.607
Birefringence	0.010
Optic Char./Sign	Uniaxial
Hardness	5
Specific Gravity	2.8
Crystal System	Tetragonal
Habit	Tetragonal dipyramids
Lustre	Vitreous, greasy
Colour Range	Colourless, bluish-green, green, white
Pleochroism	–
Cleavage	Basal
Fracture	Conchoidal
Dispersion	–
Sources	Australia, Austria, Belgium, Brazil, Canada, France, Spain, USA
Transparency	Transparent–translucent
Class	Phosphates

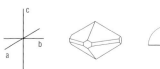

APOPHYLLITE

$KFCa_4Si_8O_{12}(OH)_{16}$

Apophyllite (*ah-POFF-ee-lite*) is a collective name in general use for minerals of the fluorapophyllite–hydroxyapophyllite series of which fluorapophyllite is by far the most abundant and colourful member. Translated from early Greek the name means 'to leaf apart', referring to the way the crystals flake apart when heat-

ed. Fine crystals are recovered from cavities in basalts (vesicles) that held trapped gases when the lava was molten. Associated minerals may include calcite, quartz, prehnite, and datolite. Apophyllite also occurs in cavities in gneiss and limestone.

Euhedral crystals in apophyllite generally exhibit one of two major crystal habits. The rectangular prism capped by a steep four-sided pyramid is a form that is treasured by collectors especially if it is doubly terminated. The unusual feature of this form is that the faces of the terminal pyramids are not in alignment with the prism faces. They are rotated by 45° and plunge down the prism edges to produce diamond shapes as opposed to the typical tetrahedral triangles as seen on zircon crystals.

In the other major habit the prism faces terminate in flat faces or pinacoids that are perpendicular to the length of the crystal. If the prisms are short and blocky these pinacoidal terminations give the crystals a cubic appearance.

The prism faces of apophyllite crystals are striated lengthwise and exhibit a vitreous lustre in contrast to the pearly lustre of the cleavage faces. The mineral fluoresces LW Blue-green (R) Yellow (O). Apophyllite is sometimes faceted as a collector's stone but the easy cleavage, brittleness and extreme heat sensitivity make it a serious challenge to the facetier.

Refractive Indices	1.530–1.538
Birefringence	0.002
Optic Char./Sign	Uniaxial/+
Hardness	4.5–5
Specific Gravity	2.3–2.4
Crystal System	Tetragonal
Habit	Tabular, prismatic, pseudo-cubic
Lustre	Vitreous, pearly
Colour Range	Colourless, greenish, grey, flesh red, white, yellowish
Pleochroism	–
Cleavage	Perfect (x 2)
Fracture	Uneven
Dispersion	High
Sources	Brazil, China, Finland, Germany, Iceland, India, Italy, Mexico, USA, Scotland, Sweden, Austria
Transparency	Transparent
Class	Silicates

TOP: *Apophyllite crystal from India*
BOTTOM: *Green apophyllite crystal*

SCHEELITE

CaWO$_4$

Refractive Indices	1.918–1.934
Birefringence	0.014–0.016
Optic Char./Sign	Uniaxial/+
Hardness	4.5–5
Specific Gravity	5.9–6.1
Crystal System	Tetragonal
Habit	Pseudo-octahedral
Lustre	Adamantine
Colour Range	Brown, greenish-grey, orange, red, yellow, white, colourless
Pleochroism	Definite
Cleavage	Perfect
Fracture	Conchoidal, uneven, brittle
Dispersion	0.026
Sources	Australia, Brazil, Canada, Mexico, Namibia, South Africa, USA, Zimbabwe
Transparency	Transparent–translucent
Class	Tungstates

Scheelite (*SHE-lite*) occurs in granite, skarns, pegmatites, and hydrothermal deposits. Associated minerals are apatite, cassiterite, epidote, fluorite, garnets, molybdenite, quartz, schorl, topaz and vesuvianite. It was named after Swedish chemist, K.W. Scheele, the discoverer of tungsten. Molybdenum can readily substitute for tungsten, and scheelite forms a replacement series with the molybdenate mineral powellite. Relatively pure scheelite will fluoresce bright blue under short-wave ultraviolet light, while powellite exhibits a golden-yellow fluorescence. Specimens of the tetragonal dipyramidal crystals formed by both scheelite and powellite are very popular with collectors. A deposit in the Gamsberg area of Namibia yielded huge orange scheelite crystals and transparent gem rough. A magnificent gem weighing 58 carats was faceted from this material.

■ A fine yellow scheelite may resemble a fancy diamond except for its double refraction.

EKANITE

ThCa$_2$Si$_8$O$_2$0

Refractive Indices	1.568–1.580
Birefringence	0.012
Optic Char./Sign	Uniaxial/–
Hardness	4.5
Specific Gravity	3.08–3.30
Crystal System	Tetragonal
Habit	Tetragonal bipyramids
Lustre	Vitreous
Colour Range	Green, red, yellow, light brown
Pleochroism	–
Cleavage	Distinct
Fracture	Uneven
Dispersion	–
Sources	Canada, Italy, Russia, Sri Lanka, Tajikstan, USA
Transparency	Translucent
Class	Silicates

Ekanite (*EK-an-ite*) was named in 1961 for F.L.D. Ekanayake, who discovered it in 1953 in a gravel pit in Sri Lanka. It is metamict calcium thorium silicate. Subsequently discovered specimens were polished as cabochons and revealed a four-rayed star. However, they also revealed a marked degree of radioactivity and this has restricted them to specialized collections housed under controlled conditions. Specimen-quality red ekanite crystals are found at Rouville, Quebec, Canada.

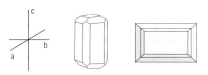

BOLÉITE

Pb(CuAg)Cl$_2$(OH)$_2$H$_2$O

Refractive Indices	2.03–2.04
Birefringence	0.010
Optic Char./Sign	Uniaxial/–
Hardness	3–3.5
Specific Gravity	5.05
Crystal System	Tetragonal
Habit	Pseudo-cubic
Lustre	Vitreous–pearly
Colour Range	Deep indigo blue
Pleochroism	–
Cleavage	Perfect
Fracture	Uneven
Dispersion	0.071
Sources	Australia, Chile, England, France, Germany, Greece, Iran, Italy, Mexico, UK, USA
Transparency	Transparent–opaque
Class	Chlorides

Boléite (*BO-lay-ite*) is a rather scarce mineral that is found in relatively few copper deposits. It was named for the type locality Boleo in Baja California, Mexico. It may be mistaken for a cubic mineral since it frequently assumes a pseudo-cubic habit with an apparent simple cube comprising three interpenetrant crystals that are oriented at right angles to each other. Look for the notches or interpenetrant angles present in many of these specimens to discover their twinned nature. The pseudo-cubes rarely exceed one centimetre (0.39 inches) in size. Specimens are attractive and very popular with collectors. They generally consist of a scattering of intense blue crystals bedded in a white clayey matrix or loose individual twinned crystals. Soft, cleavable and twinned boleite is a difficult material to work and faceted stones are rarely encountered in collections.

PHOSGENITE

$Pb_2(CO_3)Cl_2$

Refractive Indices	2.114–2.140
Birefringence	0.026
Optic Char./Sign	Uniaxial/+
Hardness	2.5–3
Specific Gravity	6–6.3
Crystal System	Tetragonal
Habit	Prismatic, tabular, massive
Lustre	Adamantine
Colour Range	Brownish-yellow, greenish-white, grey, pinkish-white, colourless
Pleochroism	Weak
Cleavage	Distinct (x3)
Fracture	Conchoidal
Dispersion	Strong
Sources	England, Greece, Italy, Morocco, Namibia, USA
Transparency	Transparent–translucent
Class	Carbonates

Phosgenite (*FOZ-gen-ite*) is relatively rare. Unusually for a carbonate mineral, it crystallizes in the tetragonal system. It forms as the result of oxidation of lead minerals and owes its exceptionally high lustre to its lead content. Phosgenite exhibits a yellow fluorescence under long-wave ultraviolet light. Associated minerals include anglesite, cerussite, galena and limonite. Facet quality rough is rare. The cleavages can be problematic when cutting cabochons.

TAAFFEITE

$BeMgAl_4O_8$

Taaffeite (*TARF-ite*) is a very rare gem mineral that was first discovered as a cut stone. In 1945 a light mauve stone, described as a spinel, was offered to Count Taaffe, of Dublin, Ireland, an amateur gemologist and collector. When the count examined it he detected signs of double refraction. He bought the stone and sent it to the London gem laboratory where it was found to be a beryllium magnesium aluminate. Taaffeite was the first mineral found to contain both beryllium and magnesium as essential constituents. By 1967 the source of the mineral had still not been discovered and there were still only four known taaffeite specimens, all cut stones. Tiny waterworn fragments were eventually found in the gem gravels of Sri Lanka. In 1995 important deposits of gem gravel were found at Tunduru in southern Tanzania. Diggers from the established workings at Songea rushed to the new find. During this phase the author worked with many kilos of the gem concentrate from Tunduru and found the bulk of it to be comprised of pyrandine garnets, dravite tourmaline and a wide range of spinel. Corundum, chrysoberyl and other

Refractive Indices	1.717–1.723
Birefringence	0.004
Optic Char./Sign	Uniaxial/–
Hardness	8
Specific Gravity	3.60–3.61
Crystal System	Hexagonal
Habit	Prismatic
Lustre	Vitreous
Colour Range	Lilac, pink, violet
Pleochroism	Weak
Cleavage	–
Fracture	Conchoidal
Dispersion	0.020
Sources	China, Sri Lanka, Tanzania
Transparency	Transparent–translucent
Class	Aluminates

interesting and unusual minerals accounted for less than 10 percent by weight of the total production. One of the waterworn pebbles had the appearance of an attractive light pink spinel but on checking with the polariscope it was found to be doubly refractive. The ovoid pebble weighed slightly over 1.5g. A window was quickly polished into the frosted surface and this served to confirm doubling and refractive indices of 1.718 – 1.722. This first African taaffeite was then cut yielding a beautiful lilac-pink oval brilliant of 2.12cts. There have also been finds of small grains of low-grade taaffeite in association with fluorite in China.

■ There have been a few subsequent taaffeite finds from the Tunduru region of Tanzania.

PEZZOTTAITE

$Cs(Be_2Li)Al_2Si_6O_{18}$

Refractive Indices	1.601–1.620
Birefringence	0.009–0.011
Optic Char./Sign	Uniaxial/–
Hardness	8.0–8.5
Specific Gravity	2.97–3.06
Crystal System	Trigonal
Habit	Tabular
Lustre	Vitreous
Colour Range	Pink, reddish-purple, raspberry red
Pleochroism	Pink-orange/pinkish-purple
Cleavage	Imperfect
Fracture	Conchoidal, very brittle
Dispersion	–
Sources	Afghanistan, Madagascar
Transparency	Transparent–translucent
Class	Silicates

■ Pezzottaite is a new gem variety.

Pezzottaite is a caesium-rich late-stage beryllium mineral that occurs as isolated crystals in vugs in granitic pegmatites associated with amazonite feldspar, cleavelandite, quartz and schorl. It was first discovered at the Sakavalana Mine, Ambatovita, Madagascar in 2002 and named in honour of Dr Federico Pezzotta for his work on the granitic pegmatites of that island.

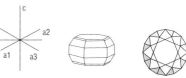

BERYL

$Be_3Al_2(SiO_3)_6$

Refractive Indices	1.560–1.599
Birefringence	0.005–0.009
Optic Char./Sign	Uniaxial/–
Hardness	7.5–8
Specific Gravity	2.65–2.85
Crystal System	Hexagonal
Habit	Prismatic
Lustre	Vitreous
Colour Range	Blue, colourless, green, orange, pink, red, yellow
Pleochroism	Definite
Cleavage	Indistinct
Fracture	Conchoidal
Dispersion	0.014
Sources	Afghanistan, Brazil, Madagascar, Malawi, Mozambique, Namibia, Nigeria, Tanzania, USA, Zambia, Zimbabwe
Transparency	Transparent–translucent
Class	Silicates

Beryl (*BER-ill*) occurs in pegmatite dykes, mica schists and hydrothermal veins often associated with feldspar, topaz, tourmaline and smoky quartz. It is an allochromatic mineral, which means that it is colourless in its purest form, the following varieties being coloured by traces of metallic elements. A tough mineral, it also has very low heat sensitivity.

Aquamarine (AKWA-mar-ine), meaning 'water of the sea', is the sea-green to sky-blue variety of beryl that owes its hues to traces of iron. Large prismatic crystals of exceptional clarity occasionally occur in pegmatitic cavities. However, the largest faceted aquamarine is thought to be a greenish, rectangular step-cut gem of 2,594 carats owned by Pala Properties International of California. Sources of aquamarine include Afghanistan, Brazil, Kenya, Madagascar, Mozambique, Namibia, Nigeria, Russia, Tanzania, USA, Zambia, and Zimbabwe.

Bixbite is a rare intense red beryl named for Maynard Bixby, a well-known mineral collector who first discovered it in the Thomas Mountain range, Utah, USA. The limited production currently reaching the market originates from the Violet Mine in the Wah Wah Mountains of Utah. Bixbite crystallizes in association with orthoclase feldspar, spessartine garnet and topaz under conditions of low pressure and high temperature along fractures or within cavities and porous areas of rhyolitic magmas at or near the surface. The red colour of bixbite is thought to be due to the substitution of manganese for aluminium in the beryl structure. A doubly terminated crystal in matrix in the J.F. Barlow Collection, Wisconsin, USA that measures 26 x 8mm (1.02 x 0.3 inches) is one of the largest and finest specimens found to date. Faceted stones seldom exceed 0.50 ct in weight.

Golden Beryl, Yellow and Greenish-yellow Beryl. The term heliodor is still widely used for beryl of a greenish-gold colour

TOP: *Etched aquamarine crystal*

LEFT: *An aquamarine necklace*

LEFT: *Red beryl from Utah*

especially in Germany and Namibia. Probably the largest cut golden beryl in existence is the flawless, slightly greenish-gold emerald cut gem of 2,054 carats on display in the Hall of Gems, Washington, D.C. Sources of golden beryl/heliodor are Brazil, Madagascar, Namibia, Russia, Sri Lanka and Zimbabwe.

Goshenite The colourless form of beryl was named for the source at Goshen, Hampshire County, Massachusetts, USA. The Lily Pond Mine at Goshen produced absolutely colourless beryl, a form that is relatively uncommon. Sources of goshenite are China, Madagascar, Mozambique, Namibia, and the USA.

Green Beryl A bright clean variety that is usually coloured by iron. It exhibits a light yellow-green to mid-green hue without the hint of blue that would result in it being termed aquamarine.

Emerald owes its intense green colour to the presence of traces of chrome. However, this definition of emerald is the subject of a long-standing dispute over the role of vanadium as a chromophore. Can an intense green beryl that is coloured by vanadium be described as emerald? 'Yes', say advocates of Pliny's definition that 'emerald is the grass green variety of beryl'. 'No', say those who support a more scientifically based definition 'emerald is the chrome rich variety of beryl'. Followers of this school of thought make use of the term vanadian beryl to describe green beryls that are coloured by vanadium.

ABOVE: *A faceted beryl colour suite*

Emerald does not occur in pegmatitic cavities an environment that is most favourable to other members of the beryl family. However, this is no surprise since chrome is an element that is lacking in granitic pegmatites. The majority of emerald deposits are formed when the mineral-rich liquid solutions associated with pegmatitic intrusions move out under pressure and permeate the schists of the surrounding contact metamorphic zone. In this environment it is possible for the beryl crystals to pick up the trace of chrome that gives them their emerald green colour. The fabulous emerald occurrence of Muzo in Colombia is an exception. In this deposit most of the emeralds are found in veins of white calcite that were hydrothermally emplaced in a huge body of limestone and black shale. Some crystals may occur in the dolomites and pockets are occasionally discovered in the black shale itself. Originally discovered and worked by the Indians Muzo was producing superb emeralds long before the Spanish conquistadors set foot in South America. High in the Andes the Chivor Mine was also discovered and worked by the Indians. Chivor emeralds often exhibit remarkable clarity but they display a somewhat lighter bluish-green that is not as highly regarded as the richly saturated green of Muzo emerald.

The dispute over nomenclature was revived in 1963 when green beryl was discovered near Salininha, Brazil. The London

College of Science and Technology found the material to be vanadian beryl but the Gemological Institute of America certified it as emerald. This fired enthusiasm for emerald prospecting in Brazil and important finds were made at Carnaiba, Socoto, Itabira, Novo Era and Santa Terezinha de Goias.

Africa was the world's earliest source of emerald. Often referred to as Cleopatra's emerald mines the occurrences at Jebel Zabara and Jebel Sikait were worked over 3,800 years ago long before that lady ruled Egypt.

In 1956 emeralds of a superb colour were discovered in the Mweza Hills of Zimbabwe. The natives believed that a mischievous spirit they called Sandawana haunted the area. They told the discoverers, Bob Contat and Corrie Oosthuizen, that Sandawana must have smiled on them. Bob and Corrie liked the idea and decided to market the stones they produced as Sandawana Emeralds. The stones held their colour down to the smallest of sizes and the name Sandawana soon became synonymous with the most intense and finest colour of emerald.

In 1963 the author took a number of emerald crystals to Europe. These had been recovered from a deposit near the Kafubu stream to the west of Luanshya, Zambia. Unlike Colombian stones the material did not 'pink' under the colour filter because it had an iron content that suppressed the chrome emission. The presence of iron was also responsible for the specific gravity and refractive indices being slightly higher than normal. Despite the fact that the material had already been analysed to establish that both chrome and vanadium were present it was rejected as being 'merely green beryl' in both London and Idar Oberstein. Finally almost a year later the stones were accepted as emeralds. Numerous new finds were made and the Kafubu Emerald Fields became an important source of fine emeralds and a significant economic factor in Zambia.

Emerald sources: Afghanistan, Australia, Austria, Brazil, Bulgaria, Canada, Colombia, Egypt, India, Madagascar, Mozambique, Nigeria, Norway, Pakistan, Russia, South Africa, Tanzania, USA, Zambia, Zimbabwe.

■ The sale of an emerald (a stone dedicated to Venus) in Babylon is the earliest recorded gem sale.

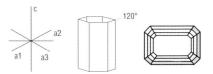

LEFT: *A green beryl crystal*

PAINITE

$CaZrBAl_9O_{18}$

Painite (*PAIN-ite*). In 1951 a 1.7 gram (0.06 oz) deep red hexagonal crystal was found in gem gravels near Mogok, Myanmar. Analysis revealed that traces of chromium, vanadium and iron influenced its colour. A second, somewhat larger, dark red crystal was later found in the same area. It is now displayed in the British Museum of Natural History. Painite was recognized as the rarest gem material on Earth, and for decades these were the only two known specimens.

Refractive Indices	1.787–1.816
Birefringence	0.029
Optic Char./Sign	Uniaxial/–
Hardness	7.5
Specific Gravity	4.01–4.03
Crystal System	Hexagonal
Habit	Tabular
Lustre	Vitreous
Colour Range	Pink, orange-red, deep red, brown
Pleochroism	Orange-red/light purple
Cleavage	–
Fracture	Conchoidal
Dispersion	–
Sources	Myanmar
Transparency	Transparent
Class	Aluminates

■ Painite is extremely rare but some recent finds have been made in Myanmar.

TOP: *Painite crystals*
BELOW: *Faceted painite*

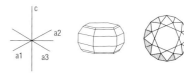

The source of the original crystals is said to be the Sinhalite Mine, a small working near the village of Ohngaing and a short distance north-northwest of Mogok. New discoveries have revealed an association between painite and ruby. Numerous very small rubies are actually attached to the specimen painite #11. The painite is stated to occur in the weathered contact zone between leucogranite and marble.

Other recent finds include two deposits in the Mogok area and a completely new locality at Namya in northern Myanmar. The material from the latter source is generally lighter in tone, red to pink in colour and distinctly dichroic. The strongest reds are seen when looking down the 'C' axis. Painite fluoresces a weak red under long-wave and a moderate red under short-wave ultraviolet light.

The total production of crystals and fragments now numbers in the thousands. Several hundred stones have been faceted but euhedral crystals and pieces of quality facet rough are still very rare.

JEREMEJEVITE

$Al_6(BO_3)_5(F,OH)_3$

Jeremejevite (*YE-re-me-jev-ite*) is a rare gem mineral that crystallizes out of hydrothermal solutions in vugs in granitic pegmatites in association with albite, gypsum, quartz and tourmaline. It forms elongated tapering crystals usually zoned in light hues. Deeper cornflower blue crystals are extremely rare. Initially it was mistaken for beryl and jeremejevite was named in honour of P.V. Eremeev (Jeremejev in German) the Russian

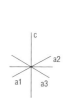

mineralogist and crystallographer who first recognized the species. Gem rough recovered from the deposit on the Namibian coastline north of Swakopmund has produced attractive colourless, blue and yellowish faceted stones that seldom exceed one carat in weight.

Refractive Indices	1.644–1.653
Birefringence	0.013
Optic Char./Sign	Uniaxial/–
Hardness	7–7.5
Specific Gravity	3.27–3.29
Crystal System	Hexagonal
Habit	Long prismatic
Lustre	Vitreous
Colour Range	Colourless, brown, blue, purple, light yellow
Pleochroism	Distinct
Cleavage	Nil
Fracture	Conchoidal
Dispersion	Distinct
Sources	Germany, Madagascar, Namibia, Russia
Transparency	Transparent
Class	Borates

SUGILITE

$KNa_2Li_3(Fe,Mn,Al)_2Si_{12}O_{30}$

Refractive Indices	1.577–1.611
Birefringence	0.002–0.004
Optic Char./Sign	Uniaxial/–
Hardness	6–6.5
Specific Gravity	2.74
Crystal System	Hexagonal
Habit	Massive
Lustre	Vitreous, waxy
Colour Range	Brown, pink, purple, reddish, colourless, light brownish-yellow, violet
Pleochroism	–
Cleavage	Poor
Fracture	Subconchoidal
Dispersion	–
Sources	Australia, Canada, Italy, Japan, South Africa, Tajikstan
Transparency	Translucent–opaque
Class	Silicates

■ Sugilite is also known as Wesselite.

LEFT: *Rough and polished sugilite*

Sugilite (*SUG-il-ite*) was named in honour of Ken-ichi Sugi, the petrologist who first discovered it on Iwagi Island, Shikoku, Japan in 1944. Associated minerals include aegirine, pectolite, poudretteite and polylithionite. The mineral remained somewhat obscure until the discovery of compact seams of intense purple massive sugilite in the Wessels Manganese Mine near Hotazel, South Africa. In 2002 a second source of gem-grade sugilite was discovered in the nearby N'Chwaning II manganese mine. With its superb colour and good working properties, this material enjoys a strong demand for manufacture into cabochons, beads, and ornamental objects. Stones faceted from the very limited production of semi-transparent rough command relatively high prices. Crystal specimens are very rare.

CANCRINITE

$Na_7CaAl_6Si_6O_{24}(CO_3)_2$

Cancrinite (*CAN-crin-ite*) is found in plutonic and other intrusive igneous rocks. It was named after the Russian Count Georg Cancrin (1774–1845). This complex mineral is one of the rarer members of the feldspathoid group. Associated with nephelite, quartz and sodalite, cancrinite typically occurs in a massive form but it has been found as hexagonal crystals with a perfect prismatic cleavage. Cabochons that are sold as cancrinite usually prove to be quartz with cancrinite inclusions; however, a fibrous variety of semi-opaque yellow cancrinite found at Bancroft and at French River, Canada, has been cut into cabochons and beads.

Refractive Indices	1.491–1.524
Birefringence	0.012–0.025
Optic Char./Sign	Uniaxial/–
Hardness	5 -6
Specific Gravity	2.42–2.50
Crystal System	Hexagonal
Habit	Massive
Lustre	Vitreous–pearly
Colour Range	Blue, green, orange, pink, reddish, white, yellow
Pleochroism	–
Cleavage	Perfect prismatic
Fracture	Conchoidal
Dispersion	–
Sources	Canada, Finland, India, Norway, Russia, USA
Transparency	Transparent–translucent
Class	Silicates

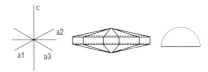

AFGHANITE

$(Na,Ca,K)^8(Si,Al)_{12}O_{24}(SO_4,Cl,CO_3)_3(H_2O)$

Refractive Indices	1.523–1.529
Birefringence	0.006
Optic Char./Sign	Uniaxial/+
Hardness	5.5–6
Specific Gravity	2.55–2.65
Crystal System	Hexagonal
Habit	Barrel, massive
Lustre	Vitreous
Colour Range	Colourless, blue
Pleochroism	–
Cleavage	Perfect
Fracture	Conchoidal
Dispersion	–
Sources	Afghanistan (Sar-e-Sang, Badakhshan), Germany, Italy
Transparency	Transparent–translucent
Class	Silicates

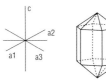

Afghanite (*AF-gan-ite*) is named for the source. It forms fine hexagonal sapphire-blue crystals and is associated with the sodalite group of minerals. It has the potential to produce attractive gems but to date gem rough appears to be virtually unobtainable and good crystal specimens are rare.

MILARITE

$K_2O.4CaO.4BeO.Al_2O_3.24SiO_2.H_2O$

Milarite (mill-ARE-ite) is a complex beryllium aluminium silicate that occurs in granitic pegmatites. The small pieces of facet rough that have been cut to date have all originated from a single African source.

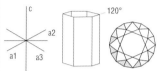

Refractive Indices	1.529–1.532
Birefringence	0.003
Optic Char./Sign	Uniaxial/–
Hardness	5.5–6
Specific Gravity	2.55–2.61
Crystal System	Hexagonal
Habit	Prismatic
Lustre	Vitreous
Colour Range	Colourless, pale-green, yellow
Pleochroism	–
Cleavage	Imperfect
Fracture	Conchoidal to uneven, brittle
Dispersion	–
Sources	Africa, Brazil, Namibia, Switzerland, USA
Transparency	Transparent–translucent
Class	Silicates

■ Milarite is a rare, yellow, barrel-shaped beryllium silicate.

NEPHELINE

$(Na,K)AlSiO_4$

Refractive Indices	1.528–1.549
Birefringence	0.005
Optic Char./Sign	Uniaxial/–
Hardness	5.5–6
Specific Gravity	2.55–2.67
Crystal System	Hexagonal
Habit	Massive, hexagonal
Lustre	Vitreous–greasy
Colour Range	Blue, brown, green, grey, red, off-white
Pleochroism	–
Cleavage	Imperfect
Fracture	Sub-conchoidal, brittle
Dispersion	–
Sources	Canada, Germany, Italy, Russia, USA
Transparency	Transparent–semi-opaque
Class	Silicates

■ Elaeolite, a massive green variety of Nepheline, is cut and stones may be chatoyant.

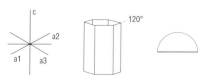

Nepheline (*NEFF-he-lean*) is a rock-forming mineral generally associated with albite, apatite, biotite, calcite, cancrinite and sodalite. Its name, derived from the Greek word for 'cloud', is an allusion to the 'milky' translucency of most specimens. Occasionally, however, colourless material is found that is sufficiently transparent to be faceted.

APATITE

$Ca_5(F,Cl)(PO_4)_3$

Refractive Indices	1.63–1.65
Birefringence	0.004
Optic Char./Sign	Uniaxial/–
Hardness	5
Specific Gravity	3.15–3.22
Crystal System	Hexagonal
Habit	Prismatic
Lustre	Vitreous–
Colour Range	Blue, colourless, green, pink, violet, yellow
Pleochroism	Green: weak Blue: strong
Cleavage	Poor (x 2)
Fracture	Conchoidal
Dispersion	0.016
Sources	Afghanistan, Brazil, Madagascar, Mexico, Myanmar, Sri Lanka, USA
Transparency	Transparent–translucent
Class	Phosphates

■ The green variety of Apatite is termed 'asparagus stone'.

The name apatite (*APA-tite*) is derived from the Greek meaning 'I am misleading', probably a reference to the mineral's resemblance to beryl. Crystals of gem quality occur in pegmatites or hydrothermal veins. Most gem material belongs to the sub-variety fluorapatite. Another sub-variety that may be faceted is termed manganapatite since some of the calcium has been replaced by manganese. This material has a deeper blue-green colour and higher refractive indices. Afghanistan produces superb apatite crystal specimens. Violet crystals are found in Maine, USA. Deep sapphire-blue facet rough occurs in the Phalaborwa Mine, South Africa. Large bottle-green facet rough originates from Zimbabwe. Madagascar produces gem rough in a wide range of hues including electric blue and neon green. The material has an absorption spectra of Å5855, Å5772, Å5742 (yellow-green) and Å5120, Å5070, Å4910 (blue), and fluoresces LW Violet (R) Yellow (O) Orange (O) White (O) SW/LW Green (O). The material is relatively soft, brittle and highly heat sensitive. It may be somewhat difficult to cut but the wide variety of colour it exhibits makes a range of faceted apatites an interesting addition to any collection. Translucent material with parallel acicular inclusions may be cut into cabochons that show a distinct cat's-eye effect.

TOP: *Apatite suite*
BOTTOM LEFT: *Terminated apatite crystal*
BELOW: *Apatite cat's-eye*

BASTNASITE

$(Ce,La,Y)CO_3F$

Refractive Indices	1.717 – 1.818
Birefringence	0.101
Optic Character	Uniaxial +
Dispersion	Nil
Hardness	4–4.5
Specific Gravity	4.7–5
Crystal System	Hexagonal
Habit	Short prisms, Tabular rounded
Lustre	Vitreous, pearly
Colour Range	brown, grey, tan, pink, white, yellow
Pleochroism	Weak
Cleavage	Distinct – basal, Poor – prismatic
Fracture	Uneven
Sources	Balkans, Canada, Greece, Hungary, Malawi, Norway, Sweden, Turkey, USA
Transparency	Translucent to opaque
Class	Carbonates

Bastnasite was named after its type locality, the Bastnas Mine, Riddarhyttan, Sweden. Despite the fact that it is one of the more widespread rare earth carbonates bastnasite remains a scarce mineral and it has yet to be discovered in significant concentrations. It is found in bauxite deposits, carbonatites and rarely in unusual granites. There have also been reports of hydrothermal sources. Associated minerals include albite, analcime, apatite, barite, brookite, calcite, dolomite, fluorite, hematite, monazite, parisite, quartz, rhodochrosite, rutile, serandite, siderite, zircon. Usually encountered as mineral specimens, gem rough and cut stones are seldom seen.

■ Bastnasite is an important ore of cerium and other rare earth metals.

ZINCITE

$(Zn,Mn)O$

Zincite (*ZINK-ite*), a red oxide of zinc, occurs in metamor-phosed weathered ore deposits. Natural crystals are rare and it usually appears in a massive form, as subhedral granules or as finely dissemi-nated particles. The zincite crystals that often occur as a furnace product during smelt-ing are termed 'serendipitous crystals'. Naturally occurring transparent crystals and cleav-age fragments are rare. They may be cut as deep-red faceted gems. Sub-translucent to opaque material is cut as cabochons.

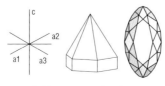

Refractive Indices	2.013–2.029
Birefringence	0.016
Optic Char./Sign	Uniaxial/+
Hardness	4–4.5
Specific Gravity	5.43–5.7
Crystal System	Hexagonal
Habit	Granular
Lustre	Sub-adamantine
Colour Range	Orange, red, yellow
Pleochroism	Strong
Cleavage	Perfect (x1)
Fracture	Sub-conchoidal
Dispersion	Low
Sources	Australia, Italy, Poland, Spain, USA
Transparency	Translucent
Class	Oxides

BREITHAUPTITE

NiSb

Refractive Indices	–
Birefringence	–
Optic Char./Sign	–
Hardness	3.5–4.0
Specific Gravity	7.54–8.23
Crystal System	Hexagonal
Habit	Massive reniform
Lustre	Metallic
Colour Range	Copper-red, light brownish-red
Pleochroism	Nil
Cleavage	Nil
Fracture	Uneven
Dispersion	Nil
Sources	Argentina, Australia, Austria, Canada, France, Germany, Sardinia, Canada
Transparency	Opaque
Class	Sulphides

Breithauptite (*BREE-thowp-tite*) occurs in hydrothermal calcite veins in association with cobalt, nickel and silver. It is sometimes cut as cabochons with a strong colour and high lustre.

MIMETITE

$Pb_5(AsO_4)_3Cl$

Mimetite (*MIM-eh-tite*) is so named because it closely resembles or 'mimes' pyromorphite. It is a somewhat uncommon mineral that is found in altered lead deposits. Associated minerals are wulfenite, limonite, calcite, barite and galena. It is closely related to vanadinite and pyromorphite and these three minerals form an unusual chemical series in which the substitutions take place in the basic chemical units or anions, rather than, as is usually the case, in the cations. Mimetite the arsenate (AsO4) is generally yellow, pyromorphite (PO4) the phosphate green, and vanadinite (VO4) the vanadate red. Bright orange cabochons have been cut from material originating from Mapimi, Mexico. Transparent but somewhat included facet rough from Tsumeb, Namibia, has been faceted into gems over 1.00 ct in weight.

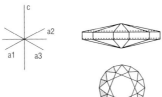

Refractive Indices	2.120–2.144
Birefringence	0.015
Optic Char./Sign	Uniaxial/–
Hardness	3.5–4
Specific Gravity	7.0–7.25
Crystal System	Hexagonal
Habit	Prismatic, massive, botryoidal, globular, reniform
Lustre	Adamantine–resinous
Colour Range	Colourless, brown, grey, green, orange, yellow, white
Pleochroism	–
Cleavage	Imperfect
Fracture	Sub-conchoidal
Dispersion	–
Sources	Australia, Bolivia, France, Germany, Morocco, Mexico (Mapimi), Namibia (Tsumeb), USA (Arizona)
Transparency	Transparent–translucent
Class	Phosphates

PYROMORPHITE

$Pb_5(PO_4)_3Cl$

Refractive Indices	2.042–2.059
Birefringence	0.010
Optic Char./Sign	Uniaxial–
Hardness	3.5–4
Specific Gravity	6.5–7.1
Crystal System	Hexagonal
Habit	Prismatic, pyramidial, tabular
Lustre	Vitreous–resinous
Colour Range	Brown, green, orange, yellow, colourless, grey, white
Pleochroism	–
Cleavage	Imperfect
Fracture	Sub-conchoidal, brittle
Dispersion	–
Sources	Australia, Bulgaria, Canada, China, Czech Republic, England, France, Germany, Kazakhstan, Mexico, S. Africa, Spain, USA, Zambia
Transparency	Transparent–translucent
Class	Phosphates

Pyromorphite (*PIE-roh-morph-ite*) is a mineral of secondary origin. It frequently occurs in lead ore-bodies but seldom in significant quantity. Associated minerals include cerussite, galena, limonite and other secondary lead deposit minerals. It is very unusual as a cut stone.

■ Pyromorphite's name comes from the Greek *pyr* (fire) and *morph* (form).

COVELLITE

CuS

Covellite (*COVE-ell-ite*) is a striking mineral with its vivid iridescent blues. It is found in association with other copper sulphides such as bornite, chalcocite and chalcopyrite and with the oxide cuprite in copper ore-bodies. It often forms as an intergrowth with chalcocite. Massive material can be cut into brilliant blue cabochons.

Refractive Indices	1.45–2.62
Birefringence	1.17
Optic Char./Sign	Uniaxial
Hardness	1.5–2
Specific Gravity	4.6–4.76
Crystal System	Hexagonal
Habit	Tabular, massive, foliated
Lustre	Metallic
Colour Range	Indigo–midnight blue
Pleochroism	–
Cleavage	Perfect
Fracture	Uneven, brittle
Dispersion	–
Sources	Austria, Canada, Chile, Germany, Italy, Serbia, USA, Zambia
Transparency	Opaque
Class	Sulphides

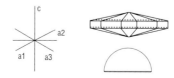

MOISSANITE

SiC

Moissanite (*MWA-san-ite*) was created in the laboratory 12 years before it was discovered in nature. The inventor, Eugene G. Acheson, patented his process for the synthesis of silicon carbide in 1893 giving his product the trade name Carborundum.

In 1905, while working on fragments of meteoric iron at Diablo Canyon in Arizona, Nobel laureate Dr. Ferdinand H. Moissan discovered small green platelets of silicon carbide: the mineral was subsequently named in his honour.

Natural moissanite is very rare, its occurrence being limited to metallic meteorites and minute traces in kimberlites. It is classed as a native element despite being a chemical compound! That is because its bonding resembles that of diamond and it does not conform to any other mineral class. It has not been found in sufficient size to facet. (*See* Chapter 7, synthetic gems).

Refractive Indices	2.65–2.69
Birefringence	0.040
Optic Char./Sign	Uniaxial
Hardness	9.25
Specific Gravity	3.1–3.3
Crystal System	Trigonal
Habit	Tabular
Lustre	Adamantine
Colour Range	Green, near colourless
Pleochroism	Nil
Cleavage	Nil
Fracture	Nil
Dispersion	0.104
Sources	USA (Canyon Diablo, Arizona)
Transparency	Transparent–translucent
Class	Native elements

■ Moissanite is a 'space age' mineral that was first discovered in a meteorite.

CORUNDUM

Al$_2$O$_3$

Corundum (*cor-UN-dum*) is usually found in granular limestone, gneiss, mica or chlorite schists. Associated minerals include diaspore, garnet, kyanite, spinel and tourmaline. Corundum also occurs as a primary constituent of aluminous igneous rocks. It is the second hardest natural mineral, a fact that can be attributed

Refractive Indices	1.759–1.779
Birefringence	0.008–0.009
Optic Char./Sign	Uniaxial/–
Hardness	9
Specific Gravity	3.96–4.01
Crystal System	Trigonal
Habit	Tabular, barrel-shaped
Lustre	Vitreous–adamantine
Colour Range	Red, black, blue, brown, colourless, colour-change, green, pink, violet, yellow
Pleochroism	Strong
Cleavage	Nil
Fracture	Conchoidal
Dispersion	0.018
Sources	Afghanistan, Australia, Brazil, Cambodia, India, Kashmir, Kenya, Madagascar, Malawi, Mozambique, Myanmar, Nigeria, Tanzania, Thailand, USA, Vietnam
Transparency	Transparent–opaque
Class	Oxides

in part to the strong oxygen-aluminium bonds. These short bonds pull the oxygen and aluminium atoms close together, making corundum crystals quite dense for a mineral composed of two comparatively light elements. Most corundum is of industrial grade. Blue-grey in colour and virtually opaque, the mineral is crushed to various grit sizes and used as an abrasive.

Tough, hard and heavy, transparent corundum inevitably ends up in placer deposits and nearly all gem corundum is recovered from gem gravels. The rare and sought-after corundum varieties, ruby and sapphire, are among the most highly prized of gems.

Ruby is the name given to transparent to translucent intense red corundum. Gem corundum in any other colour or shade of the spectrum is sapphire. In its purest form corundum would be transparent and colourless but this rarely happens in nature. Natural 'white' sapphire usually exhibits faint hints of grey, blue, green or yellow when compared with a colourless synthetic sapphire.

Ruby owes its superb hue to traces of chromium. The finest stones originate from Myanmar: these are the famous 'Burmese' rubies of Mogok in upper Burma. Occasionally the mines of the Taita-Taveta region of southern Kenya will produce rubies of a similar hue. The ruby mined in Thailand tends to have purplish or brownish tones but modern heat treatment effectively eliminates these unfavourable hues. Thailand is a major centre for the processing and marketing of corundum gems from many sources. Gem ruby of a good colour is also produced in neighbouring Cambodia and Vietnam. Low-grade, virtually opaque ruby that exhibits a weak star-effect is mined in Mysore, India. Ruby is also mined in Tanzania, Malawi and Madagascar.

Sapphire gets its rich blue hue from the presence of combined traces of titanium and iron. The prime colour is the fabled cornflower blue of sapphires from Kashmir. They originate from a small valley at a height of 4572 m (15,000 feet) in the northwest Himalayas that lies under deep snow for most of the year. The corundum occurs in a pegmatite vein associated with euclase, garnet, kyanite and tourmaline. During the brief period the deposit is accessible the production is usually limited to recovering loose sapphires from pockets of kaolin. Very fine blue sapphire is also produced from Myanmar. Sri Lanka produces a wide range of sapphire: exceptional blues, gentle pinks and lively yellows and produces star stones that are often of the highest quality. There is a small production of attractive stones, especially lively blues, from Montana USA. Australian deposits have produced considerable quantities of sapphire. The best golden yellows and greens are usually of Australian origin. Some good blues have come from Australia, especially after heat-treatment.

ABOVE: *A ruby from Thailand*

■ Rubies are also called 'RatnaRaj' a name that means 'King of Gems'.

ABOVE: *A blue sapphire from Sri Lanka*

The blue sapphire from Anakie, Queensland tends to be somewhat inky and the lighter blues from Invarell, New South Wales can be a little steely. Very fine blue sapphire is originating from Madagascar. African sources are also producing some excellent sapphire. A deposit in southwest Kenya produces a light blue that cuts into lively calibrated stones. There is still some production from Malawi, particularly in the region of Chimwadzulu. The alluvial gravels of the Umba valley, Songea and Tunduru in Tanzania are producing a wonderful colour range of sapphires, including some that have the rare padparadschah orange-pink colour and others that exhibit the phenomenon of colour-change.

LEFT: *A golden-yellow sapphire*
ABOVE: *A blue sapphire ring*
BELOW LEFT: *A pink-purple sapphire*

■ *Padparadschah* – Lotus Blossom in Sanskrit – is a rare orange-pink variety of sapphire.

PHENAKITE

Be_2SiO_4

Phenakite (*FEN-ah-kite*). The name, derived from a Greek word for 'deceiver', alludes to the mineral's deceptive resemblance to quartz. A rare beryllium mineral, it is found in pegmatitic pockets in association with apatite, beryl, cassiterite, chrysoberyl, feldspars, quartz and topaz. Phenakite is one of the few silicate minerals to crystallize in the trigonal system. Crystals of phenakite may be somewhat lacking in colour and dispersion but with their hardness, lack of distinct cleavage, rarity and high degree of lucidity they can make lively interesting gemstones.

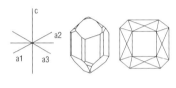

Refractive Indices	1.654–1.670
Birefringence	0.015
Optic Char./Sign	Uniaxial/+
Hardness	7.5–8
Specific Gravity	2.9–3.0
Crystal System	Trigonal
Habit	Prismatic, rhombohedral
Lustre	Vitreous
Colour Range	Colourless, white, tints of brown, pink or yellow, bluish, pinkish-red
Pleochroism	–
Cleavage	Distinct
Fracture	Brittle
Dispersion	0.015
Sources	Brazil, Namibia, Norway, Poland, Russia, USA, Zimbabwe
Transparency	Transparent–translucent
Class	Silicates

■ The faceted oval phenakite (569ct) exhibited in the Smithsonian, Washington, USA, was cut from the largest rough found to date: a pebble that had a mass of 1,470ct.

SIMPSONITE

$Al_4(TaNb)_3O_{13}(OH)$

Simpsonite (*SIMP-son-ite*) is a very rare mineral named after E.S. Simpson (1875-1939), government mineralogist of Western Australia, where it was first discovered in 1938 in the Tabba Tabba pegmatite. Colourful, bright and durable it has the potential to become a very popular gemstone if it were not for a lack of facet rough.

Refractive Indices	2.025–2.045
Birefringence	0.020
Optic Char./Sign	Uniaxial/–
Hardness	7–7.5
Specific Gravity	6.68–6.82
Crystal System	Trigonal
Habit	Tabular, short prismatic
Lustre	Adamantine
Colour Range	Brown, orange, yellow, white
Pleochroism	Nil
Cleavage	Indistinct
Fracture	Brittle
Dispersion	Nil
Sources	Australia, Brazil, Canada, Russia, Zaire Zimbabwe
Transparency	Transparent–translucent
Class	Tantalates

■ Alto de Gis, Rio Grande do Norte, is said to be the sole source of gem simpsonite in Brazil.

TOURMALINE

$Na(Li,Al)_3Al_6Si_6O_{18}(BO_3)_3(OH)_4$

Tourmaline (*TOUR-mah-leen*) occurs in granitic pegmatites, granites, gneiss and contact metamorphic zones. It occurs in the form of inclusions in beryl, feldspar, quartz and zircon. It is found in association with albite, apatite, beryl, cassiterite, feldspar, garnet, lepidolite, scapolite, spodumene and topaz. The chemical composition and physical properties of tourmaline vary to some extent with colour. The pink and red varieties from lithium-rich pegmatites have a lower density, usually around 3.03, than the dark green and blue varieties that generally average about 3.10. Varietal names that are still widely used include achroite (colourless), dravite (brown), indicolite (blue), liddicoatite (polychromatic), rubellite (red), siberite (violet), schorl (black), tsilaisite (yellow/brown) and verdelite (green). Brazil is the source of Paraiba tourmaline. This material is usually heat-treated to produce the famous electric blue and fluorescent green hues. Tourmaline frequently exhibits two or more colours in a single crystal. In bi-colour or parti-colour tourmalines the crystal changes colour along its length. Crystals may also exhibit concentric zones of colour when viewed parallel to their 'C' axis. Crystals with a red centre, a white or colourless inner and a green outer are called watermelon tourmaline. Liddicoatite, named in honour of Richard Liddicoat the renowned American gemologist, is a fascinating polychromatic variety of calcium-rich lithium tourmaline discovered in Madagascar. An emerald-green variety of tourmaline that occurs in Tanzania is marketed as chrome tourmaline regardless of the fact that in a large proportion of the specimens tested the dominant chromophore has proved to be vanadium. Some of these vanadian tourmalines exhibit a marked colour change, appearing deep emerald-green in daylight and intense red under incandescent light. Tourmaline exhibits pyro-electricity (it acquires an electric charge when heated) and piezo-electricity (it builds up an electric charge when it is rubbed). Tourmaline can be cut as attractive cat's-eye cabochons when it contains oriented fine needle-like inclusions or hollow tubes.

Refractive Indices	1.622- 1.643
Birefringence	0.018 –0.020
Optic Char./Sign	Uniaxial/–
Hardness	7–7.5
Specific Gravity	2.98–3.20
Crystal System	Trigonal
Habit	Longitudinal striae, hemimorphic
Lustre	Vitreous
Colour Range	Blue, brown, colourless, green, pink, red, violet, yellow, black
Pleochroism	Strongly dichroic
Cleavage	Nil
Fracture	Sub-conchoidal
Dispersion	0.017
Sources	Afghanistan, Australia, Brazil, Democratic Republic of Congo, Italy, Kenya, Madagascar, Mozambique, Myanmar, Namibia, Nigeria, Pakistan, Russia, Sri Lanka, Tanzania, USA, Zambia, Zimbabwe
Transparency	Transparent–opaque
Class	Silicates

TOP LEFT: *Tourmaline on feldspar*
TOP RIGHT: *Pink tourmaline and lepidolite crystals*
ABOVE: *Green tourmaline from Zambia*

■ Paraiba tourmaline is characterized by the presence of a trace of copper in its composition.

QUARTZ

SiO_2

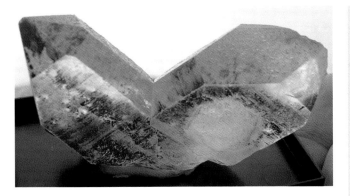

Refractive Indices	1.543–1.554
Birefringence	0.009
Optic Char./Sign	Uniaxial/+
Hardness	7
Specific Gravity	2.65–2.66
Crystal System	Trigonal
Habit	Prismatic
Lustre	Vitreous
Colour Range	Brown, black, colourless, green, pink, violet, white, yellow, orange, purple
Pleochroism	Weakly dichroic
Cleavage	Nil
Fracture	Conchoidal
Dispersion	0.013
Sources	Australia, Brazil, Democratic Republic of Congo, India, Madagascar, Malawi, Mexico, Namibia, Russia, Uruguay, USA, Zaire, Zambia, Zimbabwe
Transparency	Transparent–translucent
Class	Oxides

■ A gypsy's crystal ball should ideally be made of clear rock crystal.

Quartz (*KWOR-tz*) is the most widespread of minerals occurring in igneous, sedimentary and metamorphic environments. The source list to the right is limited to a cross-section of those countries that currently produce significant amounts of gem quartz. Crystals of colourless quartz or rock crystal are abundant and almost inevitably the first specimens encountered by the tyro collector. Fine crystal specimens of rose quartz are so rare that they rate among the most treasured possessions of a handful of fortunate collectors. The diversity of this mineral is such that entire collections are devoted to its many sub-varieties. Small doubly terminated quartz crystals are often referred to by such misleading names as 'desert diamonds' or 'herkimer diamonds'. When colourless quartz is full of fine fractures, the thin films of air may interfere with the passage of light producing a show of rainbow colours. This type of material is known as rainbow quartz. Quartz crystallizing from hydrothermal solutions often encloses crystals of minerals such as beryl, rutile and tourmaline that form at higher temperatures. Clear quartz containing long slender crystals of golden rutile is called rutilated quartz or more poetically 'Venus hair stone' or 'Flèches d'amour' ('arrows of love'). Quartz containing green actinolite fibres is referred to as 'Thetis hair stone'. When quartz is so densely packed with actinolite that it appears solid green, it is known as prase. Dumortierite quartz exhibits a strong blue colour because it is full of inclusions of dumortierite. Quartz crystals with internal cavities containing water and air bubbles are very collectible and are known as en-hydros. White or 'milky' quartz is packed with innumerable minute cavities containing water or liquid carbon dioxide. Cabochons are sometimes cut from white quartz veins especially if they carry visible traces of gold. More than 40 different minerals are reported to have occurred as quartz inclusions.

Quartz crystals may exhibit a brown colouring that is frequently distributed in alternating light and dark parallel bands or zones that follow the crystal outline. If the material is somewhat smoky in hue it is termed smoky quartz and if it is so dark that it is virtually black it is called morion. Moderate heat usually induces a lightening of the smoky colour in quartz. Material from some sources, for example the southern Democratic Republic of Congo, converts to an attractive golden citrine hue when heated. Citrine, the golden-yellow variety of quartz, is relatively scarce in nature and the majority of commercial material is obtained by the heat treatment of amethyst or smoky quartz.

Crystals of **amethyst**, the purple to violet variety of quartz, are encountered in vugs located in hydrothermal quartz veins. Alternatively, amethyst crystals are often found lining the central cavities of the agate geodes often associated with basalt flows. The name is believed to be derived from the Greek word Amethustos, which can be translated as 'not drunken' (see bullet point). Many fine examples of amethyst are mounted in the rings of bishops. In the 19th century Russian production set the hallmark for superb amethyst and even today fine violet material with distinct underlying port-wine tones may be described as Siberian amethyst. Brazil and Zambia are currently the major producers of gem-quality amethyst.

Rose quartz is generally filled with very fine inclusions. The best material, including the rare rose quartz crystal specimens, comes from the Jequitinhona Valley, Brazil. Material from Madagascar may produce a fine six-rayed asterism if the stones are correctly oriented and cut as high-domed cabochons. Massive material, suitable for beads, spheres and ornamental work, is mined in Namibia and the central provinces of India.

At its best, **quartz cat's-eye** may bear a fair resemblance to precious chrysoberyl cat's-eye. The distinct streak of light or 'eye' that is evident in this material is the product of numerous parallel asbestos fibres. The finest honey-coloured or brownish material is found in the gem gravels of Sri Lanka.

Tiger's-eye is a quartz pseudomorph after the blue asbestos known as crocidolite. The principal source of this material is in Griqualand West, South Africa, and the pervasive hydrous iron oxide or limonite of this region is responsible for its typical attractive golden brown colour. The material exhibits a fascinating and constantly shifting light effect since the alternating silky gold and brown bands keep reversing their appearance with the slightest change in position of the light source or of the stone. In a modified form of this material known as tiger iron, swathes and bands of silvery-black hematite have intruded that break up and diversify the patterns. Variegated blue and gold

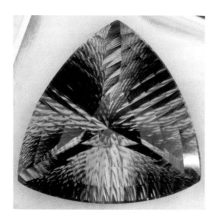

ABOVE: *A fancy cut amethyst*

■ Legend tells that amethyst acquired its magnificent colour when a remorseful Bacchus poured a libation of wine over colourless quartz.

■ Citrine quartz gained popularity as the poor-man's topaz.

■ Rose quartz crystals are much rarer than diamonds.

BELOW: *An amethyst and aquamarine ring*

material, sometimes termed 'zebra' is the result of incomplete limonite staining. When the material is plain blue it is called hawk's-eye; the very scarce plain green material is known as falcon's-eye. Heating of the gold-coloured material results in the limonite being converted to hematite thus producing the red-coloured material that is marketed as bull's-eye. An intriguing brecciated form of tiger's-eye occurs

near Outjo in Namibia. This very attractive and relatively scarce material has been termed riebeckite. In Southern Africa it is always referred to as Pietersite after the Windhoek gem dealer Sid Pieters who first introduced it to the market.

Quartzite is a metamorphic rock that has formed either through the bonding of small grains of quartz through heat and pressure or at lower temperatures and pressures through gradual silica cementation. In green aventurine quartz, the included crystals of platy, chrome-rich fuchsite mica are responsible for its colour and also for the reddish residual glow seen under the Chelsea filter. There are large deposits in Zimbabwe where it is quarried for use as 'emerald quartzite' paving. India is an important producer and the principal source of aventurine quartz cabochons and beads.

'Swazi green' quartzite is a compact, very fine-grained material that is found in an attractive range of medium to intense greens. It can be used for cabochons and spheres but a large proportion of the production is tumbled and used in the manufacture of ornamental gemstone trees.

Eosite is a close-grained bluish-white quartzite with veins and splotches of brownish-red. It carries inclusions of small cubic pyrites crystals. It is carved into small ornaments for sale in Idar-Oberstein, Germany.

Buddstone is an attractive green and white metamorphosed chert that owes its colour to inclusions of chlorite, epidote and fuchsite. It exhibits complex swirling patterns, the result of extensive folding and distortion. The material takes a good finish, making interesting cabochons, beads, eggs and other ornamental objects. It became known as buddstone because it was originally discovered by Billy Budd in the Barberton district of South Africa.

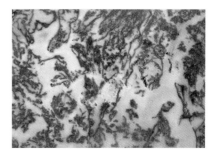

CHALCEDONY

SiO$_2$

Technically, the name chalcedony (*kal-SID-oh-nee*) may be applied to any variety of crypto-crystalline quartz. In practice, unless qualified, the term refers to translucent, self-coloured, dove-grey material.

Blue chalcedony occurs in pure ethereal blues or hues modified by degrees of lilac or grey. Lapidaries and jewellery designers alike enjoy its integrity as a working medium and its subtle colouring. Material from the deposit at Otjoruharui, in northern Namibia is known as 'African Blue': it ranges from a light blue-grey to a superb pure blue. There are smaller deposits in California and Nevada but Oregon produces the most sought-after American blue chalcedony.

Chrysocolla chalcedony. Also known as 'gem silica' in the USA, this scarce, blue-green to blue variety occurs in the oxidized zone of copper ore-bodies in Arizona, USA; the 'Copperbelt' of Central Africa; and Namibia. Its durability and superb colour make it one of the most sought-after and costly forms of chalcedony.

Chrysoprase is an attractive apple-green form of chalcedony that is coloured by nickel. One of the most prized forms of chalcedony, significant sources of this material include Australia, Brazil, Russia, Tanzania and the USA.

Carnelian, the warm reddish-orange variety of chalcedony, owes its hue to traces of iron. It is frequently heat-treated to enrich its reddish tones. It also occurs with bands of white in a layered form. India, Namibia, South Africa and Zimbabwe are significant sources. It is carved into objets d'art or engraved as intaglios or cameos in both its self-coloured and layered forms.

M'torolite. Chrome is responsible for the deep emerald green hue of this unusual chalcedony. To date it has been found only in the hills of the mineral-rich Great Dyke formation of Zimbabwe above the chrome-mining town of M'toroshanga.

Onyx was the name traditionally given to chalcedony that exhibited parallel black-and-white layers. In modern usage it is most frequently applied to the plain black cabochon cut stones that are popular for men's rings or cuff links.

Sard is a plain brownish-red material. When parallel bands of white contrast with the brownish-red body colour it is referred to as sardonyx. Layered stones such as the traditional onyx and sardonyx are an ideal medium for the art of cameo, intaglio and relief carving.

Refractive Indices	1.544–1.553
Birefringence	N/a
Optic Char./Sign	N/a
Hardness	7
Specific Gravity	2.651
Crystal System	N/a
Habit	Crypto-crystalline
Lustre	Waxy to resinous
Colour Range	Full spectrum
Pleochroism	N/a
Cleavage	N/a
Fracture	Conchoidal
Dispersion	N/a
Sources	Australia, Brazil, India, Madagascar, Namibia, USA
Transparency	Translucent–opaque
Class	Silicates

TOP: *Blue chalcedony*
ABOVE: *Silicified chrysocolla*

Agate

The name agate is derived from that of an early source, the Achates River (now the Drillo) in Sicily. Agate is a multi-hued form of chalcedony in which the colours are distributed in an incredible diversity of patterns; some of the better-known varieties are listed below.

Agate is popular with lapidaries since it has very good working properties and takes an excellent finish. Attractive and extremely tough, it lends itself to a wide range of ornamental and practical uses. Workshops in the twin towns of Idar-Oberstein, Germany, produce agate jewellery, bowls, various ornaments and carvings, together with a wide range of utensils fitted with agate handles. India, an important source of agate, has a long history of working this tough material. Craftsmen there make carvings and cabochons and hand-drill agate beads and pebbles to make up long strands of 'beggar beads'.

Varieties of Agate

Banded agate. Agate with parallel bands of colour. This is a common form of agate of worldwide occurrence. NB A large proportion of the more exotically coloured banded agate offered for sale has been dyed.

Blue agate. Distinct blues are seldom seen in agate. Uncommon but found in Namibia, Tanzania and the USA.

Blue Lace agate. This variety has light and medium blue bands with white lacework. Found in Malawi, Namibia and Tanzania.

Chatoyant agate. Very finely layered agate exhibiting a cat's-eye effect. Uncommon but found in South Africa.

Dendritic agate. Agate with black inclusions of manganese oxide resembling the forms of ferns and trees. Found in India, the USA and Zimbabwe.

Enhydros agate. Agate with a hollow centre containing water. Found in Australia, Brazil, India and Uruguay.

Eye agate. Agate with concentric bands in the shape of an eye. Found in India.

Fire agate. A very translucent agate containing iridescent spheroids of limonite. Found in Mexico.

Fortification agate. Banded agate with patterns resembling the floor of a castle. Widespread.

Fossil agate. Forms when dead organic material is replaced, molecule by molecule, by silica. The process is so gradual that the new agate retains the shape and markings of the wood, coral, shell, dinosaur bone, etc. Widespread.

Iris agate. Very finely banded, highly translucent agate. Cut in thin slabs, it exhibits spectral hues when viewed in transmitted light. Found in the USA.

TOP: *Picture agate*
MIDDLE: *Blue Lace agate*
BOTTOM: *Fortification agate*

Mexican Lace agate (also called Crazy Lace agate). Complex and often zigzag lace patterns.

Mosaic agate.Brecciated agate. Widespread.

Moss agate (or Mocha Stone in the USA). Translucent chalcedony with mossy or fern-like inclusions. Found in India, South Africa, the USA and Zimbabwe.

Oolitic agate. Agate containing numerous small round grains that resemble ooliths.

Orbicular agate. This material contains numerous spherical inclusions. Slabbing often reveals that the spheres contain many concentric circles in colours that contrast with the body of the stone.

Plume agate. Plume-like patterns in various colours. Found in the USA (Oregon and Texas) and Zimbabwe.

Ribbon agate. Wide ribbons of colour run through this material. Found in Zimbabwe.

Ruin agate. So-called because the patterns in this agate resemble a skyline of ruined buildings.

Sagenitic agate. Translucent chalcedony containing radiating patterns of acicular inclusions.

Scenic agate (or landscape agate) forms patterns resembling scenery. The agate from Yellowstone, Montana, is the world's best.

Tempskya agate. Fossilized tree fern. Found in the USA (Idaho and Pacific Northwest).

Thunder-egg agate. Thunder eggs are hard nodules that remain after the decomposition of softer volcanic rocks. Most of them have hollow central cavities that have gradually filled with silica in the form of agate or chalcedony, known as thunder-egg agate. Occurs in the USA (Oregon and New Mexico).

Turritella agate. Numerous fossilized shells embedded in an opaque black chalcedony. Although known as an agate, it would be more correct to class this material as a jasper. Found in the USA (Wyoming).

Zebra agate. This variety has sharply contrasting black-and-white stripes. Found in India (Baroda).

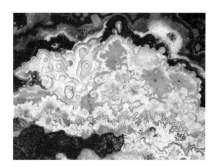

TOP: *Crazy Lace agate*
ABOVE: *Moss agate*
BELOW: *Rough jasper*

Jasper

Jasper is an opaque form of chalcedony with solid hues. Specimens that display a combination of jasper and agate characteristics are termed jasp-agates.

Jaspers are usually cut as cabochons or carved. They take an excellent polish and are hardy enough for all jewellery applications. Various forms of this material are also frequently made into decorative objects, such as ashtrays or bookends. Jaspers are found all over the world but particular colours and patterns may originate from a specific area.

Varieties of Jasper

Algae jasper. Bright red jasper with a cellular structure. Found in the USA (Minnesota).

Banded Ironstone. This variety of jasper features contrasting bands of bright red jasper and metallic black specular hematite. Marketed as *Jaspilite* in the USA, it is found in South Africa, the USA and Zimbabwe.

Bloodstone. Dark green jasper with red blood-like spots. Found in India, Madagascar, the USA and Zimbabwe.

Brecciated jasper is jasper fractured by movements in the Earth's crust and then bonded with the chalcedony that formed in the cracks. Found in South Africa and the USA.

Bruneau Canyon jasper. The picture jasper (see below) from this source enjoyed great demand, since it frequently exhibited what appeared to be blue skies. A dam has submerged the mining site and specimens of this material are rare. Named after the Bruneau River, Idaho, USA.

Dinosaur bone. Perfectly fossilized dinosaur bones, complete with colourful jasper-filled cell structures. Found in the USA (Colorado and Utah).

Egyptian jasper. Red jasper with white or grey spherical inclusions. Found in Egypt and the USA.

Fossilized wood. The cells of this wood have been completely replaced by silica either in the microcrystalline form of chalcedony or in the amorphous hydrated form of opal. Also referred to as petrified or silicified wood. Widespread.

Mookaite. Inconsistent in the nature of its silicification from opalite to jasper. Patterns vary and hues are pink, purple, red, white and yellow. Found in Mooka, Western Australia.

Morgan Hill jasper. Warm brown jasper with red and white patterns. The variety poppy jasper, which has red orbicular patterns, is a collectors item. Found in the USA (California).

Nunkirchen jasper. Grey or brown jasper that is dyed blue and marketed as 'Swiss lapis'. Found in Germany.

Orbicular jasper. Jasper containing numerous spherical inclusions. Found in Madagascar and the USA.

Picture stone Jaspers or jasp-agates that appear to embody pictures of landscapes (sometimes known as scenic jasper), birds, fish, faces, etc. Fine specimens are uncommon but come from widespread sources.

Puddingstone . A conglomerate in which rounded pebbles of jasper are bonded in a translucent white quartz matrix. This material is popular in China for carving snuff bottles. Widespread.

Ribbon jasper. Banded jasper with broad ribbon-like stripes of colour. Widespread.

Zebra jasper. Dark brown jasper with light brown stripes. Found in India.

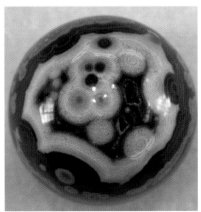

TOP: *Brecciated jasper*
MIDDLE: *Morgan Hill poppy jasper*
BOTTOM: *Orbicular jasper*

BENITOITE

BaTi(Si$_3$O$_9$)

Benitoite (*Ben-EAT-oh-ite*) was discovered at the beginning of the 20th century and given the name of the sole source in San Benito County, California, USA. A tough, magnificent gem mineral, it commonly exhibits a strong blue fluorescence under short-wave ultraviolet light, and has no heat sensitivity. Unfortunately, the deposit was soon worked out and the gem is now very rare. The only available facet rough takes the form of small fragments recovered from the sporadic reworking of the old dumps at the San Benito Mine. Benitoite and other rare associated minerals were formed at this location when hydrothermal solutions carrying relatively high concentrations of unusual elements such as barium, titanium, caesium, niobium, and lithium, filled fractures in a serpentine rock. The deposit has produced incredible mineral specimens in which triangular blue benitoite crystals emerge from a bed of snowy-white natrolite together with rods of red-black neptunite and clusters of yellow-brown joaquinite crystals.

Refractive Indices	1.757–1.804
Birefringence	0.047
Optic Char./Sign	Uniaxial/+
Hardness	6–6.5
Specific Gravity	3.65–3.68
Crystal System	Trigonal
Habit	Bi-pyramidal
Lustre	Vitreous
Colour Range	Light to dark blue, colourless, yellowish
Pleochroism	Very strong
Cleavage	Nil
Fracture	Conchoidal
Dispersion	0.039–0.046
Sources	USA (San Benito County, California)
Transparency	Transparent–translucent
Class	Titanates

■ Benitoite is a gem that embodies the colour of a sapphire and the fire of a diamond.

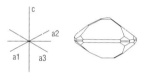

HEMATITE

Fe$_2$O$_3$

The name hematite (*HEM–ah-tite*) is derived from the Greek root *ema* meaning 'blood', either with reference to the red powder of its streak or to the blood red slurry produced when it is ground with water employed as a coolant. A relatively common ore of iron, hematite occurs in hydrothermal veins. Most gem-quality material originates from the north of England. Hematite is usually cut in the form of tablets, intaglios, cabochons or beads.

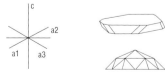

Refractive Indices	2.94–3.22
Birefringence	0.28
Optic Char./Sign	Uniaxial/–
Hardness	5.5–6.5
Specific Gravity	4.9–5.3
Crystal System	Trigonal
Habit	Rhombohedral
Lustre	Metallic
Colour Range	Metallic black, Steel grey
Pleochroism	Nil
Cleavage	Poor
Fracture	Uneven, tough
Dispersion	Nil
Sources	England, Germany, Scandinavia, USA
Transparency	Opaque
Class	Oxides

■ Grinding with water will produce a plentiful flow of 'blood' from hematite.

WILLEMITE

Zn_2SiO_4

Willemite (*WILL-em-ite*), zinc silicate, was named in honour of King William I of Belgium. It is a relatively rare secondary mineral from primary zinc deposits that forms in association with calcite, franklinite and greenockite. Willemite is best known among collectors for its remarkable luminescent properties. Under short-wave ultraviolet light it exhibits an intense green fluorescence and it may also phosphoresce. Phosphorescent minerals continue to glow for some time after the ultraviolet source is removed. Rough is usually small and seldom exceeds two grams (0.07 oz). Clean crystals of this rare mineral have been faceted as interesting gems.

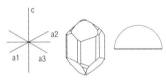

Refractive Indices	1.691 –1.725
Birefringence	0.028
Optic Char./Sign	Uniaxial/+
Hardness	5.5
Specific Gravity	3.9–4.2
Crystal System	Trigonal
Habit	Prismatic
Lustre	Vitreous, resinous
Colour Range	Usually colourless, greenish, brownish, yellowish, black, blue-grey, pink, red, white
Pleochroism	Nil
Cleavage	Distinct
Fracture	Sub-conchoidal
Dispersion	Low
Sources	Belgium, Canada, Greenland, Namibia, USA
Transparency	Transparent–translucent
Class	Silicates

■ Willemite is an important ore of zinc.

EUDIALYTE

$Na_4(CaCeFeMn)_2ZrSi_6O_{17}(OH,Cl)_2$

Refractive Indices	1.598–1.613
Birefringence	0.004
Optic Char./Sign	Uniaxial
Hardness	5–5.5
Specific Gravity	2.9
Crystal System	Trigonal
Habit	Distorted rhombohedra, tabular
Lustre	Vitreous
Colour Range	Blue, brown, pink, violet-red, yellow, green, orange, carmine red
Pleochroism	Weak
Cleavage	Poor basal
Fracture	Uneven
Dispersion	Nil
Sources	Australia, Brazil, Canada, Czech Republic, Greenland, Madagascar, Morocco, Norway, Russia, USA
Transparency	Transparent–translucent
Class	Silicates

Eudialyte (*YOU-dia-lite*) is a relatively rare cyclosilicate mineral. Associated minerals include aegirine, albite, calcite, nepheline, natrolite and quartz. Its attractive colouring ensures its popularity with collectors despite the fact that it seldom forms good crystals.

The massive eudialite that is occasionally available from the mineral-rich Kola Peninsula of Russia makes attractive cabochons and spheres.

DIOPTASE

H_2CuSiO_4

Refractive Indices	1.644–1.709
Birefringence	0.053–0.056
Optic Char./Sign	Uniaxial/+
Hardness	5
Specific Gravity	3.28–3.35
Crystal System	Trigonal
Habit	Prismatic, rhombohedral
Lustre	Vitreous
Colour Range	Emerald green
Pleochroism	Weakly dichroic
Cleavage	Perfect (x3)
Fracture	Sub-conchoidal
Dispersion	0.022
Sources	Chile, Democratic Republic of Congo, Namibia, Russia, USA, Zaire
Transparency	Transparent–translucent
Class	Silicates

Dioptase (*dye-OP-tase*) is a relatively rare mineral that occurs in comparatively few copper deposits. Crystal tips may be clear enough to facet small stones. Facet rough seldom exceeds 0.2 grams (0.007 oz). Dioptase is one of the few minerals that can challenge the hue of a fine emerald. It exhibits marked cleavage and it is rather too soft to be worn as a ring-stone but small crystal specimens are sometimes mounted for wear in pendants or brooches. Good crystal specimens of dioptase are standouts in any mineral collection. Associated minerals are calcite, cerussite, chrysocolla, dolomite and limonite.

LEFT TOP: *A dioptase cluster*
LEFT BOTTOM: *Dioptase crystals on calcite*

■ Dioptase, or 'Emerald copper', is more attractive as crystal specimens than as cut stones.

GASPÉITE

(Ni,MgFe)CO$_3$

Refractive Indices	1.160–1.830
Birefringence	0.220
Optic Char./Sign	Uniaxial/-
Hardness	4.5–5
Specific Gravity	3.7
Crystal System	Trigonal
Habit	Massive, rhombohedral
Lustre	Vitreous–dull
Colour Range	Pale green to apple green
Pleochroism	Nil
Cleavage	Perfect (3x)
Fracture	Uneven
Dispersion	Nil
Sources	Australia (Tasmania), Bosnia, Germany, Greece, Italy, S. Africa, Zimbabwe
Transparency	Translucent
Class	Carbonates

Gaspéite was first discovered on the Gaspé peninsula, Quebec, Canada. It is a secondary mineral that occurs in the vicinity of nickel sulphide deposits in association with millerite, pentlandite, and other nickel minerals. It was considered to be a rarity, found in very few localities and occasionally cut as a cabochon for serious collectors. Now all of that has changed thanks to recent finds in Western Australia. Gaspéite is becoming a popular ornamental mineral mounted as cabochons in sterling silver jewellery or carved into sculptures and objets d'art.

SMITHSONITE

ZnCO$_3$

Smithsonite (*SMITH-son-ite*) was named for James Smithson (1765–1829), the English mineralogist who financed the founding of the Smithsonian Institution in Washington, D.C. Smithsonite forms in dry climates as a weathering product of primary sulphide zinc ores such as sphalerite. Specimens from the Tsumeb mine in northern Namibia are particularly colourful

Refractive Indices	1.625–1.850
Birefringence	0.225
Optic Char./Sign	Uniaxial/–
Hardness	4–4.5
Specific Gravity	4.42–4.44
Crystal System	Trigonal
Habit	Botryoidal, rhombohedral
Lustre	Pearly–vitreous
Colour Range	Apple-green, blue-green, blue, brown, colourless, lavender, orange, pink, red, white, yellow, grey, purple
Pleochroism	Nil
Cleavage	Perfect (x3)
Fracture	Uneven
Dispersion	Nil
Sources	Belgium, Greece, Mexico, Namibia, Poland, USA, Zambia
Transparency	Transparent–translucent
Class	Carbonates

because they tend to carry traces of cobalt. The Kelly Mine, Magdalena, New Mexico has produced incredible blue-green botryoidal specimens. Associated minerals are those typically found in oxidation zones of zinc sulphide deposits: cerussite, dolomite, hemimorphite, limonite, mimetite and wulfenite. The high density, good cleavage, crystal habit, lustre, reaction to hot hydrochloric acid and high hardness for a carbonate are conclusive factors in distinguishing smithsonite from other minerals.

■ Cabochon-cut massive pieces of smithsonite are marketed as 'bonamite'.

RHODOCHROSITE

$MnCO_3$

Refractive Indices	1.596–1.816
Birefringence	0.218
Optic Char./Sign	Uniaxial/–
Hardness	3.5–4
Specific Gravity	3.45–3.70
Crystal System	Trigonal
Habit	Rhombohedral, massive
Lustre	Vitreous–resinous
Colour Range	Brown, pink, red, white, yellow
Pleochroism	Weakly dichroic
Cleavage	Perfect (x3)
Fracture	Brittle
Dispersion	Nil
Sources	Argentina, Canada, England, Germany, Peru, South Africa, USA
Transparency	Transparent–opaque
Class	Carbonates

Rhodochrosite (*row-doe-CROW-site*) is a name derived from the Greek *rhodon*, meaning 'rose', and *chrosis*, meaning 'colouring'. This very colourful and relatively unusual carbonate forms in the oxidized zone of manganese deposits in association with calcite, fluorite, manganite, quartz, rhodonite and spessartine. The principal source of the pink and white, banded stalactitic material is the San Luis silver mine in the mountains of Argentina. This mine was originally worked for silver and copper by the Incas, hence the alternative name Rosinca for this massive stalactitic form of rhodochrosite. A cross-section cut through these stalactites reveals concentric bands in various shades of pink. This attractive material is employed for numerous ornamental purposes.

Magnificent crystal specimens and facet-grade rough have originated from the Kalahari Manganese Fields of South Africa.

■ Trade names for rhodochrosite include Rosinca and Inca Rose.

Crystal habits exhibited by rhodochrosite from the N'Chwaning 1 Mine include large transparent scalenohedra with rounded or curved faces, flat terminated scalenohedra, 'wheat-sheaf' bundles of crystals and perfectly formed, intense red, crystal spheroids. Associated minerals include hausmannite, manganite and quartz. Damaged crystals provide great facet rough. Some of the outstanding gems cut from this material weigh in excess of 20 carats.

The Sweet Home Mine in Colorado, USA, has produced superb sharp rhombohedral crystals of rhodochrosite with a fine rose colour. Twinning is fairly typical of rhodochrosite in forms that include contact and penetration twins. Massive rhodochrosite occurs in botryoidal, globular, stalactitic, layered, nodular, vein-filling and granular forms.

ABOVE LEFT: *A rhodochrosite cluster*
LEFT: *Polished rhodochrosite specimen*

MAGNESITE

MgCO$_3$

Magnesite (*MAG-nes-ite*) is the product of low-grade metamorphism of magnesium-rich rocks through contact with carbonate-rich solutions. It is most frequently found in a massive form that may be lamellar, fibrous, coarse or granular; seldom encountered in crystal form; and transparent gem rough is very rare. The limited amount of facet rough on offer usually originates from Brazil. The rare crystals take the form of rhombohedrons or hexagonal prisms with pinacoidal terminations.

Associated minerals include calcite, dolomite, aragonite, strontianite and serpentine. When dealing with rough, an acid test has proved to be the simplest method of distinguishing between calcite and magnesite. The magnesium ion acts as a blocker that prevents the magnesite from reacting readily with cold acids in contrast to the strong reaction that is seen when calcite is brought into contact with dilute hydrochloric acid.

The massive material is cut into cabochons. Transparent faceted stones are seldom seen and mostly limited to specialized collections.

Refractive Indices	1.515–1.717
Birefringence	0.192–0.202
Optic Char./Sign	Uniaxial/–
Hardness	3.5–4.5
Specific Gravity	2.98–3.02
Crystal System	Trigonal
Habit	Rhombohedral, massive
Lustre	Vitreous–silky
Colour Range	Colourless, yellowish, greyish, brown, white
Pleochroism	Nil
Cleavage	Perfect (x3)
Fracture	Conchoidal
Dispersion	Nil
Sources	Austria, Brazil, Canada, China, Greece, Italy, Spain, Sweden, Korea, USA
Transparency	Transparent–Opaque
Class	Carbonates

DOLOMITE

CaMg(CO$_3$)$_2$

Dolomite (*DOLL-oh-mite*), named for French mineralogist Déodat de Dolomieu, is a carbonate of calcium and magnesium. It is normally rhombohedral in crystal habit, but some crystals may exhibit sufficiently curved growth, possibly as a result of twinning, to form saddle shapes. These forms are known as classical dolomite and they represent a unique crystal habit. Fine pink crystal specimens occur in rare instances when some of the magnesium has been replaced by cobalt. Associated minerals include barite, calcite, fluorite and quartz.

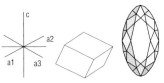

Refractive Indices	1.502–1.681
Birefringence	0.179
Optic Char./Sign	Uniaxial/–
Hardness	3.5–4
Specific Gravity	2.8–2.9
Crystal System	Trigonal
Habit	Rhombohedral, massive
Lustre	Vitreous, pearly
Colour Range	Colourless, brown, greenish, pink, reddish
Pleochroism	Nil
Cleavage	Perfect (x3)
Fracture	Sub-conchoidal
Dispersion	Low
Sources	Canada, Spain, Switzerland, USA (New Mexico: facet rough)
Transparency	Transparent–opaque
Class	Carbonates

■ Massive North American pieces of dolomite are called 'wonderstone'.

KUTNOHORITE

Ca(Mn,Mg,Fe)(CO3)$_2$

Kutnohorite (*KUT-no-hor-ite*) is a rare carbonate mineral that forms radiating sprays of crystals. It was named after the type locality near Kutna Hora in the Czech Republic. A member of the dolomite group, it is difficult to distinguish from dolomite except for its higher density. It often occurs in association with calcite and rhodochrosite. Compact material from the Wessels Mine, Hotazel, South Africa can be cut to yield attractive light pink cabochons.

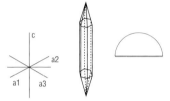

Refractive Indices	1.535–1.727
Birefringence	0.192
Optic Char./Sign	Uniaxial/–
Hardness	3.5–4
Specific Gravity	3.10–3.12
Crystal System	Trigonal
Habit	Rhombs, Massive
Lustre	Vitreous–dull
Colour Range	Pink, white, yellow, light brown
Pleochroism	Nil
Cleavage	Perfect (3x)
Fracture	Conchoidal
Dispersion	Nil
Sources	Argentina, Australia, Canada, Czech Republic, Italy, South Africa, USA
Transparency	Translucent
Class	Carbonates

SIDERITE

FeCO$_3$

Siderite (*SID-er-ite*) is named from the Greek word for iron, *sideros*. This iron carbonate is found in hydrothermal ore veins, as layers in sandstone and limestone, and in both metamorphic and igneous rocks. It forms a replacement series with the manganese carbonate rhodochrosite. Exceptional crystal specimens have originated from Bohemia, Cornwall in England, France, Germany and Switzerland. Gemmy amber-coloured crystal specimens of arsenio-siderite were recovered from the Tsumeb copper mine in northern Namibia. Transparent material yields attractive faceted collectors' gems. Massive material is occasionally cut as cabochons.

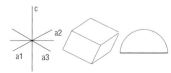

Refractive Indices	1.570/1.633–1.785/1.875
Birefringence	0.215–0.240
Optic Char./Sign	Uniaxial/–
Hardness	3.5–4.5
Specific Gravity	3.83–3.96
Crystal System	Trigonal
Habit	Rhombohedral, massive, botryoidal, globular
Lustre	Vitreous
Colour Range	Brown, grey, green, russet, white, yellowish
Pleochroism	Nil
Cleavage	Perfect
Fracture	Uneven
Dispersion	Strong
Sources	Austria, Belgium, Bolivia, Canada, Czech Republic, France, Italy, Greenland, Namibia, New Zealand, Peru, Portugal, Spain, UK, USA
Transparency	Transparent–opaque
Class	Carbonates

■ Siderite is also known as Chalybite, a facet rough from Pinasquevia, Portugal.

MILLERITE

NiS

Millerite (*MILL-er-ite*) is a nickel sulphide that forms sprays of acicular crystals in hydrothermal replacement deposits or cavities in dolomite and limestone. It is one of the small group of minerals found in iron-nickel meteorites. The clusters of bright metallic crystals make attractive specimens. For the lapidary, Rossing, Namibia, appears to be the sole source of rather turbid yellowish-green facet rough.

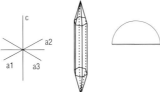

Refractive Indices	Nil
Birefringence	Nil
Optic Char./Sign	Nil
Hardness	3–3.5
Specific Gravity	5.3–5.5
Crystal System	Trigonal
Habit	Radiating Acicular, fibrous masses
Lustre	Metallic
Colour Range	Brassy yellow, yellowish-green, grey
Pleochroism	Nil
Cleavage	Perfect
Fracture	Uneven, brittle
Dispersion	Nil
Sources	Canada, England, Czech Republic, Germany, Namibia, S. Africa, USA, Wales
Transparency	Semi-opaque–Opaque
Class	Sulphides

CALCITE

CaCO$_3$

The name calcite (*KAL-site*) is derived from the Greek word for lime, *chalix*. Limestones are massive bodies of sedimentary calcite that frequently contain identifiable coral and shell fossils. Attractive material is used for cabochons and carved ornaments, wall tiles, paving slabs and building blocks for architectural purposes. Ornamental marbles are metamorphosed forms of limestone.

Calcium carbonate is virtually insoluble in pure water. However, once natural water has percolated through limestone it contains enough carbon dioxide to form soluble calcium bicarbonate. Droplets of this water gradually deposit calcium carbonate to extend stalactites or fall to the cave floor to build stalagmites. When pairs meet they form fluted columns. Calcite deposited around hot springs exhibits banded patterns of colouration and is often used for ornamental purposes. Calcite specimens may exhibit fluorescence, phosphorescence, thermoluminescence and/or triboluminescence. Rhombs of clear colourless calcite known as Iceland spar are excellent for demonstrating double refraction. Golden yellow and colourless calcite is faceted, and an attractive pink variety, cobalti-calcite, is cabochon-cut for collectors.

Refractive Indices	1.486–1.660
Birefringence	0.172
Optic Char./Sign	Uniaxial/–
Hardness	3
Specific Gravity	2.71
Crystal System	Trigonal
Habit	Scalenohedrons, rhombohedrons, stalactite
Lustre	Vitreous–resinous
Colour Range	Blue, black brown, colourless, green, grey, orange, pink, red, white, yellow
Pleochroism	Nil
Cleavage	Perfect x 3
Fracture	Conchoidal
Dispersion	e ray–0.008 o ray–0.017
Sources	Brazil, England, Germany, Iceland, Mexico, Namibia, USA
Transparency	Transparent–translucent
Class	Carbonates

CINNABAR

HgS

Cinnabar (*SIN-ah-bar*) occurs in veins, in rocks of sedimentary origin, limestone, sandstone and shales. The mineral has been the main ore of mercury throughout the centuries. Some deposits used by the Romans are still mined today. Good size, well-formed crystals are scarce, crusts and crystal complexes being more common. Its formation is frequently massive, or in capillary needles. Euhedral crystals are uncommon, but modified rhombohedrons, and prismatic formations sometimes occur. So, too, do twinned specimens; they are considered classics by collectors. Associated minerals are dolomite, pyrite, quartz, realgar and stibnite. It has very high sensitivity to heat. Massive material is cut as cabochons and clean faceted stones are spectacular.

Refractive Indices	2.91–3.27
Birefringence	Strong
Optic Char./Sign	Uniaxial/+
Hardness	2–2.5
Specific Gravity	8.0–8.2
Crystal System	Trigonal
Habit	Tabular, prismatic
Lustre	Adamantine–sub-metallic
Colour Range	Black, brick-red, brown, cinnamon-red, grey, scarlet
Pleochroism	Nil
Cleavage	Perfect (x3)
Fracture	Uneven–splintery
Dispersion	Nil
Sources	China, Italy, Mexico, Russia, Spain, USA
Transparency	Transparent–Opaque
Class	Sulphides

■ Cinnabar is the main source of mercury. The name comes from the Persian for dragon's blood.

PYRAGYRITE

Ag$_3$SbS$_3$

Pyrargyrite (*PYRE-are-jyr-ite*) is a popular collector's mineral. It is usually found in the same ore veins as argentite, calcite, galena, proustite, sphalerite, silver and silver sulphides. Crystals can be very attractive but they are reactive to light and may darken with too much exposure. Fine specimens should be stored in closed containers with minimal exposure to light. Pyrargyrite is seldom transparent enough to facet.

Refractive Indices	2.881–3.084
Birefringence	0.2+ very strong
Optic Char./Sign	Uniaxial/–
Hardness	2.5
Specific Gravity	5.77–5.86
Crystal System	Trigonal
Habit	Prismatic
Lustre	Adamantine, sub-metallic
Colour Range	Dark-red to reddish-black
Pleochroism	Strong
Cleavage	Indistinct (x3)
Fracture	Conchoidal
Dispersion	Strong
Sources	Bolivia, Canada, Chile, Czech Republic, Germany, Mexico, USA
Transparency	Translucent–semi-opaque
Class	Sulphides

PROUSTITE

Ag3AsS3

Proustite (*PROW-stite*) is a rare stone and a very unusual type of sulphide since it is neither metallic nor opaque. It cuts into spectacular faceted stones that make wonderful display pieces but they are too soft to be worn in items of jewellery. It is a much rarer mineral than the closely related pyrargyrite, with which it is associated in silver ore-bodies.

Refractive Indices	2.790–3.088
Birefringence	0.297
Optic Char./Sign	Uniaxial/–
Hardness	2–2.5
Specific Gravity	5.57–5.64
Crystal System	Trigonal
Habit	Rhombohedral, scaleno hedral, prismatic
Lustre	Adamantine, sub-metallic
Colour Range	Orange-red, scarlet, deep red
Pleochroism	Strong
Cleavage	Distinct (x3)
Fracture	Conchoidal to uneven, brittle
Dispersion	Weak
Sources	Chile, Czech Republic, France, Germany, Mexico, USA
Transparency	Transparent–opaque
Class	Sulphides

■ Proustite is mined and smelted as an ore of silver.

STICHTITE

Mg₆Cr₂CO₃(OH)₁₆–4H₂O

Stichtite (*STICK-tite*) is a rare mineral that, unlike most other carbonates, forms in compact masses or micaceous aggregates. Associated minerals are serpentine and chromite. Stichtite is purplish pink to purplish rose-red in colour. It is usually associated with serpentine in a green and purplish pink combination that makes for attractive specimens or ornamental stone carvings.

Refractive Indices	1.516–1.545
Birefringence	Nil
Optic Char./Sign	Uniaxial/–
Hardness	1.5–2.5
Specific Gravity	2.16
Crystal System	Trigonal
Habit	Massive, micaceous, foliated, lamellar
Lustre	Greasy–pearly
Colour Range	Lilac with green serpentine veins, rose pink
Pleochroism	Distinct
Cleavage	Perfect (x1)
Fracture	Uneven
Dispersion	Nil
Sources	Australia, Canada, South Africa
Transparency	Transparent–opaque
Class	Carbonates

CHRYSOBERYL

$BeAl_2O_4$

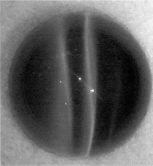

Refractive Indices	1.742–1.757
Birefringence	0.009
Optic Char./Sign	Biaxial/+
Hardness	8.5
Specific Gravity	3.68–3.78
Crystal System	Orthorhombic
Habit	Tabular, twins
Lustre	Vitreous–adamantine
Colour Range	Brown, green, yellow
Pleochroism	Strong
Cleavage	Fair
Fracture	Conchoidal
Dispersion	0.015
Sources	Brazil, Myanmar, Sri-Lanka, Russia, Tanzania, Zimbabwe
Transparency	Transparent–translucent
Class	Oxides

Chrysoberyl (*CHRIS-oh-ber-ill*) occurs in pegmatites and mica schists and being very tough it is often encountered in alluvial deposits. It is usually yellow, yellowish-green, golden yellow or brown and worked with diamond powder it can be cut into fine gemstones of remarkable clarity and high lustre that are very lively and durable.

Alexandrite is a rare and much sought after variety of chrysoberyl. It was first discovered in the Ural Mountains of Russia in 1830. It exhibits the military colours of Imperial Russia, green by day and red in artificial light so it was very fitting that the discovery of the new gem, named in his honour, should be announced on the birthday of the Tsar Alexander II. There have been finds in Sri Lanka and Brazil but demand for this extremely rare stone has always exceeded the supply.

Alexandrite chrysoberyl may form pseudo-hexagonal cyclic twins and this is the habit typical of the crystals recovered from the schists of the Novello Claims near Masivingo, Zimbabwe. Alexandrite from Lake Manyara, Tanzania, has a moderate colour change and its hues often lack intensity. The rare pieces of rounded water-worn facet rough recovered from the alluvial gravels at Tunduru in southern Tanzania tend to exhibit stronger, more desirable colours. Associated minerals include garnet, feldspar and mica.

Cat's-eye: When chrysoberyl is filled with microscopic parallel needle-like inclusions, it is cut as a cabochon to bring out its chatoyancy. This is the true cat's-eye or cymophane and no other chatoyant gem can match it.

An ancient superstition about cat's-eye is that the stone is always wakeful and protective of its owner. Take two penlights, hold them over the stone then move them to angle away from one another and the 'eye' will open. If a single penlight is held at a 45° angle and directed at the side of a cat's-eye stone it will reveal the striking 'milk and honey' effect.

TOP LEFT: *A cat's-eye chrysoberyl*
TOP RIGHT: *A cat's-eye chrysoberyl, with eye open*

■ Chrysoberyl's name derives from the Greek words *chrysos*, meaning gold, and *beryllos*, meaning beryl.

TOPAZ

$Al_2SiO_4(F,OH)_3$

Refractive Indices	1.629–1.637
Birefringence	0.008
Optic Char./Sign	Biaxial/+
Hardness	8
Specific Gravity	3.4–3.65
Crystal System	Orthorhombic
Habit	Prismatic
Lustre	Vitreous
Colour Range	Blue, colourless, gold, greenish, pink, red, violet, yellow
Pleochroism	Distinct
Cleavage	Perfect, basal
Fracture	Conchoidal
Dispersion	0.014
Sources	Australia, Brazil, Japan, Madagascar, Mexico, Myanmar, Namibia, Nigeria, Pakistan, Russia, Sri Lanka, USA, Zimbabwe
Transparency	Transparent–translucent
Class	Fluo-silicates

LEFT: *A range of topaz colours*

■ In early times all yellow stones were called topazes.

BELOW: *Irradiated 'Swiss blue' topaz and diamond earrings*

Topaz (*TOE-paz*) occurs in cavities in acid igneous rocks such as granite and rhyolite, in pegmatite dykes and in contact metamorphic zones. Associated minerals include brookite, cassiterite, fluorite, mica, quartz and tourmaline. The name topaz has a very long history but it may be that in the distant past it referred to a totally different stone. Pliny links the name, through the Greek word *topazos* 'to seek', with a mysterious gem island in the Red Sea. He is probably referring to Zeberget, an important source of the stone we know today as peridot. An alternative derivation sees the Sanskrit word *tapas* meaning 'fire' as a likely root for the name. The vast majority of topaz is colourless and the cut stones are often sold as 'silver topaz'. Deposits of natural blue topaz are fairly widespread, the best material coming from Brazil, Russia and Zimbabwe. The low cost and range of hues available in irradiated topaz has seriously affected the market for natural blue stones. Natural pink topaz has always been very rare, and pink stones either in jewellery or offered on the internet are almost certainly heat-treated yellow Brazilian goods. Recent production from the Democratic Republic of Congo has included some very interesting topaz specimens that are virtually identical to the imperial topaz from Ouro Preto, Minas Gerais, Brazil. Topaz builds up a distinct electrical charge from heat or friction that it will retain for several hours. In some Brazilian crystals gently stroking with the finger, or applying pressure down the 'C' axis with the crystal held between finger and thumb is all that is needed to electrify them.

LAWSONITE

$H_4CaAl_2Si_2O_{10}$

Refractive Indices	1.665–1.686
Birefringence	0.019 –0.021
Optic Char./Sign	Biaxial/+
Hardness	7–8
Specific Gravity	3.08–3.09
Crystal System	Orthorhombic
Habit	Prismatic
Lustre	Vitreous
Colour Range	Light blue, colourless, grey, pinkish, white
Pleochroism	Distinct
Cleavage	Perfect (2x)
Fracture	Uneven
Dispersion	Strong
Sources	Italy, USA
Transparency	Transparent–translucent
Class	Silicates

Lawsonite is a metamorphic mineral occurring in crystalline schists associated with serpentine or as a secondary mineral in altered gabbros and diorites. Associated minerals include epidote, garnet, quartz and sphene. The rare faceted stones are usually small, although a cut stone of two carats has been reported.

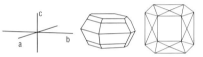

FIBROLITE (SILLIMANITE)

Al_2SiO_5

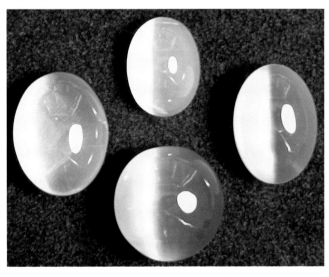

Refractive Indices	1.658–1.678
Birefringence	Strong
Optic Char./Sign	Biaxial/+
Hardness	6–7
Specific Gravity	3.14–3.25
Crystal System	Orthorhombic
Habit	Prismatic
Lustre	Vitreous+
Colour Range	Blue, brown, colourless, green, grey
Pleochroism	Distinct
Cleavage	Perfect (x1)
Fracture	Uneven
Dispersion	0.015
Sources	Kenya, India, Myanmar, Sri Lanka, USA
Transparency	Transparent–translucent
Class	Silicates

The name fibrolite (*FI-bro-lite*) refers to the massive fibrous sub-variety of the gem that can be cut into very fine chatoyant cabochons. The transparent faceted gems are more frequently

■ Fibrolite was first discovered in 1824.

referred to as sillimanite, a name that was given to the mineral in the USA to honour the oil-petroleum work of Yale professor Benjamin Silliman.

Fibrolite occurs in schists, gneisses and granites, in association with andalusite and corundum. The majority of gem rough is recovered from alluvial deposits. Sri Lanka produces colourless, grey and russet-brown cat's-eyes and fine blue-violet gems occur in the famous gravel deposits of Mogok in Myanmar. Tends to form long slender crystals that lack distinct terminations. Good matrix specimens are rare.

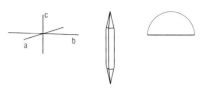

GRANDIDIERITE

$(Mg,Fe^{2+})Al_3(BO_3)(SiO_4)O_2$

Refractive Indices	1.602–1.639
Birefringence	0.037
Optic Char./Sign	Biaxial/–
Hardness	7.5
Specific Gravity	2.976
Crystal System	Orthorhombic
Habit	Nil
Lustre	Vitreous
Colour Range	Bluish-green– Greenish-blue
Pleochroism	Strong
Cleavage	Good (x2)
Fracture	Uneven
Dispersion	Very strong
Sources	Algeria, Antarctica, Canada, Germany, Greenland, Italy, Madagascar, Malawi, New Zealand, Norway, South Africa, Slovak Republic, USA
Transparency	Transparent–translucent
Class	Silicates

■ The only known occurrence of facet grade grandidierite is in southern Madagascar.

Grandidierite (*GRAN-did-ierite*) is a rare accessory mineral found in association with andalusite, corundum, fibrolite, garnet, iolite, kornerupine, sapphirine, serendibite, sinhalite and spinel in pegmatites and gneisses. Good-size crystals up to eight centimetres (3.12 inches) in length and limited amounts of facet-grade rough occur in Madagascar. The stone was named for Alfred Grandidier (1836–1912), the French explorer who was an authority on that island.

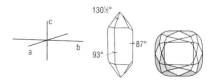

ANDALUSITE

Al_2SiO_5

Refractive Indices	1.633–1.644
Birefringence	0.007–0.013
Optic Char./Sign	Biaxial/–
Hardness	7–7.5
Specific Gravity	3.1–3.2
Crystal System	Orthorhombic
Habit	Square prisms
Lustre	Vitreous
Colour Range	Brown–green–red
Pleochroism	Strong: Green–russet brown
Cleavage	Distinct (x3)
Fracture	Uneven
Dispersion	0.016
Sources	Brazil, Canada, Madagascar, Russia, Spain (Andalusia), Sri Lanka, USA
Transparency	Transparent–opaque
Class	Silicates

Andalusite (*and-ah-LOO-site*) was named after the Spanish province in which it was first discovered. The prismatic crystals occur in a metamorphic environment and they are often associated with corundum, garnet, iolite and tourmaline. They seldom attain large sizes and euhedral crystals are very rare. Brazil produces the largest and finest rough: in fact, flawless cut stones in excess of five carats are most unusual from any other source. Fine, disoriented needles of rutile are the most typical inclusion to be found in andalusite. Andalusite is regarded as a collector's gem and hence seldom mounted in jewellery despite its pleasant autumnal colours and interesting pleochroism. Out of the ordinary, available and reasonable in both durability and price this 'laid-back' stone deserves higher regard from the jewellery trade than it currently receives. The gem has a weak green or yellowish-green (SW) fluorescence and an absorption spectra of Å5505 4550 4360, low heat sensitivity and is somewhat brittle. It is identifiable in the field from its habit, colour and pleochroism.

Mangan-andalusite, also known as viridine, is a bright green variety. Its iron and manganese content, positive optic sign and distinctly higher refractive indices have resulted in some authors considering it to be a separate species. Gemmy rough is small but when it cut it yields attractive intense green stones.

Chiastolite is an opaque variety of andalusite that is of very widespread occurrence. When a crystal is cut through, its cross-section will usually reveal an off-white body colour and a blackish diagonal cross that consists of dark carbonaceous impurities. These crystals are often sectioned, polished and worn as amulets.

■ Chiastolite, known as lapis crucifer, was treasured as an amulet by early Christians.

TOP LEFT: *Marquise-cut andalusite and step-cut mangan-andalusite*

TOP RIGHT: *Rough andalusite crystal*

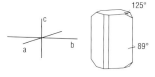

IOLITE

$Mg_2Al_4Si_5O_{18}$

Iolite (*EYE-oh-lite*) – a name derived from the Greek for 'violet' – is a gem that was also rather misleadingly termed 'water sapphire'. Its most remarkable feature is its trichroism: it reveals a deep violet-blue looking down the length of the prism, but when viewed through the sides the hues are blue-grey or yellowish-brown. It is not particularly popular with mineral collectors since it does not make showy specimens and is seldom encountered in crystal form. Facet rough generally takes the form of water-worn pebbles or irregular fragments of seam material. Oriented correctly it yields attractive deep blue faceted gems. 'Bloodshot iolite' originates from Sri Lanka. It contains innumerable thin platelets of hematite or goethite that give the stone a distinct red colour when viewed at certain angles.

Refractive Indices	1.52–1.57
Birefringence	0.008–0.012
Optic Char./Sign	Biaxial/–
Hardness	7–7.5
Specific Gravity	2.58–2.66
Crystal System	Orthorhombic
Habit	Massive
Lustre	Vitreous
Colour Range	Brownish, grey, blue-violet
Pleochroism	Strong. trichroic
Cleavage	Distinct
Fracture	Sub-conchoidal
Dispersion	0.017
Sources	India, Madagascar, Myanmar, Namibia, Sri Lanka, Zimbabwe
Transparency	Transparent–translucent
Class	Silicates

■ When navigating through fog and mist, the Vikings used a thin sliver of Iolite to determine the position of the sun.

STAUROLITE

$Fe_2Al_9Si_4O_{22}(OH)_2$

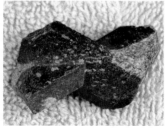

Staurolite (*STAR-oh-lite*) – from the Greek *stauros* (cross) and *lithos* (stone) – forms in interpenetrant twin crystals. Many intersect at 60°, but those that form a right-angled cross are used as amulets. A metamorphic mineral, staurolite occurs in association with almandine, kyanite and micas. Rough material transparent enough to facet brilliant red gems is very rare. A zinc-rich variety of staurolite was found to be yellowish-green in colour under fluorescent light and red-brown in incandescent light. Compared with common staurolite it had a slightly higher density (3.79) and lower refractive indices at 1.721–1.731.

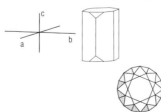

Refractive Indices	1.736–1.746
Birefringence	0.01
Optic Char./Sign	Biaxial/+
Hardness	7–7.5
Specific Gravity	3.7–3.8
Crystal System	Orthorhombic
Habit	Interpenetrant twins
Lustre	Vitreous–resinous
Colour Range	Black, brown, red
Pleochroism	Distinct
Cleavage	Poor
Fracture	Sub-conchoidal
Dispersion	Nil
Sources	Brazil, France, Italy, Scotland, USA
Transparency	Translucent–opaque
Class	Silicates

■ Twinned crystals of staurolite were known as 'baptismal stones' in parts of Europe and employed as amulets at baptisms.

BORACITE

$Mg_6Cl_2B_{14}O_{26}$

Boracite (*BOR-ah-site*) is an interesting borate with low heat sensitivity that occurs in association with minerals such as gypsum, anhydrite and halite that also form as a result of evaporation. Matrix clusters can be very attractive as mineral specimens. While it occurs in pleasant colours and has the clarity and hardness required of a gemstone it is restricted to the category of a collector's stone because of its slight solubility in water. Faceted stones weighing more than one carat are quite rare.

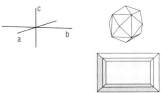

■ Boracite is remarkably hard for an evaporite that is slightly soluble in water.

Refractive Indices	1.658–1.673
Birefringence	0.011
Optic Char./Sign	Biaxial
Hardness	7–7.5
Specific Gravity	2.9–3
Crystal System	Orthorhombic
Habit	Pseudo-cubic, octahedrons, dodecahedrons, tetrahedrons
Lustre	Vitreous - sub-adamantine
Colour Range	Blue, colourless, pale green, grey, pink, violet, yellowish
Pleochroism	Nil
Cleavage	Poor
Fracture	Conchoidal, brittle
Dispersion	Nil
Sources	Germany, UK, USA
Transparency	Transparent–translucent
Class	Borates
Comments	Weak fluorescence under short-wave ultraviolet. Strongly piezo-electric and pyro-electric.

DANBURITE

$CaB_2Si_2O_8$

Danburite (*DAN-burr-ite*) was first found in a dolomite formation associated with microcline and oligioclase feldspars in Connecticut, USA. The original source is now buried beneath the city of Danbury. Other minerals frequently associated with danburite are quartz, cassiterite, dolomite, fluorite and ruby corundum.

Danburite is little known as a gemstone but its popularity with knowledgeable collectors is growing. Its crystals have excellent clarity and they are easy to cut into brilliant attractive gems. Japanese production is limited to a small quantity of light-brown facet rough from Kyushu Island. The majority of the available rough, in the form of bright slender crystals, originates from Charcas, San Luis Potosi, Mexico. The terminations of these crystals are frequently too thin to cut and pieces of clean facet grade material exceeding 5 grams (0.17 oz) are rare.

Refractive Indices	1.63–1.636
Birefringence	0.006
Optic Char./Sign	Biaxial/–
Hardness	7–7.25
Specific Gravity	2.97–3.02
Crystal System	Orthorhombic
Habit	Prismatic
Lustre	Vitreous
Colour Range	Colourless, brown, light yellow, pink
Pleochroism	Weak
Cleavage	Indistinct
Fracture	Sub-conchoidal
Dispersion	0.017
Sources	Japan, Madagascar, Mexico, Myanmar, Switzerland, USA
Transparency	Transparent–translucent
Class	Silicates

DUMORTIERITE

$Al(AlO)_7(B,OH)(SiO_4)_3$

Refractive Indices	1.678–1.689
Birefringence	0.011
Optic Char./Sign	Biaxial/–
Hardness	7
Specific Gravity	3.26–3.36
Crystal System	Orthorhombic
Habit	Prismatic, massive
Lustre	Vitreous, dull
Colour Range	Violet-blue, pink, brown
Pleochroism	Crystals are pleochroic
Cleavage	Nil
Fracture	Uneven, hackly
Dispersion	Nil
Sources	France, Mozambique, USA, Zimbabwe
Transparency	Translucent–semi-opaque
Class	Silicates

Dumortierite (*DO-mort-ierite*) was named for the French pale-ontologist Eugéne Dumortier. It is found in aluminium-rich metamorphic rocks and in contact metamorphic zones. Associated minerals include andalusite, kyanite, lazulite, muscovite, pyrophyllite, sillimanite and staurolite. A boro-silicate mineral, it is widely employed as an ornamental stone in its massive form. The deep violet to blue colour lends itself to the manufacture of attractive cabochons, beads, spheres, eggs and other ornamental objects.

■ The material sold as gem dumortierite is usually quartz with dumortierite inclusions.

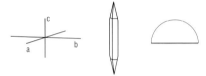

HAMBERGITE

$Be_2(OH)BO_3$

Hambergite (*HAM-berg-ite*) occurs as an accessory mineral in granitic pegmatites typically associated with apatite, beryl, danburite, feldspar, fluorite, quartz, spodumene or zircon. It was named in honour of Swedish mineralogist Axel Hamberg (1863–1933). Madagascar is an important source for facet-grade rough of this rare mineral. Rough pieces seldom exceed 4 grams (0.14 oz). Flawless gems are unusual and the perfect cleavages frequently cause problems for the facetier.

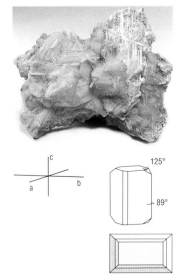

Refractive Indices	1.55–1.63
Birefringence	0.080
Optic Char./Sign	Biaxial/+
Hardness	7.5
Specific Gravity	2.365
Crystal System	Orthorhombic
Habit	Prismatic
Lustre	Vitreous
Colour Range	Colourless, greyish, yellowish
Pleochroism	Nil
Cleavage	Perfect (x2)
Fracture	Uneven brittle
Dispersion	0.015
Sources	Madagascar, Myanmar, Norway, Russia, USA
Transparency	Transparent–translucent
Class	Borates

PERIDOT

$(Mg,Fe)_2SiO_4$

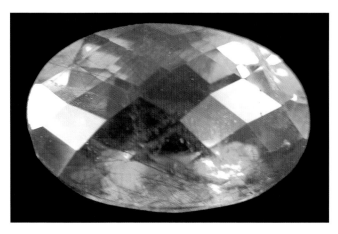

Refractive Indices	1.654–1.689
Birefringence	0.036
Optic Char./Sign	Biaxial/+
Hardness	6.5–7
Specific Gravity	3.25–3.45
Crystal System	Orthorhombic
Habit	Prismatic, massive
Lustre	Vitreous
Colour Range	Green, yellow-green, olive
Pleochroism	Weak
Cleavage	Imperfect
Fracture	Conchoidal
Dispersion	0.020
Sources	Brazil, Egypt, Ethiopia, Kenya, Mexico, Myanmar, Pakistan, USA
Transparency	Transparent–translucent
Class	Silicates

■ Peridot is found on Topazios, an island in the Red Sea. It was probably originally named topaz.

TOP: *Oval, chequer-board cut peridot*
LEFT: *A selection of peridot jewellery*

Peridot (*PER-ih-doe*) is the gem variety of olivine. It is an idiochromatic mineral since iron is not only an essential element in its composition but also the chromophore responsible for its colour. However, analysis of peridot specimens of the finest colour usually reveals a relatively low iron content, with nickel and chromium present as trace elements. Peridot has been mined as a gemstone for thousands of years. The Roman historian Pliny the Elder recorded a verbal tradition that the Egyptians were mining green stone from the Isle of Zabargad in the Red Sea in about 1500 BC. The well-formed crystals from Zabargad (also called Zeberget or the Isle of St. John) occur in a vein of nickel ore that runs through an altered and metamorphosed peridotite rock. In most other sources gem peridot occurs as nodules that have been eroded out of their matrix and worn down to somewhat rounded pebbles. This is certainly true of the gem rough that originates from Arizona, USA, a major source of this gem. Specimens of euhedral crystals in matrix are scarce. Iron-nickel meteorites are probably the most unusual source of peridot; some such material has been faceted and mounted in items of jewellery.

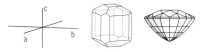

SINHALITE

$MgAlBO_4$

Sinhalite (*SIN-ha-lite*) is a rare mineral that until recently was known only in the form of alluvial rough from gem gravels in Sri Lanka. First discovered in 1952, its value is restricted by its uninspiring olive-green colour, but there is a limited production

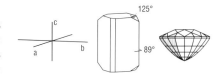

of cut stones from Sri Lanka that is sought after by collectors of the rare and unusual. Studies of a water-worn crystal from Mogok in Myanmar afforded the first morphological data for this species. An occurrence of pale pink to brownish pink chrome-sinhalite has been reported from northeast Tanzania.

Refractive Indices	1.667–1.705
Birefringence	0.038
Optic Char./Sign	Biaxial/–
Hardness	6.5
Specific Gravity	3.47–3.49
Crystal System	Orthorhombic
Habit	Waterworn
Lustre	Vitreous
Colour Range	Brown, golden-brown, olive-green, greenish-yellow
Pleochroism	Strong
Cleavage	Distinct (x2)
Fracture	Conchoidal
Dispersion	0.017
Sources	Myanmar, Sri Lanka, Tanzania
Transparency	Transparent–translucent
Class	Borates

■ The name sinhalite is derived from *Sinhala*, the Sanskrit name for Sri Lanka.

KORNERUPINE

$MgAl_2SiO_6$

Refractive Indices	1.665–1.678
Birefringence	0.013
Optic Char./Sign	Biaxial/–
Hardness	6.5–7
Specific Gravity	3.28–3.35
Crystal System	Orthorhombic
Habit	Elongated prisms
Lustre	Vitreous
Colour Range	Colourless, brown, green, pink, white, yellow
Pleochroism	Trichroic
Cleavage	Distinct (x2)
Fracture	Conchoidal
Dispersion	0.018
Sources	Australia, Greenland, Kenya, Madagascar, Myanmar, Sri Lanka
Transparency	Transparent–translucent
Class	Silicates

Kornerupine (*cor-ne-ROO-peen*) originates in regional metamorphic environments but the rare pieces of gem rough that are found normally occur with andalusite, chrysoberyl, diopside, garnet, iolite, ruby, sapphire, spinel, topaz and zircon as water-worn pebbles in parcels of gem rough that have been recovered from alluvial gravels. Intense green, strongly pleochroic material is found in Madagascar. Asteriated material occurs in Myanmar and some of the attractive light green material from the Taita Hills of southern Kenya will yield chatoyant cabochons.

■ An asteriated kornerupine has been reported from Mogok.

PREHNITE

$Ca_2 Al_2 Si_3 O_{10}(OH)_2$

Refractive Indices	1.616–1.649
Birefringence	0.033
Optic Char./Sign	Biaxial/+
Hardness	6–6.5
Specific Gravity	2.8–2.95
Crystal System	Orthorhombic
Habit	Nodular
Lustre	Vitreous–waxy
Colour Range	Colourless, green, grey, white
Pleochroism	Nil
Cleavage	Good
Fracture	Uneven
Dispersion	Nil
Sources	Australia, Austria, Canada, China, France, Germany, India, Namibia, Scotland, South Africa, USA
Transparency	Transparent–opaque
Class	Silicates

Prehnite (PRAY-nite) is usually deposited from hydrothermal solutions often occurring as thick crystalline crusts lining cavities in mafic igneous rocks. It creates radial spheres, nodules, stalactites and epimorphs over epidote, laumontite and other pre-existing minerals. Associated minerals include calcite, datolite, epidote, fluorapophyllite, laumontite, pectolite, quartz and stilbite.

Well-developed individual crystals are rare. Faceted gems are seldom fully transparent and they tend to exhibit a somewhat 'sleepy' appearance, meaning they lack the 'fire' of more lively gems. Most gemmy prehnite rough is cut as cabochons or carved.

■ Discovered by Colonel H. von Prehn (1733–1785) in Cape Province, South Africa.

MARCASITE

FeS_2

Refractive Indices	Nil
Birefringence	Nil
Optic Char./Sign	Nil
Hardness	6–6.5
Specific Gravity	4.85–4.90
Crystal System	Orthorhombic
Habit	Bladed, prismatic, tabular
Lustre	Metallic
Colour Range	Brassy yellow with a greenish tint
Pleochroism	Nil
Cleavage	Poor
Fracture	Uneven, brittle
Dispersion	Nil
Sources	China, France, Mexico, Peru, Russia, USA
Transparency	Opaque
Class	Sulphides

The fact that the name marcasite (*MARK-ah-seet*) is derived from the Arabic word for pyrite is one of several causes of confusion between these two minerals. Marcasite and pyrite are polymorphs. The 'marcasite' of the jewellery trade is actually pyrite, the more stable, cubic form of iron sulphide. The less stable marcasite is of little importance to the gem and ornamental stone trades, but makes an interesting inclusion in the sagenitic agate from Nipomo, California.

■ Stainless steel is sometimes substituted for pyrites in inexpensive costume jewellery.

TANTALITE

$(Fe,Mn)(Ta,Nb)_2O_6$

Tantalite (*TAN-tal-lite*), the iron tantalate, forms a replacement series with the niobium tantalate columbite and in combination they form columbo-tantalite, an economic mineral that commonly occurs in lithium-rich granitic pegmatites. Associated minerals include albite, amblygonite, apatite, beryl, cassiterite, lepidolite, spodumene and tourmaline. An important ore of the scarce metallic elements niobium and tantalum, colombo-tantalite is essentially opaque black and has occasionally been cut as cabochons. Manganotantalite is formed when manganese virtually eliminates the iron element from the formula. It is an intense red transparent material that is capable of yielding superb gems when faceted. If antimony replaces the iron in columbo-tantalite, then stibiotantalite is formed. This is a heavier mineral with a density of 7.46. It is brighter than columbo-tantalite, with refractive indices of 2.39–2.46, and somewhat softer, with a hardness of 5.5–6. It can be cut into bright fiery golden-brown gems that bear some resemblance to sphalerite.

Refractive Indices	2.190–2.457
Birefringence	0.083
Optic Char./Sign	Biaxial/+
Hardness	6–6.5
Specific Gravity	5.3–8.0
Crystal System	Orthorhombic
Habit	Prismatic
Lustre	Sub-metallic
Colour Range	Black, brown, red
Pleochroism	Sometimes strong
Cleavage	Distinct (x2)
Fracture	Sub-conchoidal
Dispersion	Nil
Sources	Canada, Finland, Madagascar, Mozambique, Norway, USA, Zimbabwe
Transparency	Translucent–opaque
Class	Tantalates

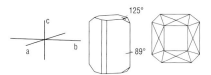

ZOISITE

$Ca_2Al_3(SiO_4)_3(OH)$

Refractive Indices	1.68–1.72
Birefringence	0.008–0.010
Optic Char./Sign	Biaxial/+
Hardness	6–7
Specific Gravity	3.15–3.36
Crystal System	Orthorhombic
Habit	Prismatic
Lustre	Vitreous
Colour Range	Blue, brown, green, pink, reddish, violet
Pleochroism	Strong
Cleavage	Distinct
Fracture	Conchoidal
Dispersion	0.0196
Sources	Austria, India, Mexico, Mozambique, Tanzania, USA
Transparency	Transparent–translucent
Class	Silicates

■ The tanzanite mines at Merelani were originally worked for graphite.

TOP: *Oval brilliant tanzanite 12.07ct*
LEFT: *Tanzanite rings*

OPPOSITE PAGE
TOP LEFT: *A variety of zoisite colours*
TOP RIGHT: *A blue zoisite crystal*
BOTTOM LEFT: *A clino-zoisite cabochon*
RIGHT MIDDLE AND BOTTOM: *A tanzanite heart and pear*

Zoisite (*ZOE-site*) and its relative clino-zoisite belong to the structurally complex epidote group of minerals. Zoisite occurs most frequently in crystalline schists that have formed through the dynamic metamorphism of basic igneous rocks. Associated minerals include calcite, corundum, the garnet varieties andradite and grossular, and hornblende and quartz. The mineral suddenly came to the fore as a gem material with the dramatic discovery in 1967 of large transparent intense violet-blue crystals near Arusha, northern Tanzania. The blue crystals were identified as zoisite. Attractive green zoisite combined with ruby crystals was already being mined at Longido, and there was some russet-brown to grey-green zoisite associated with the graphite mined in the Merelani Hills. The search for the source of the blue crystals ended below outcrops of the graphite ore-body. Specimens of the dull coloured zoisite from the mine were sent to the company in Germany that was cutting the blue crystals. They pre-formed several stones and then subjected them to heat treatment. The russet brown stones changed to a superb violet-blue colour. The stones that had originally been brownish-grey-green changed to a somewhat steely blue. The stones are now marketed under the trade name 'Tanzanite'.

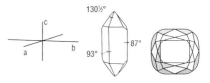

The largest tanzanite crystal to date weighs 16,839 carats (3.4 kilos) and the largest cut tanzanite 242 carats.

Before 1967 there were already three members of the zoisite group that had found minor niches in the world of gems:

Thulite is a pleasant pink or mottled pink-and-white variety that was initially found in Norway and named after Thule, the ancient name for that country. It is also found in Austria, Australia and the USA. Used for cabochons and as an ornamental stone it has a hardness of 6, density of 3.1 and refractive index of 1.70.

Anyolite – a name derived from *anyoli*, the Masai word for green – is an ornamental stone mined near Longido, Tanzania. It comprises massive emerald-green, chrome-rich zoisite that combines with black amphibole to form the matrix for large, vividly coloured ruby crystals. Incredible sculptures and a wide range of objets d'art have been worked from this strikingly colourful material.

Saussurite is a compact green variety that is frequently mottled with flecks of white and occasionally carries inclusions of black metallic spinel. It has frequently been employed as a jade substitute.

BROOKITE

TiO$_2$

Refractive Indices	2.583–2.741
Birefringence	0.122
Optic Char./Sign	Biaxial/+
Hardness	5.5–6
Specific Gravity	3.87–4.08
Crystal System	Orthorhombic
Habit	Tabular–platy
Lustre	Adamantine–sub-metallic
Colour Range	Dark brown, greenish black, reddish, yellowish
Pleochroism	Nil
Cleavage	Indistinct
Fracture	Sub-conchoidal
Dispersion	Strong
Sources	Austria, England, France, Russia, Switzerland, USA, Wales
Transparency	Translucent–opaque
Class	Oxides

Brookite (*BROOK-ite*) occurs in granite, porphyry, gneiss, chlorite and mica schists associated with anatase, rutile, quartz, feldspar, chalcopyrite, hematite and sphene. It forms a polymorphic group with rutile and anatase. The platy crystals of brookite assume a pseudo-hexagonal form in contrast to the rod-like or needle-like forms of rutile. Seldom occurring in sizes or shapes suitable for working, brookite is rarely faceted as a gemstone.

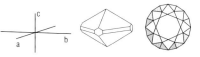

ENSTATITE

(Mg,Fe)SiO$_3$

Enstatite (*EN-stah-tite*) is found in both metamorphic and igneous rocks. It has also been identified in some meteorites. Associated minerals include augite, feldspars and garnets. It forms a solid solution series with hypersthene and ferrosilite. Enstatite-hypersthene specimens show an increase in both density and refraction directly related to the proportion of iron in their com-

Refractive Indices	1.663–1.673
Birefringence	0.009–0.011
Optic Char./Sign	Biaxial/+
Hardness	5.5
Specific Gravity	3.26–3.28
Crystal System	Orthorhombic
Habit	Prismatic, lamellar
Lustre	Vitreous, pearly
Colour Range	Colourless, green, olive-green, grey, brown
Pleochroism	Nil
Cleavage	Prismatic (x2)
Fracture	Conchoidal
Dispersion	Weak
Sources	Austria, India, Myanmar, South Africa, Tanzania, USA
Transparency	Transparent–opaque
Class	Silicates

position. The hand spectroscope may reveal a single clear-cut absorption line at 5060Å. Transparent brown faceted stones from Mysore, India sold as enstatite have a specific gravity of 3.30, refractive indices of 1.669–1.680 and negative optical sign:

therefore they are much closer to hypersthene than to enstatite in their composition. An iron rich sub-variety from Austria with a bronze-like sub-metallic lustre is sold as Bronzite. Chrome enstatite is an emerald green sub-variety that is coloured by a trace of chrome. Glassy green enstatite material from Sri Lanka yields chatoyant cabochons. Green material with oriented inclusions has produced six-rayed star cabochons.

NATROLITE

$Na_2Al_2Si_3O_{10}-2H_2O$

Refractive Indices	1.473–1.502
Birefringence	0.012–0.013
Optic Char./Sign	Biaxial/+
Hardness	5.5–6
Specific Gravity	2.21–2.26
Crystal System	Orthorhombic
Habit	Slender prismatic
Lustre	Vitreous
Colour Range	Colourless, white, tinted-brown and yellow, green, red
Pleochroism	Nil
Cleavage	Perfect (x2)
Fracture	Irregular, brittle
Dispersion	Weak
Sources	Canada, India, USA
Transparency	Transparent–translucent
Class	Silicates

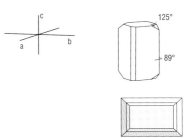

Natrolite (*NA-tro-lite*) produces some fine crystal specimens but it is often seen at its best as an accessory to other minerals. Fine, clean, radiating sprays of natrolite crystals enhance the beauty of many associated minerals including apophyllite, benitoite, neptunite, stilbite and other zeolites. Natrolite is rarely available in the form of colourless facet rough and the massive white material is of no interest to the lapidary.

CHLORASTROLITE

Ca2(Mg,Fe)Al$_2$(SiO$_4$)(Si$_2$O$_7$)(OH)$_2$·H$_2$O)

Chlorastrolite (*klor-AST-roh-lite*) is a name derived from two Greek words: *chloros*, meaning green, and *astros*, meaning star. Lake Superior, and especially the shoreline of the Isle Royale, is the source of light blue-green material. Deeper greens occur in the basalts of Houghton and Keweenaw Counties, Michigan, USA. Chlorastrolite occurs in cavities in amygdaloidal basalt tending to fill the smaller voids, few of which are larger than a pea. It is widely used in brooches, tiepins and other jewellery items that are not subjected to heavy wear. Mottled light and dark green in colour, it forms a network of radiating stellate structures with individual segments exhibiting a degree of chatoyancy. This pattern is responsible for its popular name, 'turtleback'. Associated minerals include agate, datolite, prehnite and thomsonite. Chlorastrolite is a variety of pumpellyite. Uigite, a variety of chlorastrolite, occurs on the Isle of Skye off the west coast of Scotland.

Refractive Indices	1.65–1.66
Birefringence	0.010
Optic Char./Sign	Nil
Hardness	5–6
Specific Gravity	3.18–3.23
Crystal System	Orthorhombic
Habit	Radial fibrous
Lustre	Silky–pearly
Colour Range	Light to dark green with white banding
Pleochroism	Nil
Cleavage	Nil
Fracture	Splintery–granular
Dispersion	Nil
Sources	USA (Michigan)
Transparency	Translucent–opaque
Class	Silicates

■ Chlorastrolite is the state stone of Michigan, USA.

SAMARSKITE

(YCeUFe)$_3$(NbTaTi)$_5$O$_{16}$

Samarskite occurs in granitic pegmatites associated with columbite, tantalite, euxenite, feldspars, fergusonite, gadolinite, monazite, quartz and zircon. The lustrous jet-black crystals are rare and make interesting cabinet specimens. However, they contain rare earth metals and are sufficiently radioactive to damage other specimens and people. In view of the dangers, the popularity of samarskite cabochons as jewellery stones is almost incomprehensible.

Refractive Indices	Nil
Birefringence	Nil
Optic Char./Sign	Isotropic
Hardness	5–6
Specific Gravity	4.30–5.87
Crystal System	Orthorhombic
Habit	Prismatic, massive
Lustre	Vitreous–sub-metallic
Colour Range	Dark brown to velvet black
Pleochroism	Nil
Cleavage	Poor
Fracture	Conchoidal, brittle
Dispersion	Nil
Sources	Brazil, Madagascar, Norway, Russia, Sweden, USA
Transparency	Nearly opaque
Class	Oxides

 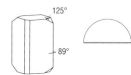

PLANCHÉITE

$Cu_8Si_8O_{22}(OH)_4.H_2O$

Planchéite is named for J. Planché, who first collected specimens of the copper mineral from the Congo region. Planchéite occurs as rosettes, spherules or radiating sprays of feathery acicular crystals in association with numerous colourful secondary copper minerals such as dioptase, cerussite, chrysocolla and conichalcite. The lapidary may find it needs some care to avoid undercutting. It is worth a little extra time since it can make very attractive cabochons.

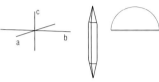

Refractive Indices	1.645–1.715
Birefringence	0.070
Optic Char./Sign	Biaxial +
Hardness	5.5
Specific Gravity	3.6–3.8
Crystal System	Orthorhombic
Habit	Fibrous radial
Lustre	Vitreous–silky
Colour Range	Blue, very light blue, turquoise
Pleochroism	Distinct
Cleavage	Nil
Fracture	Fibrous
Dispersion	Relatively strong
Sources	Argentina, Congo-Zaire, Democratic Republic of Congo, France, Germany, Italy, Namibia, Norway, South Africa, UK, Zambia
Transparency	Translucent–opaque
Class	Silicates

■ Planchéite was formerly known as Shattuckite.

GOETHITE

FeO(OH)

Goethite (*GUR-tite*) was named after Johann von Goethe, the German philosopher, poet and playwright. It used to have a reputation for being a rather dull item but this is far from true today with a fine variety of specimens available. Good pieces may consist of a radiating cluster of deep black crystals or massive stalactites that exhibit a rainbow of iridescent colours. Goethite also occurs in many striking forms as an inclusion in quartz crystals. The gem rough that is traded as cacoxenite is actually tufts of golden-yellow goethite needles in amethyst. Interesting free forms are often polished from this material.

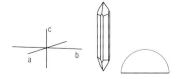

Refractive Indices	2.26–2.398
Birefringence	0.138
Optic Char/Sign	Biaxial –
Hardness	5–5.5
Specific Gravity	4.27 – 4.29
Crystal System	Orthorhombic
Habit	Botryoidal, stalactitic, bladed, columnar
Lustre	Adamantine, metallic, silky, dull, earthy
Colour Range	Black, brown, russet, yellow
Pleochroism	Visible
Cleavage	Perfect (1x)
Fracture	Uneven, splintery, brittle
Dispersion	Relatively strong
Sources	Australia, Brazil, Canada, Czech Republic, France, Germany, Italy, Mexico, South Africa, UK, USA
Transparency	Opaque
Class	Hydroxides

ABOVE LEFT: *Goethite crystal cluster*
ABOVE RIGHT: *Goethite and quartz crystal cavity*

THOMSONITE

$NaCa_2Al_5Si_5O_{20}-6H_2O$

Thomsonite (*TOM-son-ite*) is one of the more unusual zeolites. A secondary mineral resulting from the breakdown of feldspars, it occurs in cavities in igneous rocks, especially lava flows. Associated minerals are calcite, chabazite, natrolite, quartz and stilbite. It is brittle, very rarely forms crystals, and occurs mostly as mottled or banded massive material. Tightly compacted acicular radiating clusters can be cut into interesting cabochons.

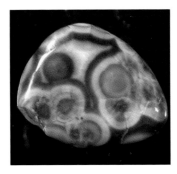

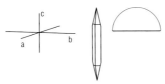

Refractive Indices	1.511–1.545
Birefringence	0.005–0.015
Optic Char./Sign	Biaxial +
Hardness	5–5.5
Specific Gravity	2.3–2.4
Crystal System	Orthorhombic
Habit	Spherical concretions
Lustre	Vitreous, pearly, porcellaneous
Colour Range	Brown, green, red, white, yellow, colourless
Pleochroism	Nil
Cleavage	Perfect (x2)
Fracture	Uneven
Dispersion	Distinct–strong
Sources	Germany, Italy, Scotland, USA
Transparency	Translucent–opaque, transparent
Class	Silicates

■ Thomsonite forms spherical aggregates that bear a resemblance to agate.

HEMIMORPHITE

$Zn_4Si_2O_7(OH)_2-H_2O$

Refractive Indices	1.614–1.636
Birefringence	0.022
Optic Char./Sign	Biaxal +
Hardness	4.5–5
Specific Gravity	3.4–3.5
Crystal System	Orthorhombic
Habit	Bladed, botryoidal
Lustre	Vitreous
Colour Range	Brown, colourless, blue-green, green, white, yellow, light blue
Pleochroism	Distinct
Cleavage	Perfect
Fracture	Sub-conchoidal, brittle
Dispersion	Nil
Sources	England, France, Italy, Mexico, Namibia, Siberia, USA, Zambia
Transparency	Transparent–translucent
Class	Silicates

Hemimorphite (*HEMI-morph-ite*) literally means 'half shape', a reference to the contrasting terminations at opposite ends of a crystal. Hemimorphite occurs in two very different forms: either as fan-shaped aggregates of thin, colourless, bladed crystals, or as blue to blue-green botryoidal crusts that resemble smithsonite or prehnite. These crusts often exhibit bands of colour and the material is sometimes fashioned into cabochons. Associated minerals include calcite, limonite and smithsonite.

CONICHALCITE

CaCu(AsO$_4$)(OH)

Refractive Indices	1.730–1.846
Birefringence	0.041–0.046
Optic Char./Sign	Biaxial +/-
Hardness	4.5
Specific Gravity	4.1
Crystal System	Orthorhombic
Habit	Fibrous, massive
Lustre	Vitreous, greasy
Colour Range	Green, yellow-green, blue-green
Pleochroism	Nil
Cleavage	Nil
Fracture	Nil
Dispersion	Very strong
Sources	Russia (Siberia), Spain, USA
Transparency	Sub-translucent–opaque
Class	Arsenates

Conichalcite (*CONE-ih-kal-site*) is a massive material composed of radiating spherules that can be cut into interesting cabochons.

LITHIOPHILITE

Li(Mn,Fe)PO$_4$

Lithiophilite, (*LITHIO-phy-lite*) is a scarce primary phosphate mineral. It is found in phosphate-rich peg-matites. Lithiophilite alters readily to other colourful and gemmy phosphate minerals such as dickinsonite, eosphorite, fairfieldite, purpurite and vivianite. Associated miner-als include albite, amblygonite, beryl, lepidolite, quartz and spodumene. It forms a series with triphylite. Triphylite is difficult to obtain in facet grade but it may be cut into interesting green to pink colour change gems.

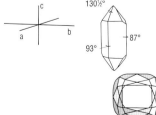

Refractive Indices	1.669–1.682
Birefringence	0.013
Optic Char./Sign	Biaxia/+
Hardness	4–5
Specific Gravity	3.34
Crystal System	Orthorhombic
Habit	Massive
Lustre	Vitreous, resinous
Colour Range	Greenish-brown, reddish-brown, pinkish
Pleochroism	Strong
Cleavage	Near perfect basal
Fracture	Uneven
Dispersion	Weak
Sources	Australia, Brazil, Canada, Germany, India, Namibia, Poland, Portugal, USA
Transparency	Transparent–translucent
Class	Phosphates

PURPURITE

MnPO4

Refractive Indices	1.85–1.92
Birefringence	0.070
Optic Char./Sign	Biaxial/+
Hardness	4–4.5
Specific Gravity	3.4
Crystal System	Orthorhombic
Habit	Massive
Lustre	Vitreous–sub-metallic
Colour Range	Purple–red, pink
Pleochroism	Strong
Cleavage	Good
Fracture	Uneven
Dispersion	Relatively strong
Sources	Australia, France, Namibia, USA
Transparency	Translucent–opaque
Class	Phosphates

Purpurite (*PURR-pure-ite*) is the manganese-rich end member and heterosite the iron-rich end member of a phosphate series. Purpurite has a colour that is so striking that this alone would ensure its popularity with the gem and mineral fraternity if it were not such a rarity. It is an alteration product of another rare mineral, lithiophilite. The gradual replacement that has taken place molecule by molecule results in a pseudomorph or 'false shape'. The mineral now has the chemistry of purpurite but retains the crystal shape and symmetry of lithiophyllite.

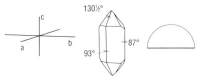

VARISCITE

$AlPO_4 \cdot 2H_2O$

Refractive Indices	1.55–1.59
Birefringence	0.031
Optic Char./Sign	Biaxial/-
Hardness	3.5–5
Specific Gravity	2.2–2.57
Crystal System	Orthorhombic
Habit	Massive
Lustre	Waxy
Colour Range	Bluish-green, colourless, red, yellow-green, white
Pleochroism	–
Cleavage	–
Fracture	Uneven
Dispersion	–
Sources	Australia, Belgium, Brazil, France, Germany, Senegal, Spain, UK, USA
Transparency	Sub-translucent–opaque
Class	Phosphates

Variscite (*VARE-iss-ite*) is a richly coloured and patterned hydrous aluminium phosphate. It lends itself to the manufacture of attractive cabochons and small objets d'art or it can be milled into beads. The name is derived from Variscia, the region in Germany where the mineral was first discovered. Alternative names include Amatrice and Utahlite. Associated minerals are apatite, chalcedony, crandallite, limonite and wardite.

SCORODITE

$FeAsO_4-2H_2O$

Scorodite (*SKO-row-dite*) is a rare and colourful secondary arsenate that forms in the upper oxidation zones of arsenic-rich ore bodies. It is associated with adamite, arsenio-siderite, arseno-pyrite, limonite and olivenite. Scorodite may also occur as a precipitate on the outer rim of hot springs. The bright greens and blues displayed by this mineral ensure that crystal specimens are sought after display items.

Refractive Indices	1.74–1.92
Birefringence	0.160
Optic Char./Sign	Biaxial/+
Hardness	3.5–4
Specific Gravity	3.1–3.3
Crystal System	Orthorhombic
Habit	Octahedral, prismatic
Lustre	Sub-adamantine
Colour Range	Blue. Brown, colourless, green, white, yellow
Pleochroism	Nil
Cleavage	Poor
Fracture	Conchoidal
Dispersion	Relatively strong
Sources	Algeria, Austria, Brazil, Canada, England, Greece, Mexico, Namibia, USA
Transparency	Transparent–translucent
Class	Arsenates

■ Scorodite is soluble in hydrochloric acid.

■ Scorodite gives off a garlic-like smell when heated.

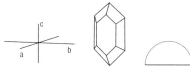

WAVELLITE

$4AlPO_4.2Al(OH)_3.9H_2O$

Refractive Indices	1.520–1.561
Birefringence	0.025–0.026
Optic Char./Sign	Biaxial/+
Hardness	3.5–4
Specific Gravity	2.31–2.36
Crystal System	Orthorhombic
Habit	Spherical aggregates
Lustre	Vitreous
Colour Range	Black, brown, green, white, yellow
Pleochroism	Nil
Cleavage	Perfect
Fracture	Uneven
Dispersion	Nil
Sources	Czech Republic, France, Germany, USA
Transparency	Transparent, translucent
Class	Phosphates

Wavellite (*WAVE-ell-ite*) is a secondary aluminium phosphate that is found in ore deposits, especially in association with limonite and phosphorite. Crystals are rare and the mineral usually forms clusters of green spherical aggregates. In Arkansas, USA, wavellite occurs in a beige-coloured chert matrix and it is often coated with bright green variscite, another aluminium phosphate. Broken spherules reveal a radiating structure of fine bright crystals usually coloured by traces of vanadium in a shade of green that might range from deep emerald through bright green and apple green to pastel green. The mineral is occasionally found in other colours including yellow and black. Wavellite is cut as interesting cabochons, slabs and other ornamental objects.

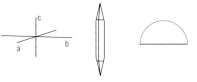

CELESTITE

$SrSO_4$

Refractive Indices	1.621–1.633
Birefringence	0.009–0.010
Optic Char./Sign	Biaxial/+
Hardness	3–3.5
Specific Gravity	3.96–4.00
Crystal System	Orthorhombic
Habit	Tabular, prismatic
Lustre	Vitreous
Colour Range	Blue, colourless, orange, yellow
Pleochroism	Weakly trichroic
Cleavage	Perfect (x 2)
Fracture	Uneven
Dispersion	Nil
Sources	Canada, England, Germany, Madagascar, USA
Transparency	Transparent–translucent
Class	Sulphates

Celestite (*sell-EST-ite*) occurs in sandstones and limestone and is commonly associated with barite, calcite, dolomite, fluorite, gypsum, halite and sulphur. It usually fluoresces chalky-blue under short-wave ultraviolet light. Celestite is typically pale blue or colourless, but a quarry in Ontario, Canada, produces orange material.

Brown, yellow and greenish specimens have also been reported. The mineral forms as tabular and prismatic crystals and may also occur in pseudo-hexagonal trillings. It can be massive, grainy, nodular, radiating, or take the form of numerous lustrous crystals lining geodes: the last-named habit, particularly prevalent in Madagascar, is very popular with crystal collectors. The mineral's cleavage and brittleness make it difficult to facet. Cut stones in excess of 10 carats are unusual.

■ Celestite geodes from Madagascar make superb cabinet specimens.

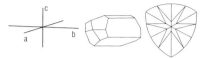

CERUSSITE

PbCO$_3$

Refractive Indices	1.804–2.078
Birefringence	0.274
Optic Char./Sign	Biaxial/–
Hardness	3–3.5
Specific Gravity	6.5+
Crystal System	Orthorhombic
Habit	Prismatic (striated lengthwise)
Lustre	Adamantine+
Colour Range	Black, blue-green, colourless, grey, white, yellow
Pleochroism	Nil
Cleavage	Distinct
Fracture	Conchoidal
Dispersion	0.051
Sources	Australia, Democratic Republic of Congo, Germany, Morocco, Namibia, USA
Transparency	Transparent–translucent
Class	Carbonates

The name cerussite (ser-YOU-site) is derived from the Latin for white lead, *cerussa*. This mineral is found in the oxidation zone of lead deposits, usually in association with galena, barite, calcite and anglesite. The high lustre and interesting twinned forms of cerussite specimens ensure their lasting popularity in crystal collections. Cerussite exhibits three basic types of twinning: elbow- or chevron-shaped twins, cyclic twins and reticulated twins. Elbow twinning is the most common form. Cyclic twins may form star shapes with six 'spokes' extending from the central star. Specimens of reticulated twinning are usually very intricate, forming superb complex structures of interconnecting beams. Cerussite's high sensitivity to heat makes cold dopping essential. Facet cutting is not very difficult but finishing is tricky and the stones should be polished on a wax lap.

■ Damaged crystals of Cerussite from Tsumeb in Namibia afford excellent facet rough.

TOP: *Doubly terminate crystal*
BOTTOM: *Parallel twin crystals*

ADAMITE

$Zn_3As_2O_8 \cdot Zn(OH)_2$

Refractive Indices	1.708–1.744
Birefringence	0.025
Optic Char./Sign	Biaxial/+/–
Hardness	3.5
Specific Gravity	4.34–4.35
Crystal System	Orthorhombic
Habit	Radiating clusters
Lustre	Sub-adamantine
Colour Range	Colourless, green, violet, yellow
Pleochroism	Nil
Cleavage	Distinct (x 1)
Fracture	Conchoidal
Dispersion	Strong
Sources	Algeria, Chile, Greece, France, Mexico, Namibia, USA
Transparency	Transparent–translucent
Class	Arsenates

Adamite (*A-dam-ite*) is a rare mineral occurring in the form of drusy interlocking crystals in the oxidized zone of zinc ore-bodies. The lustrous clusters of bright lime-green radiating crystals exhibit dramatic fluorescence under both long- and short-wave ultraviolet light.

TOP: *Fan-shaped adamite cluster*
LEFT: *Adamite on matrix, Namibia*

Adamite crystal groups are popular collector's items. Rare larger single crystals unsuitable for specimens but having some clarity can be made into attractive faceted stones.

WITHERITE

$BaCO_3$

Refractive Indices	1.529–1.677
Birefringence	0.148
Optic Char./Sign	Biaxial/–
Hardness	3–3.75
Specific Gravity	4.27–4.35
Crystal System	Orthorhombic
Habit	Massive
Lustre	Vitreous
Colour Range	Colourless, yellow, white
Pleochroism	Nil
Cleavage	Distinct (x1)
Fracture	Uneven
Dispersion	Low
Sources	Canada, England, Japan, USA
Transparency	Transparent–translucent
Class	Phosphates

Witherite (*WITHER-ite*) occurs in veins frequently associated with galena. Crystals are always twinned and massive material is usually 'sleepy'. Facetable pieces are generally small and gem rough seldom exceeds five grams (0.17 oz). The translucent material is sometimes cut as cabochons.

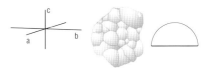

ANHYDRITE

$CaSO_4$

Refractive Indices	1.571–1.614
Birefringence	0.043
Optic Char./Sign	Biaxial/+
Hardness	3.5
Specific Gravity	3.0
Crystal System	Orthorhombic
Habit	Tabular
Lustre	Vitreous
Colour Range	Blue, colourless, grey, violet, white
Pleochroism	Weak
Cleavage	Perfect (x3)
Fracture	Uneven
Dispersion	0.013
Sources	Canada, Germany, Mexico, Peru, USA
Transparency	Transparent–translucent
Class	Sulphates

Anhydrite (*an-HIDE-rite*) does not form directly, but is the result of the de-watering of the rock-forming mineral gypsum ($CaSO_4$-$2H_2O$). This loss of water produces a reduction in volume of the rock layer and can cause the formation of cavities in which the anhydrite is often associated with calcite and halite. It may also occur as a pseudomorph after halite. Good mineral specimens of anhydrite are very rare. Nevertheless, anhydrite showing a good blue colour in well-formed crystals has been found in Mexico and Peru. Salt mines appear to be the only source of small crystals and irregular fragments of clean facet-grade rough.

It fluoresces LW Blue (R) LW Red. SW Pink, is very highly heat sensitive and brittle. It is rarely seen either in faceted stones or as cabochons since the material ranges from very difficult to virtually impossible to cut.

ARAGONITE

CaCO₃

Refractive Indices	1.530–1.686
Birefringence	0.155
Optic Char./Sign	Biaxial/–
Hardness	3.5–4
Specific Gravity	2.93–2.95
Crystal System	Orthorhombic
Habit	Acicular
Lustre	Vitreous
Colour Range	Brown, grey, reddish, white, yellow
Pleochroism	Strong
Cleavage	Distinct x 1
Fracture	Sub-conchoidal
Dispersion	Low
Sources	Austria, England, France, Mexico, Morocco, Namibia, Spain, USA
Transparency	Transparent–translucent
Class	Carbonates

■ Aragonite is a polymorph of calcite, meaning that it has the same chemical composition but a different physical structure.

Aragonite (*ah-RAG-on-ite*) is a polymorph of calcite. Calcite is the more stable form and when aragonite is heated to 400°C it will spontaneously convert to calcite. Aragonite fluoresces SW Green-white (R) Pink (C) White (C) SW/LW Red (O) Tan (O), LW Pink (O) White (O), has a moderate heat sensitivity and is very brittle. It is probably best known for its occurrence in the form of pseudo-hexagonal twin crystals. Specimens of these cyclic twins or trillings were first found at the original deposit in Aragon, Spain, that gave the mineral its name. Superb clusters of these cyclic twins are now available from Morocco. Typical aragonite deposits occur at hot springs, in cavities in volcanic rocks and in cave formations. These deposits may be compact, granular, massive or radially fibrous in texture. Massive material may be deposited in horizontal layers, encrusted, oolitic, stalactitic or stalagmitic. A layered sedimentary marble-like formation sometimes referred to as Mexican Onyx is used for carvings and ornamental purposes. Aragonite forms the basis of many organic gems. Coral polyps secrete aragonite and employ it as a building material. Mother-of-pearl, the lustrous inner coating that lines the shells of various shellfish, is composed of numerous layers of minute aragonite platelets; pearls are largely composed of aragonite.

ABOVE LEFT: *Aragonite crystal clusters*
BELOW: *An aragonite sphere*

SHORTITE

$Na_2Ca_2(CO_3)_3$

Shortite (*SHORE-tite*) was named for Dr Maxwell Short, Professor of Mineralogy at the University of Arizona. The type locality for this mineral is the Westvaco Mine, in the Green River formation, Sweetwater County, Wyoming, USA.

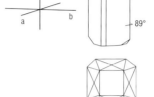

Refractive Indices	1.531–1.570
Birefringence	0.039
Optic Character	Biaxial -
Dispersion	Moderate
Hardness	3
Specific Gravity	2.605
Crystal System	Orthorhombic
Habit	Wedge-shaped, tabular, prismatic
Lustre	Vitreous
Colour Range	Colourless, light yellow, light green
Pleochroism	Nil
Cleavage	Distinct
Fracture	Conchoidal, brittle
Sources	Canada, India, Russia, Tajikistan, Uganda, USA
Transparency	Transparent
Class	Carbonates

ANGLESITE

$PbSO_4$

Anglesite (*AN-gles-ite*) occurs in the oxidized zone of lead deposits. Well-formed crystals – jutting out of the matrix like flattened blades and exhibiting the high lustre typical of lead minerals – make eye-catching cabinet specimens. The mineral gets its name from the type locality on Anglesey, an island off the north coast of Wales.

The mineral commonly fluoresces orange–yellow under both long and short-wave ultraviolet light; some specimens fluoresce chalky white under short-wave ultraviolet light. Anglesite yields very attractive faceted stones but coaxing a finished gem from this brittle, heat sensitive material can be quite a challenge. The mineral is seldom found as distinct crystals.

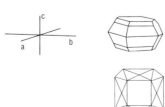

Refractive Indices	1.877–1.894
Birefringence	0.017
Optic Char./Sign	Biaxial/+
Hardness	2.75–3
Specific Gravity	6.30–6.39
Crystal System	Orthorhombic
Habit	Tabular
Lustre	Vitreous–adamantine
Colour Range	Blue, grey, green, white, yellow
Pleochroism	Nil
Cleavage	Distinct (x2)
Fracture	Conchoidal
Dispersion	0.044
Sources	Australia, England, Mexico, Morocco, Namibia, Tunisia, USA, Wales
Transparency	Transparent–opaque
Class	Sulphates

BARITE (BARYTE/BARYTES)

$BaSO_4$

Refractive Indices	1.636–1.648
Birefringence	0.012
Optic Char./Sign	Biaxial/+
Hardness	3–3.5
Specific Gravity	4.3–4.6
Crystal System	Orthorhombic
Habit	Bladed, tabular
Lustre	Vitreous
Colour Range	Blue, brown, colourless, green, red, white, yellow
Pleochroism	Nil
Cleavage	Perfect, two planes
Fracture	Uneven
Dispersion	Weak
Sources	Canada, England, France, Germany, Spain, USA
Transparency	Transparent–translucent
Class	Sulphates

■ Barite may form stalactites that can be polished as attractive ornaments.

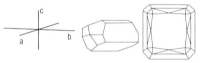

The name barite (*BAR-ite*) or alternatively baryte is derived from the Greek barys meaning heavy. The mineral is still often referred to as 'heavy ore' in the north of England. Many large transparent crystals have been found in Cumbria, England, including a single crystal recovered from the Dufton Lead Mine that weighed 45.36kg (100 lb). An even larger specimen is on display at the Elandsrand Gold Mine offices in South Africa. This euhedral crystal is warm brown in colour, measures 70 x 30 cms (27.5 x 11.8 in) and weighs 64kg (141 lb). Fine groups of barite crystals may be found in association with lead, copper, iron, zinc, gold, silver, nickel, cobalt and manganese in mineralized veins. Damaged crystals suitable for use as facet rough are not uncommon, but the easy cleavage, brittleness and heat sensitivity of this material can cause problems for the facetier. It is unusual to see cut stones in excess of 10 carats.

Bladed crystals of barite sometimes form in a concentric pattern with the crystals increasing in size as they move away from the centre. In Oklahoma, USA, these graduated crystal clusters have formed in reddish sand and the resulting flower-like formations are known as 'Desert Roses'; similar forms of barite occur in the sands near Luderitz, Namibia. Barite has a very high heat sensitivity and is brittle.

PYROPHYLLITE

AlSi$_2$O$_5$OH

Refractive Indices	1.552–1.600
Birefringence	Nil
Optic Char./Sign	Biaxial/–
Hardness	1.5
Specific Gravity	2.65–2.90
Crystal System	Orthorhombic
Habit	Radiating massive
Lustre	Greasy
Colour Range	Brown, green, white, yellow
Pleochroism	Nil
Cleavage	Basal
Fracture	Splintery
Dispersion	Nil
Sources	Belgium, Brazil, China, Mexico, Namibia, Russia, Sweden, Switzerland, USA
Transparency	Translucent–opaque
Class	Silicates

Pyrophyllite (*PIE-roff-ill-ite*) is a common early stage metamorphic mineral that is seldom encountered in the form of good mineral specimens. Associated minerals include albite, andalusite, barite, chlorite, epidote, gypsum, kyanite and quartz. Its name is derived from the Greek words for 'fire' and 'leaf'. It occurs in a fine-grained form that can be lathe-turned to produce small ornamental artefacts.

EUCLASE

BeAlSiO$_4$OH

Euclase (*YOU-clase*) is a name that refers to the easy cleavage of this mineral. Euclase is little known and relatively rare as a gemstone. Flawless gem rough above 1 gram (0.035 oz) is very rare. Its striking, distinctly monoclinic and often vividly bi-coloured striated crystals are well-known and sought after by mineral collectors. Gem rough is usually colourless,

Refractive Indices	1.652–1.672
Birefringence	0.020
Optic Char./Sign	Biaxial/+
Hardness	7.5
Specific Gravity	3.09–3.11
Crystal System	Monoclinic
Habit	Stubby prismatic
Lustre	Vitreous
Colour Range	Colourless, blue, blue-green, light green, purple, yellow
Pleochroism	Conchoidal
Cleavage	Perfect (x1)
Fracture	Nil
Dispersion	0.016
Sources	Brazil, Colombia, Kenya, Russia, Tanzania, Zimbabwe
Transparency	Transparent–translucent
Class	Silicates

sapphire blue or blue-green. Euclase is found in granitic pegmatites associated with other gem minerals such as topaz and beryl. It is easily identified by its crystal form and colouring. The perfect prismatic cleavage can be a problem for gem cutters and reduces durability, limiting the mineral's acceptance as a common gemstone. The uneven colour distribution may be used to advantage if the rough is skilfully oriented by an experienced facetier.

■ Very fine blue, gemmy crystals were produced from the Eurythmic Claim in the Urungwe district of Zimbabwe.

SAPPHIRINE

$(Mg,Al)_4(Al,Si)$

Refractive Indices	1.701–1.734
Birefringence	0.004–0.005
Optic Char./Sign	Biaxial/–
Hardness	7.5
Specific Gravity	3.42–3.48
Crystal System	Monoclinic
Habit	Tabular
Lustre	Vitreous
Colour Range	Light to dark blue, green
Pleochroism	Nil
Cleavage	Nil
Fracture	Conchoidal
Dispersion	0.019
Sources	Canada, France, Greenland, Madagascar, Norway, Sri Lanka, USA
Transparency	Transparent
Class	Silicates

Sapphirine (*SAF-fir-een*) is a rare magnesium aluminium silicate. Generally found as disseminated grains or granular aggregates, it also occurs as irregular tabular crystals. Very small blue stones are faceted for collectors.

CHONDRODITE

$((Mg,Fe)2SiO_4)_2–Mg(F,OH)_2$

The name chondrodite (*CON-drow-dite*) is derived from the Greek word for 'grain', a reference to the complex rounded individual crystals that exhibit a very granular appearance. The mineral is found in hydrothermal deposits, metamorphosed dolomitic limestones, skarn deposits and serpentine. Good crystal specimens will show numerous faces but nevertheless it is difficult to determine their symmetry. Lamellar striations are indicative of twinning. Associated minerals include biotite, calcite, diopside, graphite, magnetite, olivine, serpentine and spinel. Collectors' stones are cut from the red-brown material.

Refractive Indices	1.59–1.64
Birefringence	0.032
Optic Char./Sign	Biaxial/+
Hardness	6–6.5
Specific Gravity	3.1–3.2
Crystal System	Monoclinic
Habit	Prismatic, tabular
Lustre	Vitreous–resinous
Colour Range	Brown, red-brown, orange, yellow
Pleochroism	Trichroic
Cleavage	Distinct
Fracture	Sub-conchoidal–uneven
Dispersion	Nil
Sources	Finland, Italy, Sweden, USA
Transparency	Translucent–seldom transparent
Class	Silicates

■ Chondrodite is a member of the humite group of minerals.

GADOLINITE

$Be_2FeY_2Si_2O_{10}$

Gadolinite (*gah-DOLE-in-ite*) occurs in pegmatite veins forming rough prismatic crystals with diamond-shaped cross-sections and dome terminations. Crystals are predominantly green in colour and exhibit a good lustre. Associated minerals include monazite, fluorite, allanite and feldspar. Massive gadolinite is cut as cabochons for specialist collectors.

Refractive Indices	1.77–1.82
Birefringence	0.005
Optic Char./Sign	Biaxial/+
Hardness	6.5–7
Specific Gravity	4–4.7
Crystal System	Monoclinic
Habit	Prismatic
Lustre	Vitreous
Colour Range	Green, black, brown
Pleochroism	Nil
Cleavage	Indistinct
Fracture	Conchoidal brittle
Dispersion	Nil
Sources	Austria, China, Norway, Russia, Sweden, USA
Transparency	Green: transparent–translucent. Black: opaque
Class	Silicates

JADE, JADEITE

$NaAl(SiO_3)_2$

Refractive Indices	1.65–1.67
Birefringence	0.02
Optic Char./Sign	Biaxial/+
Hardness	6.5–7
Specific Gravity	3.3–3.5
Crystal System	Monoclinic
Habit	Fibrous, massive
Lustre	Vitreous
Colour Range	Black, blue, brown, green, lilac, mauve, orange, pink, red, violet, white, yellow
Pleochroism	Nil
Cleavage	Nil
Fracture	Uneven
Dispersion	Nil
Sources	Japan, Mexico, Myanmar, Tibet, USA
Transparency	Translucent
Class	Silicates

■ Rich emerald green Imperial Jade is called *feits'ui* in Chinese meaning 'Kingfisher plumes'.

TOP: *Carved leaf, bi-colour jadeite*
LEFT: *Oval cabochon, lavender jadeite*

Jadeite occurs in highly metamorphosed sodium-rich serpentinous rocks often in association with aragonite, calcite, nepheline, quartz, serpentine or vesuvianite. However, the majority of gem-quality jadeite is recovered in the form of loose boulders that have survived the weathering away of their matrix. The name jade is derived from the Spanish term *piedra de hijada*, meaning 'stone of the loins', and is a reference to the South American Indian custom of using the stone to treat kidney disease. It was only in about 1750 that Chinese craftsmen were first introduced to jadeite. They called this material 'new jade' to distinguish it from the nephrite and chalcedony that had been used in the creation of the ancient gemstone artworks of China. Because jadeite occurs in a wider range of hues than nephrite and takes a much better finish, it quickly became the material of choice for those who could afford it. The source of this superb material lies in remote upper Myanmar. Every boulder has to be carried by pack animals along the notorious jade trail. Armed guards are hired to protect the precious caravan from bandits on the mountain route to Chiang Mai in northern Thailand. It is here that the first deals are struck and the jade boulders change hands before continuing their long journey to Hong Kong, the world centre of the jade trade. It is amazing to think that despite the costs involved in transporting these boulders in terms of time, money, effort and all too often human lives, the boulders arrive in Hong Kong without anyone having laid eyes on the jade they may contain. The boulders are still intact, holding all their secrets within their ancient weathered rind. Experts examine the boulders looking for indications of the colour they may contain. They must determine the placing of the 'maw', a very small window a few centimetres in size, that will be polished to give potential buyers a hint of the nature of the material. If a green speck is detected in the rind this will definitely be the chosen position. The stone may have hidden fractures, lack translucency or the window may have been placed on the only patch of green in the whole stone, but despite the uncertainty it is not unusual for a boulder to fetch a price in excess of US$100,000.

Chloromelanite is a sub-variety of jadeite that is intermediate in composition between jadeite and acmite. A silicate of sodium, iron and aluminium, it is usually coloured a very dark green or black and it is often referred to as black jadeite. Its average specific gravity of 3.4 is slightly higher than that of jadeite.

Jade-albite or 'Maw-sit-sit' is a bright green chrome-jadeite/albite rock with a pattern of dark green to black veins and spots that occurs in northern Myanmar. It has an RI of 1.52-4 and an SG of 2.46–3.15. It enjoys a strong demand and is used to make attractive cabochons and carvings.

ABOVE: *Carved 'Maw-sit-sit'*

BADDELEYITE

ZrO_2

Baddeleyite (*bed-DELL-ee-ite*) is a rare zirconium mineral first discovered in the gem gravels of Sri Lanka. Its primary mode of occurrence is generally in the form of small black crystals embedded in the carbonate-rich rock of intrusive igneous pipes called carbonatites. In the early 1980s fine crystal specimens, some measuring as much as 15cm in length, were recovered from the Phalaborwa Copper Mine in northeastern South Africa. A gemmy golden-brown crystal fragment from this source was found to fluoresce intense ochre yellow under long-wave light and strong ochre-yellow under short-wave ultraviolet light. Small facet-grade pieces have been recovered as rolled pebbles from the diamond sands of Brazil. With its strong dispersion and high refractive indices this would undoubtedly be a popular stone with facetiers if gem rough were more readily

Refractive Indices	2.13–2.20
Birefringence	0.07
Optic Char./Sign	Biaxial/–
Hardness	6.5
Specific Gravity	5.5–6.0
Crystal System	Monoclinic
Habit	Tabular
Lustre	Vitreous–adamantine
Colour Range	Black, brown, colourless, yellow
Pleochroism	Distinct
Cleavage	Distinct, one plane
Fracture	Conchoidal
Dispersion	Strong
Sources	Brazil, Canada, Italy, Russia, South Africa, Sri Lanka, USA
Transparency	Transparent–translucent
Class	Oxides

JADE, NEPHRITE

$Ca_2(Mg,Fe)_5(OH)_2(Si_4O_{11})_2$

Refractive Indices	1.60–1.65
Birefringence	0.03
Optic Char./Sign	Biaxial/–
Hardness	6.5
Specific Gravity	2.90–3.02
Crystal System	Monoclinic
Habit	Massive fibrous
Lustre	Nil
Colour Range	Brown, green, white
Pleochroism	Nil
Cleavage	Nil
Fracture	Splintery
Dispersion	Nil
Sources	Canada, China, Korea, New Zealand, Siberia, Taiwan, Turkestan, USA, Zimbabwe
Transparency	Translucent
Class	Silicates

Nephrite is an amphibole and a member of the tremolite-actinolite series. A metamorphic mineral, it is commonly associated with gneisses, schist, serpentine and marble. Nephrite tends to occur in highly metamorphosed zones at contact points between rocks of dissimilar character. In Ch'unch'on, Korea, for example, the 'Baek Ok' or white jade occurs along the plane of contact between a body of dolomite-marble and the surrounding biotite schists. Nephrite is comprised of interlocking masses of fine fibrous crystals making it very tough. In its lighter coloured forms its chemical composition is close to that of tremolite, and in the darker material it is nearer to actinolite. In the South Island of New Zealand the nephrite is usually called 'green stone' and it is often carved in the form of 'Hei tiki' the traditional fertility amulets of the Maori people (these are more usually known as 'Tikki' in the case of modern pendants). While it is most frequently green in hue, oxidation of its iron content may impart some brown colouring. Chinese craftsmen make skilful use of this variation in colour when carving jade. Because of its remarkable toughness, nephrite was used in tools and weapons by many early cultures, including the Chinese in Asia, the Celts in Europe, the Indians of South and Central America and the Maoris of New Zealand.

Some nephrite from Taiwan, Alaska and Wyoming exhibits distinct chatoyancy when it is cut as high domed cabochons or beads. The material marketed as 'Snowflake jade' from Wyoming is actually a combination of tremolite amphibole and albite feldspar.

■ Rounded rough pebbles of nephrite resemble kidneys, and were called lapis nephriticus (kidney stone).

TOP LEFT AND RIGHT: *Carved nephrite*
ABOVE: *'Tikki' fertility symbol, New Zealand*

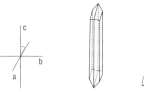

EPIDOTE

$Ca_2(Al,Fe)_3(SiO_4)_3(OH)$

Epidote (*EP-ee-dote*) is a structurally complex mineral. Crystal groups are rarely found in specimen quality but the unique pistachio colour of this material can be striking. Specimens include slender striated crystals and acicular sprays. It also occurs in fibrous, granular or massive forms. Associated minerals include actinolite, andradite, biotite, calcite and hornblende. Relatively large specimens of flawless facet rough are sometimes available but faceted stones are limited to small sizes, and appear black because of the very dark tone of the material.

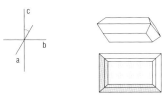

Refractive Indices	1.736–1.770
Birefringence	0.034
Optic Char./Sign	Biaxial/–
Hardness	6–7
Specific Gravity	3.3–3.5
Crystal System	Monoclinic
Habit	Prismatic, tabular
Lustre	Vitreous
Colour Range	Green, Brown, Black
Pleochroism	Strong
Cleavage	Good (1x)
Fracture	Uneven–conchoidal
Dispersion	0.030
Sources	Austria, Brazil, Italy, Mexico, USA
Transparency	Transparent–translucent
Class	Silicates

■ Chrome green epidote is known as 'Tawmawite'.

SPODUMENE

$LiAlSi_2O_6$

Refractive Indices	1.660–1.676
Birefringence	0.015
Optic Char./Sign	Biaxial/+
Hardness	6.5–7
Specific Gravity	3.13–3.20
Crystal System	Monoclinic
Habit	Prismatic
Lustre	Vitreous
Colour Range	Colourless, green, lilac, pink, white, yellow
Pleochroism	Strong
Cleavage	Perfect (x2)
Fracture	Splintery
Dispersion	0.017
Sources	Afghanistan, Brazil, Madagascar, Pakistan, USA
Transparency	Transparent–translucent
Class	Silicates

Spodumene (*SPOD-you-meen*) is a rock-forming mineral occurring in lithium-rich granites and pegmatites. Transparent gem spodumene forms euhedral crystals in pegmatite cavities in association with lepidolite, plagioclase, quartz, topaz and tourmaline.

■ Non-gem crystals of spodumene are a valuable source of lithium.

Spodumene is known under several varietal names depending on its colour. The well-known lilac-pink variety kunzite was named in honour of G.F. Kunz, the American gem expert. The rare emerald green variety hiddenite was named after A.E. Hidden, superintendent at the North Carolina mine where the deep green crystals were first discovered. Triphane is the varietal name for light yellow-green to yellow spodumene. Very fine large stones can be cut from spodumene but this material exhibits strong pleochroism and gem rough must be correctly oriented to bring out its full potential. Perfect cleavages and splintery fracture can make the faceting of large spodumene gems a distinct challenge.

PREVIOUS PAGE: *A range of spodumene*
ABOVE LEFT: *Etched green spodumene*
ABOVE: *Oval brilliant kunzite 15.02ct*

CLINOHUMITE

$(Mg,Fe^{2+})_9[(F,OH)_2(SiO_4)_4]$

Clinohumite was first discovered in boulders of metamorphosed limestone that were ejected from Mt Vesuvius. The name alludes to its monoclinic crystals. Lively orange-yellow gems have been cut from facet rough that was mined from deposits in the Pamir Mountains of Tajikistan.

Refractive Indices	1.623–1.728
Birefringence	0.028
Optic Character	Biaxial +
Dispersion	0.021
Hardness	6
Specific Gravity	3.2–3.4
Crystal System	Monoclinic
Habit	Prismatic–rounded
Lustre	Vitreous–resinous
Colour Range	Yellow, red, brown, orange
Pleochroism	Yellow–colourless
Cleavage	Poor
Fracture	Sub-conchoidal
Sources	Australia, Austria, Brazil, Canada, India, Italy, Tajikistan, Finland, Spain, USA
Transparency	Transparent–translucent
Comments	UV: Under SW light coloured stones usually exhibit tan to yellow-orange fluorescence
Class	Silicates

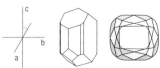

FELDSPAR (ORTHOCLASE)

KAlSi$_3$O$_8$

Orthoclase (*OR-tho-clase*). The name is taken from the Greek *orthos* ('right') and *kalo* ('I cleave'), and refers to the two cleavages present in this mineral that meet virtually at right angles. Orthoclase occurs in intrusive and extrusive igneous bodies and metamorphic rocks. An alkali feldspar orthoclase is a common component of granite rocks. Moonstone is the most important variety, especially the fine Sri Lankan orthoclase that exhibits a strong blue adularescence. Thin alternating layers of orthoclase and albite create the light interference in this material that is responsible for its 'schiller' or 'floating moon effect'. Material from the Indian deposits is found in a wide range of pastel shades. It tends to be translucent to semi-opaque and is typically cut in high domed cabochons that may either have a degree of schiller or be distinctly chatoyant. Some orthoclase exhibits weak fluorescence, bluish under long-wave light and orange under short-wave ultraviolet. Feldspar in its transparent and colourless form, termed adularia, is found in the Swiss Alps. It is sometimes faceted for collectors but it yields insipid cut stones. The facet grade yellow to golden coloured orthoclase that originates from Madagascar is much more inspiring. Superb stones are cut from this material that sometimes exceed 100 carats in weight. Coloured by iron, the absorption spectrum of this material comprises a broad diffuse band at 4480Å and a more distinct band at 4200Å.

Attractive transparent blue-green feldspar occurs in the pegmatites of the Karoi District of Zimbabwe. It is associated and frequently confused with aquamarine, another gem material that is relatively plentiful in these mica fields. Clean stones seldom exceed 5 carats in weight.

Sanidine is a glassy sub-variety of orthoclase feldspar that occurs in the German Rhineland and in USA. Colourless, beige and attractive warm-brown stones have been faceted from this material.

Refractive Indices	1.52–1.525
Birefringence	0.005
Optic Char./Sign	Biaxial/–
Hardness	6
Specific Gravity	2.56–2.59
Crystal System	Monoclinic
Habit	Tabular
Lustre	Vitreous–pearly
Colour Range	Brown, bluish, colourless, green, orange, pink, yellow
Pleochroism	Nil
Cleavage	Easy (x2)
Fracture	Uneven
Dispersion	0.012
Sources	India, Madagascar, Myanmar, Sri Lanka, Switzerland, Zimbabwe
Transparency	Transparent–translucent
Class	Silicates

■ Moonstone (*below*) is regarded as a sacred stone in India and tradition ruled that stones for sale must be displayed on a yellow cloth.

TOP: *Pear shape orthoclase 37.6ct, Madagascar*

ABOVE: *Oval moonstone cabochon, Sri Lanka*

LEFT: *Sanidine colour range, Germany*

PETALITE

LiAlSi$_4$O$_{10}$

Petalite (*PET-al-ite*) – from the Greek petalon meaning 'leaf' – occurs in lithium-rich granite pegmatites. Well-formed crystals and facet rough are rare. The mineral is usually found in its massive form and material with colour is sometimes cut as cabochons.

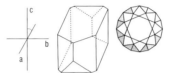

Refractive Indices	1.505–1.519
Birefringence	0.014
Optic Char./Sign	Biaxial/+
Hardness	6–6.5
Specific Gravity	2.39–2.46
Crystal System	Monoclinic
Habit	Massive
Lustre	Vitreous–pearly
Colour Range	Colourless, grey, reddish or greenish white, yellow
Pleochroism	Nil
Cleavage	Perfect
Fracture	Conchoidal, brittle
Dispersion	0.0141
Sources	Afghanistan, Sweden, USA, Zimbabwe
Transparency	Transparent–translucent
Class	Silicates

■ Rare cut petalite stones exhibit a glassy appearance (*see* left).

ACTINOLITE

Ca$_2$(Mg,Fe)$_5$(OH)$_2$(Si4O11)2

Actinolite (*ak-TIN-oh-lite*) is the iron-rich member of the tremolite–actinolite series. Its name, derived from the Greek *actinos* meaning 'ray', is a reference to the radiating habit of its crystals. It occurs in metamorphic rocks associated with epidote and quartz, has a low heat sensitivity and is moderately tough. Colourful compact material may be used for ornamental carvings or cut as cabochons (*see* jade). Material in which the needle-like crystals run parallel will yield chatoyant cabochons and fine specimens are sold as 'jade cat's-eye' in Taiwan. Chatoyant

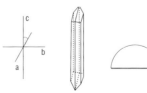

Refractive Indices	1.614–1.640
Birefringence	0.026
Optic Char./Sign	Biaxial/–
Hardness	5.5–6
Specific Gravity	3.0–3.3
Crystal System	Monoclinic
Habit	Long bladed crystals
Lustre	Vitreous
Colour Range	Green, white
Pleochroism	Distinct
Cleavage	Perfect (x 1)
Fracture	Uneven
Dispersion	Nil
Sources	Canada, China, Madagascar, New Zealand, Russia, Taiwan, USA.
Transparency	Translucent rarely transparent
Class	Silicates

rough occurs in Alaska, British Columbia and Taiwan. Single well-developed crystals are uncommon and the only source of gem-quality rough is Madagascar. Transparent actinolite can be faceted into small attractive gems.

TREMOLITE

$Ca_2Mg_5(OH)_2(Si4O_{11})_2$

Tremolite (*TREM-oh-lite*) is probably best known as a densely interwoven mat of needles in nephrite jade or as fine needle-like inclusions in quartz or emerald. However, the needles orient themselves to produce a nice sharp cat's-eye effect in cabochons cut from the compact green tremolite from Ontario, Canada.

Transparent lilac-pink hexagonite, a tremolite variety from St. Lawrence County, New York, exhibits orange fluorescence under ultraviolet light.

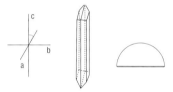

Refractive Indices	1.60–1.62
Birefringence	0.02
Optic Char./Sign	Biaxial/–
Hardness	5–6
Specific Gravity	2.9–3.3
Crystal System	Monoclinic
Habit	Prismatic
Lustre	Vitreous
Colour Range	Colourless, green, grey, lavender, lilac-pink
Pleochroism	Nil
Cleavage	Perfect (x2)
Fracture	Uneven
Dispersion	Nil
Sources	Canada, USA
Transparency	Transparent–opaque
Class	Silicates

■ Tremolite is a basic component of jade.

BERYLLONITE

$NaBe(PO_4)$

Beryllonite (*BER-ill-on-ite*), sodium beryllium phosphate, occurs in phosphate-rich pegmatites. The short prismatic to tabular crystals are frequently heavily included. The supply of facet rough is very limited and usually takes the form of limpid colourless material originating from localities in Maine, USA.

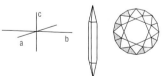

Refractive Indices	1.552–1.562
Birefringence	0.009
Optic Char./Sign	Biaxial/–
Hardness	5.5–6
Specific Gravity	2.80–2.852
Crystal System	Monoclinic
Habit	Short prisms
Lustre	Vitreous
Colour Range	Colourless, white, pale yellow
Pleochroism	None
Cleavage	Perfect
Fracture	Conchoidal
Dispersion	0.010
Sources	Afghanistan, Brazil, Canada, England, Finland, Portugal, Sweden, USA
Transparency	Transparent
Class	Phosphates

BRAZILIANITE

$NaAl_3(PO_4)_2(OH)_4$

Refractive Indices	1.603–1.623
Birefringence	0.02
Optic Char./Sign	Biaxial/+
Hardness	5.5
Specific Gravity	2.94–2.98
Crystal System	Monoclinic
Habit	Prismatic
Lustre	Vitreous
Colour Range	Colourless, yellow, yellowish-green
Pleochroism	Nil
Cleavage	Perfect, one plane
Fracture	Conchoidal
Dispersion	0.014
Sources	Brazil, USA
Transparency	Transparent–translucent
Class	Phosphates

Brazilianite (*bra-ZIL-ee-an-ite*) occurs in phosphate-rich igneous pegmatites. As its name indicates it was first discovered in Brazil. It was subsequently found at the Palermo Mine in New Hampshire, USA, where it is associated with quartz, feldspar and apatite. Brazilianite crystals are typically short, prismatic and distinctly striated. Specimen crystals and facet rough are currently sourced from Minas Gerais, Brazil and New Hampshire, USA. Brazilianite polishes well and makes an attractive gem since it has interesting green and golden hues, a vitreous lustre and relatively good hardness for a phosphate mineral. Brazilian crystals may attain several hundred carats but they are seldom free of flaws and clean faceted gems in excess of 15 carats are unusual.

DIOPSIDE

$CaMg(SiO_3)_2$

Diopside (*DYE-op-side*) has an interesting range of gemmy sub-varieties, including chrome diopside; intense green (Finland, Madagascar); fine blue violane (Italy); colourless to pale green alalite (Canada), and translucent yellow malacolite. Semi-opaque material packed with parallel acicular inclusions yields green cat's-eye

LEFT: *Star diopside*
OPPOSITE PAGE
TOP: *Chrome diopside*

cabochons. Near opaque black material with masses of intersecting oriented needle-like inclusions is often cut into star cabochons with four mobile silvery white rays. Associated minerals are actinolite, andradite, grossular, calcite, chlorite, dolomite, fluorite, olivine, phlogopite and vesuvianite.

Refractive Indices	1.664–1.694
Birefringence	0.03
Optic Char./Sign	Biaxial/+
Hardness	5–6
Specific Gravity	3.2–3.38
Crystal System	Monoclinic
Habit	Prismatic, massive
Lustre	Vitreous
Colour Range	Colourless, blue, brown, green, grey, yellow
Pleochroism	Trichroic
Cleavage	Distinct (x1)
Fracture	Conchoidal
Dispersion	Nil
Sources	Brazil, Canada, Finland, Italy, Madagascar, Myanmar, Russia, USA
Transparency	Transparent–translucent
Class	Silicates

■ A violet variety of diopside from the Italian Piedmont is called Violane.

RICHTERITE

$Na_2Ca(Mg,Fe^{2+})_5Si_8O_{22}(OH)_2$

Richterite (*RICK-ter-ite*) is an uncommon mineral belonging to the amphibole group. It occurs in bodies of contact metamorphosed limestone, igneous extrusive rocks and metasomatic deposits. The Langban Mine in Sweden is the type locality. Associated minerals are aegirine, calcite, chromite, diopside, eudialyte, fluorite, pectolite, phlogopite, quartz and sodalite. It was one of

the minerals discovered in the Canyon Diablo meteorite, Arizona, USA. It is also found sporadically in both the N'Chwaning 1 and Wessels mines of the Kalahari manganese field of South Africa, usually in association with calcite, pectolite, quartz and sugilite. Substantial pieces of massive cabochon grade material are sometimes recovered among the manganese ore. When crystals are found they are slender and prismatic with a diamond shaped cross-section.

Refractive Indices	1.605–1.641
Birefringence	Nil
Optic Char./Sign	Biaxial
Hardness	5–6
Specific Gravity	2.97–3.45
Crystal System	Monoclinic
Habit	Prismatic
Lustre	Vitreous–dull
Colour Range	Blue, brown, green, rose red, yellow
Pleochroism	Distinct
Cleavage	Perfect
Fracture	Uneven
Dispersion	Nil
Sources	Canada, Madagascar, Myanmar, South Africa, Sweden, USA
Transparency	Transparent–translucent
Class	Silicates

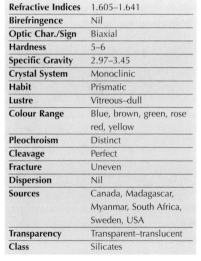

LAZULITE

$(Mg,Fe)Al_2(PO_4)_2(OH)_2$

Lazulite (*LAZE-you-lite*) is a relatively rare phosphate mineral that forms a solid solution series with the mineral scorzalite. The magnesium-rich lazulite lies at the lighter and brighter end of the scale, whereas specimens of the iron-rich scorzalite tend to be darker in tone, less transparent and higher in density. It occurs in association with andalusite, brazilianite, corundum, garnet, kyanite, quartz and rutile. Lazulite is sometimes confused with two better known and more abundant minerals: lazurite, a silicate, and azurite, a copper carbonate. An unusual aspect of lazulite is that it is more frequently encountered as euhedral crystals than in its massive form.

Refractive Indices	1.615–1.645
Birefringence	0.030
Optic Char./Sign	Biaxial/–
Hardness	5.5–6
Specific Gravity	3.1
Crystal System	Monoclinic
Habit	Pyramidal, massive
Lustre	Vitreous
Colour Range	From light sky blue to dark azure blue
Pleochroism	Strong
Cleavage	Distinct (x1)
Fracture	Uneven
Dispersion	0.014
Sources	Austria, Brazil, Canada, India, Madagascar, Sweden, Switzerland, USA
Transparency	Transparent–translucent
Class	Phosphates

DATOLITE

$HCaBSiO_5$

Datolite (*DAT-oh-lite*) occurs as a secondary mineral filling cavities in eruptive rocks in association with calcite, prehnite and diverse zeolites. Transparent crystals can be faceted into moderately brilliant stones, although brittleness is a problem when polishing. Facet grade rough seldom exceeds 2g. The massive opaque material is often suitable for cutting as cabochons.

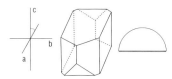

Refractive Indices	1.626–1.670
Birefringence	0.044
Optic Char./Sign	Biaxial/–
Hardness	5–5.5
Specific Gravity	2.9–3.0
Crystal System	Monoclinic
Habit	Prismatic, tabular
Lustre	Vitreous
Colour Range	Colourless, green, pink, red, violet, yellow
Pleochroism	Nil
Cleavage	Nil
Fracture	Conchoidal
Dispersion	0.016
Sources	USA (Massachusetts, New Jersey and Connecticut)
Transparency	Transparent–opaque
Class	Silicates

■ Massive pieces of datolite from Lake Superior in North America make attractive cabochons.

SPHENE (TITANITE)

$CaTiSiO_5$

Refractive Indices	1.900–2.034
Birefringence	0.134
Optic Char./Sign	Biaxial/+
Hardness	5–5.5
Specific Gravity	3.3–3.6
Crystal System	Monoclinic
Habit	Wedge-shaped prisms
Lustre	Adamantine
Colour Range	Black, brown, green, red, white, yellow
Pleochroism	Distinct
Cleavage	Indistinct
Fracture	Conchoidal
Dispersion	0.051
Sources	Austria, Canada, India, Italy, Madagascar, Pakistan, Russia, Switzerland, USA
Transparency	Transparent–translucent
Class	Titano-silicates

Sphene (*SFEEN*), a name that is derived from the Greek word for 'wedge', is an allusion to the typical crystal shape of the mineral. It occurs in plutonic igneous rocks, in certain metamorphic rocks, especially iron- and magnesium-rich schists and gneisses, and in some granular limestones. It may also be encountered in iron ore deposits. Crystals that form in vugs in granite or gneiss are often associated with adularia, apatite, chlorite and smoky quartz. An unusual variety named Greenovite that occurs in Narukot, India, and the Piedmont region of Italy owes its rose-red colouring to traces of manganese. Sphene offers an interesting variety of crystal forms for the collector. It facets into eye-catching, very brilliant, fiery gems.

■ Sphene is also known as titanite.

TRIPLITE

$Mn^{2+},Fe^{2+})_2[(F,OH) PO_4]$

The name triplite (*TRIP-lite*), derived from the Greek word *triplos* meaning 'triple', is an allusion to its three distinct cleavage directions. Stones that are cut as a challenge by experienced facetiers hold an appeal for specialised collectors.

Refractive Indices	1.650–1.680
Birefringence	0.030
Optic Character	Biaxial +
Dispersion	Relatively strong
Hardness	5
Specific Gravity	3.64
Crystal System	Monoclinic
Habit	–
Lustre	Vitreous–resinous
Colour Range	Brown, red-brown, black
Pleochroism	Distinct
Cleavage	Distinct (x3)
Fracture	Sub-conchoidal
Sources	Argentina, Australia, Austria, Brazil, Canada, Czech Republic, France, Madagascar, Mozambique, Namibia, Pakistan, Portugal
Transparency	Translucent–opaque
Class	Phosphates

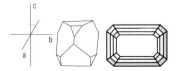

AUGELITE

$2Al_2O_3P_2O_53H_2O$

Augelite (*AWE-jell-ite*) is an extremely rare phosphate mineral found at very few locations. Identification is difficult when it is found as clear and colourless tiny crystals. Augelite occurs in granitic pegmatites and hydrothermal veins, has a low heat sensitivity and is very brittle. The best locality has been White Mountain, Mono County, California and this appears to be the only deposit on record as having produced facet grade rough.

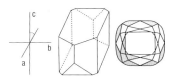

Refractive Indices	1.574–1.588
Birefringence	0.014
Crystal System	Monoclinic
Optic Char./Sign	Biaxial/+
Hardness	4.5–5
Specific Gravity	2.7
Habit	Prismatic, tabular
Lustre	Vitreous
Colour Range	Blue, colourless, pink, white, yellow
Pleochroism	Nil
Cleavage	Perfect (x 1)
Fracture	Conchoidal
Dispersion	Nil
Sources	Bolivia, Canada, Sweden, USA
Transparency	Transparent–translucent
Class	Phosphates

CHILDRENITE

(Fe, Mn)$AlPO_4(OH)_2$–H_2O

Childrenite (*CHILL-dren-ite*), a secondary mineral, was discovered in Devon, England. It is believed to be an alteration product of primary granitic phosphates in the presence of water and aluminium. Also found in ore veins, it forms a solid solution series with eosphorite. Eosphorite – (Mn, Fe)$AlPO_4$(OH)$_2$–H_2O – is less dense and pinkish to rose-red in hue due to manganese replacing some of the iron that is present in childrenite. Childrenite forms tabular or bladed individuals and lamellar aggregates in contrast to the slender crystals and rosettes formed by eosphorite. Associated minerals are chlorite, feldspar, hureaulite, lithiophilite, pyrite, quartz and triphylite. Both minerals are generally found as crystals, but facet-quality rough is rare and cut stones are usually relatively small.

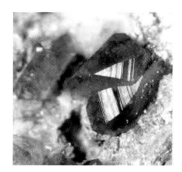

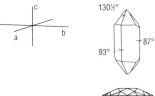

Refractive Indices	1.649–1.691
Birefringence	0.041–0.042
Optic Char./Sign	Biaxial/–
Hardness	4.5–5
Specific Gravity	3.06–3.25
Crystal System	Monoclinic
Habit	Tabular, Prismatic
Lustre	Vitreous–resinous
Colour Range	Brown, yellow-brown, dark-yellow
Pleochroism	Trichroic
Cleavage	Imperfect
Fracture	Conchoidal
Dispersion	Strong
Sources	Afghanistan, Australia, Austria, Brazil (Minas Gerais), Bolivia, Canada, England (Devon and Cornwall), France, Germany, Portugal, Sweden, USA (South Dakota)
Transparency	Transparent–translucent
Class	Phosphates

■ Childrenite is closely related to eosphorite.

CHAROITE

$K(Na,Ca)_{11}(Ba,Sr)S118O_{46}(OH,F)–nH_2O$

Charoite (*CHA-ro-ite*) is a rare mineral that has been found to date in a single location, the Chary River at Aldan in Russia. It formed as a result of the alteration of limestones induced by the close presence of an alkali-rich nepheline syenite intrusion. Heat, pressure and, more importantly, the infusion of rare elements into the rock brought about its transformation into the new mineral. Charoite is used as a gemstone in cabochon form, inlays and intarsia work, and as an ornamental stone. Its swirling patterns of interlocked crystals in lavender, lilac, violet and purple are unique and its appearance is unmistakable.

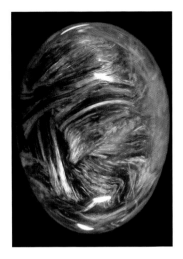

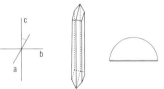

Refractive Indices	1.55–1.56
Birefringence	0.009
Optic Char./Sign	Nil
Hardness	5
Specific Gravity	2.5–2.8
Crystal System	Monoclinic
Habit	Fibrous interlocking masses
Lustre	Vitreous–pearly
Colour Range	Lilac, purple, violet, silvery-white
Pleochroism	Nil
Cleavage	Nil
Fracture	Conchoidal
Dispersion	Nil
Sources	Russia (Aldan on the Charo River, Yakutia)
Transparency	Translucent
Class	Silicate

■ Massive gemmy blocks of Charoite, up to 30cm in diameter, have been found near Chary River, Siberia.

DURANGITE

$Na(Al,F)AsO_4$

Durangite (*du-RANG-ite*) occurs in veins in alkaline rhyolite and in granitic pegmatites. It forms typical euhedral crystals up to 1cm in size. It is associated with amblygonite, cassiterite, fluorite, hematite, mimetite, tantalite and topaz. Named for the source at the Barranca tin mine, Durango, Mexico, facet rough is very rare and difficult to work because the mineral is brittle and easily fusible. It may however be faceted for specialist collectors.

Refractive Indices	1.662–1.712
Birefringence	0.050
Optic Char./Sign	Biaxial/–
Hardness	5–5.5
Specific Gravity	3.97–4.07
Crystal System	Monoclinic
Habit	Prismatic
Lustre	Vitreous
Colour Range	Orange, red-orange, red, yellow
Pleochroism	Trichroic
Cleavage	Distinct (x2)
Fracture	Uneven
Dispersion	Weak
Sources	Canada, England, Mexico, USA
Transparency	Transparent–opaque
Class	Arsenates

HERDERITE

CaBe(F,OH)PO$_4$

Herderite (*HERD-erite*) is a rather scarce phosphate mineral of limited occurrence in granite pegmatites. It forms good single crystals and interesting twins. Some specimens have been found to fluoresce a deep blue under long-wave ultraviolet light, and others exhibit a moderate green fluorescence under both long-wave and short-wave ultraviolet. Pleasant light blue and yellow gems have been faceted for collectors.

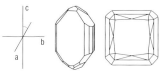

Refractive Indices	1.594–1.624
Birefringence	0.030
Optic Char./Sign	Biaxial/–
Hardness	5–5.5
Specific Gravity	2.9–3
Crystal System	Monoclinic
Habit	Prismatic
Lustre	Vitreous
Colour Range	Colourless, blue, light green, blue-green, yellow
Pleochroism	Nil
Cleavage	Indistinct (x2)
Fracture	Subconchoidal
Dispersion	Nil
Sources	Brazil, Germany, Russia, USA
Transparency	Transparent–translucent
Class	Phosphates

■ Herderite is named after S. van Herder, a mining official in Saxony.

MESOLITE

Na$_2$Ca$_2$Al$_6$Si$_9$O$_{30}$–8H$_2$O

Mesolite (*MEZ-oh-lite*) is a popular zeolite mineral that occurs in vesicular cavities in basalts and similar rocks. Ideal specimens consist of radiating sprays of acicular ice-clear crystals associated with green apophyllite, pink heulandite and drusy quartz. Mesolite is a sodium calcium zeolite that is positioned midway between natrolite (a sodium zeolite) and scolecite (a calcium zeolite). All three zeolites are closely related and may be found in association. When they occur in the form of radiating acicular clusters it is hard to distinguish between them. Generally, however, scolecite forms the larger more robust crystals, natrolite occurs in thinner crystals with pyramidal terminations, and mesolite's fibre-like crystals are usually the thinnest of the three. Massive material can be cut into cabochons with a silky lustre or in some cases a chatoyant (cat's-eye) effect.

Refractive Indices	1.505–1.506
Birefringence	0.001
Optic Char./Sign	Biaxial/+
Hardness	5–5.5
Specific Gravity	2.29
Crystal System	Monoclinic
Habit	Acicular, massive
Lustre	Vitreous
Colour Range	Colourless, white
Pleochroism	Nil
Cleavage	Perfect (x2)
Fracture	Conchoidal-uneven
Dispersion	Nil
Sources	Canada, Iceland, India, Ireland, Italy (Sicily), Scotland, USA
Transparency	Transparent–translucent
Class	Silicates

HODGKINSONITE

$Zn_2MnSiO_4(OH)_4$

Refractive Indices	1.720–1.746
Birefringence	0.022–0.026
Optic Char./Sign	Biaxial/-
Hardness	4.5–5
Specific Gravity	3.9
Crystal System	Monoclinic
Habit	Blocky prismatic
Lustre	Vitreous
Colour Range	Brown, black, lavender, orange, pink, purple, violet
Pleochroism	Nil
Cleavage	Perfect (x1)
Fracture	Uneven, brittle
Dispersion	Moderate
Sources	USA (New Jersey)
Transparency	Transparent–translucent
Class	Silicates

Hodgkinsonite (*HODGE-kin-son-ite*) is the product of metamorphism of hemimorphite and smithsonite. It was named after H. H. Hodgkinson, who discovered it in 1913. Associated minerals include barite, calcite, descloizite, spessartite, willemite and zincite. Franklin Furnace, New Jersey, USA has been the sole source of facet-quality rough. The fragments have been small and the best colours have been bright pink and lavender.

LEGRANDITE

$Zn_2AsO_4(OH)–H_2O$

Refractive Indices	1.675–1.740
Birefringence	0.060
Optic Char./Sign	Biaxial/+
Hardness	4.5–5
Specific Gravity	3.98–4.04
Crystal System	Monoclinic
Habit	Prismatic
Lustre	Vitreous
Colour Range	Colourless, straw, orange-yellow
Pleochroism	Nil
Cleavage	Poor (x1)
Fracture	Uneven
Dispersion	Strong
Sources	Australia, Brazil, Germany, Greece, Japan, Mexico, USA, Zimbabwe
Transparency	Transparent–translucent
Class	Phosphates

Legrandite (*le-GRAND-ite*) is a rare mineral that is best known by its presence in the oxidation zone of silver ore-bodies in Mexico. At the Mapimi Silver Mine near Durango, it occurs in association with adamite, aragonite, austinite, calcite, limonite, mimetite, paradamite, pyrite, smithsonite and sphalerite. Legrandite generally forms in tight clusters but occasionally single crystals are found that are large enough to yield faceted gems.

PSEUDOMALACHITE

$Cu_5(PO_4)2(OH)_4$

Pseudomalachite (*SEU-do-MAL-a-kite*) occurs as a secondary mineral in weathered hydrothermal copper deposits. This uncommon copper phosphate bears a remarkable resemblance to malachite in both colour and form. Usually radiating and spherical or botryoidal it often forms paint-like crusts. The rare crystals may attain 6mm in length, and they are typically rough and rounded. Associated minerals include libethenite, malachite, cornetite, chrysocolla and quartz.

Refractive Indices	1.791–1.867
Birefringence	0.076
Optic Char./Sign	Biaxial/–
Hardness	4.5
Specific Gravity	3.6–4.34
Crystal System	Monoclinic
Habit	Botryoidal
Lustre	Vitreous
Colour Range	Light and dark green
Pleochroism	Nil
Cleavage	Imperfect
Fracture	Conchoidal
Dispersion	Perceptible
Sources	Australia, England, Germany, Russia, USA, Zaire, Zambia
Transparency	Translucent
Class	Phosphates

■ Pseudomalachite is an oxidation product of copper ore bodies.

FRIEDELITE

$Mn_8Si_6O_{15}(OH,Cl)_{10}$

Friedelite (*FREE-del-ite*) occurs in metamorphosed manganese deposits. It is usually massive in form but it may also be found as tabular crystals. Friedelite typically exhibits a dull red fluorescence under both long- and short-wave ultraviolet light, although specimens have been reported that show bright yellow under long-wave and green under short-wave. Material from Franklin Furnace, New Jersey, USA has yielded rose-red to orange-red cabochons and faceted stones.

Refractive Indices	1.63–1.66
Birefringence	0.030
Optic Char./Sign	Biaxial
Hardness	4 -5
Specific Gravity	3.07
Crystal System	Monoclinic
Habit	Pseudo-hexagonal, tabular, massive
Lustre	Vitreous
Colour Range	Colourless, brown, pink, orange, red, russet, yellow
Pleochroism	Nil
Cleavage	Imperfect
Fracture	Uneven, tough
Dispersion	Nil
Sources	France, South Africa, Sweden, USA
Transparency	Transparent–translucent
Class	Silicates

BAYLDONITE

$(PbCu)_3As_2O8(PbCu)(OH)_2H_2O$

Bayldonite (*BAIL-done-ite*) is a complex hydrated lead copper arsenate that frequently takes the form of mamillary concretions of radiating fibrous crystals in the oxidized zone of ore deposits. It may also occur as tabular individual crystals. Associated minerals include azurite, cerussite, duftite, mimetite, quartz and wulfenite. Bayldonite was first discovered at the Penberthy Croft Mine, Cornwall, England. Fine specimens originated from the Tsumeb copper mine in northern Namibia. Can be cut into attractive cabochons.

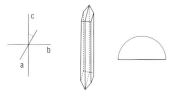

Refractive Indices	1.95–1.99
Birefringence	0.040
Optic Char./Sign	Biaxial/+
Hardness	4.5
Specific Gravity	4.35
Crystal System	Monoclinic
Habit	Mamilliary fibrous
Lustre	High resinous–sub-metallic
Colour Range	Green, yellow-green, yellow
Pleochroism	Nil
Cleavage	Nil
Fracture	Uneven
Dispersion	Relatively weak
Sources	England (Cornwall); Namibia (Tsumeb); USA (Arizona)
Transparency	Transparent–translucent
Subclass	Arsenates

■ Mammillary concretions of fibrous crystals of bayldonite can be cut as cabochons.

COLEMANITE

$CaB_3O_4(OH)_3–H_2O$

Refractive Indices	1.586–1.614
Birefringence	0.028
Optic Char./Sign	Biaxial/+
Hardness	4.5
Specific Gravity	2.42
Crystal System	Monoclinic
Habit	Stubby prismatic
Lustre	Vitreous
Colour Range	Colourless, white
Pleochroism	Nil
Cleavage	Perfect, distinct
Fracture	Uneven
Dispersion	Relatively weak
Sources	Chile, Turkey (Panderma), USA (Nevada, California)
Transparency	Transparent–translucent
Class	Borates

Colemanite (*COAL-man-ite*) is a complex secondary mineral found in evaporite deposits associated with borax, calcite, celestite, ulexite and other borate minerals. Its crystal habits are variable, including short prismatic crystals; equant crystals that appear stubby and bead-like; and crystals that are flattened and can appear bladed with terminations that are either blunted or steeply pyramidal. Colemanite is highly sensitive to heat. Clear crystals may be faceted but the massive material is seldom worked.

CREEDITE

$2CaF_2 2Al(F,OH)_3 CaSO_4 2H_2O$

Refractive Indices	1.461–1.485
Birefringence	0.024
Optic Char./Sign	Biaxial/–
Hardness	4
Specific Gravity	2.713–2.730
Crystal System	Monoclinic
Habit	Prismatic, radiating
Lustre	Vitreous
Colour Range	Colourless, orange, purple, violet, white
Pleochroism	Nil
Cleavage	Perfect
Fracture	Conchoidal, uneven
Dispersion	Strong
Sources	Bolivia, China, France, Greece, Italy, Mexico, South Africa, USA
Transparency	Transparent–translucent
Class	Sulphates

Creedite (*CREED-ite*) is a very rare sulphate mineral found as an accessory to highly oxidized ore bodies. its unique crystal form and attractive range of colours make it a nice addition to any collecion of gem minerals. However, the transparent crystals are seldom large enough to facet. Associated minerals include limonite, cassiterite, adamite and vanadinite.

DICKINSONITE

$H_2Na_6(Mn,Fe,Ca,Mg)_{14}(PO_4)_{12}H_2O$

Dickinsonite (*DICK-in-son-ite*) is a high-temperature primary mineral occurring in granitic pegmatites. It is usually associated with eosphorite, fairfieldite, lithiophilite and rhodochrosite. This mineral is sometimes faceted as a rarity for collectors of the unusual, but the finished stones are very bland.

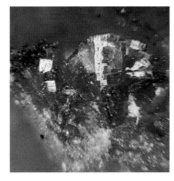

Refractive Indices	1.648–1.671
Birefringence	0.014
Optic Char./Sign	Biaxial/+
Hardness	3.5–4
Specific Gravity	3.38–3.42
Crystal System	Monoclinic
Habit	Tabular
Lustre	Vitreous
Colour Range	Yellowish-green to brownish-green
Pleochroism	Distinct
Cleavage	Perfect (x1)
Fracture	Uneven
Dispersion	Relatively strong
Sources	Australia, Czech Republic, Namibia, Rwanda, USA
Transparency	Transparent–translucent
Class	Phosphates

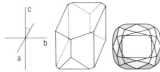

LUDLAMITE

(Fe, Mg, Mn)$_3$(PO$_4$)$_2$–4H$_2$O

Ludlamite (*LUD-lam-ite*) is a rare phosphate mineral. Of the few known localities, the most famous is the Wheal Jane Mine in Cornwall, England, where it was first discovered in 1876. The mine reopened between 1978 and 1998 and produced a number of ludlamite specimens before its final closure in 1998. Associated minerals include limonite, pyrite, siderite, triphylite and vivianite. The mineral was named for Henry Ludlam, a British collector of rare minerals. Specimens of ludlamite are typically bright green, and the crystals form beautiful sprays that are gathered at the middle like sheaves of wheat. It sometimes appears in facet quality but crystals are always small.

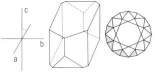

Refractive Indices	1.653–1.697
Birefringence	0.038–0.044
Optic Char./Sign	Biaxial/+
Hardness	3.5–4
Specific Gravity	3.1–3.7
Crystal System	Monoclinic
Habit	Tabular
Lustre	Vitreous
Colour Range	Colourless, shades of green
Pleochroism	Nil
Cleavage	Perfect (1x)
Fracture	Uneven
Dispersion	Relatively weak
Sources	Austria, Bolivia, Brazil, Canada, England, Germany, Japan, Mexico, Spain, USA
Transparency	Transparent–translucent
Class	Phosphates

SHATTUCKITE

2CuSiO$_3$.H$_2$O

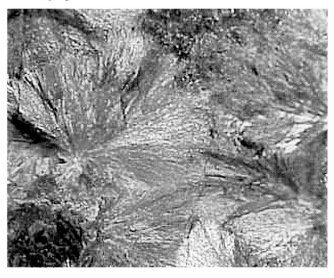

Refractive Indices	1.752–1.815
Birefringence	0.062
Optic Char./Sign	Biaxial/+
Hardness	3.5–4
Specific Gravity	3.8–4.1
Crystal System	Monoclinic
Habit	Massive, fibrous
Lustre	Silky, vitreous
Colour Range	Deep-blue
Pleochroism	Distinct
Cleavage	Perfect (x2)
Fracture	Uneven
Dispersion	Distinct to strong
Sources	Argentina, Austria, Democratic Republic of Congo, Germany, Greece, Namibia, UK, USA
Transparency	Translucent–opaque
Class	Silicates

Shattuckite (*SHAT-tuck-ite*) is a relatively rare copper silicate mineral. It was first discovered in the Shattuck Copper Mine of Bisbee, Arizona. It is virtually a tertiary mineral since it forms as an alteration product of secondary minerals. At the Shattuck Mine, it takes the form of pseudomorphs after malachite. Associated minerals are azurite, cerussite, chrysocolla and malachite. Massive shattuckite makes an attractive ornamental stone. It has a beautiful blue colour, takes a good polish, and makes nice cabochons and carvings. Aggregates of shattuckite make attractive cabinet specimens when they are found as spherules or sprays of deep blue acicular radial crystal clusters.

AZURITE

$2CuCO_3Cu(OH)_2$

Refractive Indices	1.730–1.838
Birefringence	0.108–0.110
Optic Char./Sign	Biaxial/+
Hardness	3.5–4
Specific Gravity	3.7–3.9
Crystal System	Monoclinic
Habit	Variable
Lustre	Vitreous +
Colour Range	Deep blue
Pleochroism	Distinct
Cleavage	Perfect (x1)
Fracture	Conchoidal
Dispersion	Visible
Sources	Chile, France, Mexico, Namibia, Russia, USA, Zaire, Zambia
Transparency	Translucent–opaque
Class	Carbonates

■ Azurite, malachite and cuprite combine to form the rock-like material termed bernite.

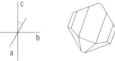

Azurite (*AZZ-your-ite*) is also known as chessylite from the famous deposit in Chessy, France. It occurs in the weathered zone of copper ore-bodies often in close association with malachite. Malachite is the more stable form and malachite

AZURITE *(continued)*

pseudomorphs after azurite retain the detail of bladed crystals or clustered radiating needles of the azurite.

Azurite specimens are always popular with collectors because of their superb colour and interesting forms. The Tsumeb copper mine in northern Namibia produced numerous fine specimen crystals. Azurite is generally employed for carving as ornamental objects or polishing as cabochons. Large pieces are too dark but small bright crystals may be faceted to yield attractive gems. It has low heat sensitivity, is brittle and effervesces on contact with hydrochloric acid. **Azurmalachite** *(AZZ-your-MAL-ah-kite)* is an attractive ornamental stone in which the vivid blue of azurite is combined with the saturated green of malachite. Azurmalachite makes striking cabochons. It may also be carved or used for small objets d'art.

TOP LEFT AND RIGHT: *Azurite on matrix*

ABOVE MIDDLE: *Azurmalachite rough*
ABOVE: *Azurmalachite cabochon*

LEFT: *Azurite cabochon*

MALACHITE

$Cu_2(CO_3)(OH)_2$

Refractive Indices	1.655–1.909
Birefringence	0.254
Optic Char./Sign	Biaxial/-
Hardness	3.5–4
Specific Gravity	3.60–4.05
Crystal System	Monoclinic
Habit	Botryoidal, stalactitic, globular
Lustre	Dull, silky, vitreous
Colour Range	Banded light and dark green
Pleochroism	Nil
Cleavage	Distinct
Fracture	Conchoidal, splintery
Dispersion	Relatively weak
Sources	Australia, Namibia, Russia, USA, Zambia, Zaire
Transparency	Translucent to opaque
Class	Carbonates

Malachite (*MAL-ah-kite*) – a name derived from the Greek word for 'mallow', a green plant of the genus Malva – is an intense green copper carbonate. While malachite frequently occurs as attractive clusters of radiating acicular crystals it is undoubtedly best known and most widely used for lapidary purposes in a massive form that may be mammiliary, botryoidal, stalactitic or globular. Since the material occurs in so many shapes and can be sawn in any direction, the variations in light and dark green banded, wavy and concentric patterns are endless. Malachite can be worked with steel tools and it readily takes a fine polish with hand buffing. Metal polish is the preferred finishing agent in the southern Democratic Republic of Congo where handcrafting malachite is a significant industry. In addition to cabochons, African masks, rounded or freely shaped beads, malachite is carved as animal souvenirs, chess pieces, and objets d'art, inlaid in chess boards, hollowed out for trinket bowls and ashtrays and even used for table tops.

■ Malachite was powdered and used for eye make up by the ancient Egyptians.

TOP: *A malachite crust*

BOTTOM LEFT: *Malachite sprays*

BELOW: *A carved malachite bowl*

Azurite is also a copper carbonate but it is not as advanced in the oxidation process as malachite and therefore not so stable. The process of oxidation that results in the gradual conversion of azurite to malachite is responsible for numerous interesting and attractive replacement specimens. The copper mine at Tsumeb in northern Namibia has produced numerous pseudomorphs of malachite after azurite. Azurmalachite (see page 163) is an extremely colourful massive material that combines the rich hues of both minerals.

HOWLITE

$Ca_2B_5SiO_9(OH)_5,$

Howlite (*HOW-lite*) is found in continental evaporite deposits with anhydrite, colemanite, gypsum and other borate and evaporite minerals. It forms in nodules that have the appearance of cauliflower heads. The black veins, interlaced throughout the nodules, add to their character. It may fluoresce blue or yellowish-white under short-wave ultraviolet light. Howlite is best known in its role as a turquoise substitute. It readily accepts the dye and makes a very convincing simulant for use in beads, cabochons and carved figurines.

Refractive Indices	1.580–1.600
Birefringence	0.020
Optic Char./Sign	Biaxial/-
Hardness	2.5–3.5
Specific Gravity	2.53–2.59
Crystal System	Monoclinic
Habit	Aggregate
Lustre	Dull sub-vitreous
Colour Range	White veined with black
Pleochroism	Nil
Cleavage	Nil
Fracture	Uneven
Dispersion	Nil
Sources	Canada, Germany, South Africa, Turkey, USA
Transparency	Translucent–opaque
Class	Silicates

LEFT: *A howlite nodule*
RIGHT: *Dyed howlite spider-web cabochon*

LEPIDOLITE

$KLi_2Al(Al,Si)3O_{10}(F,OH)_2,$

Lepidolite (*LEPI-doh-lite*) is a violet to pink variety of mica that forms in lithium-rich granitic pegmatite bodies. A typical assemblage of associated minerals would include amblygonite, feldspar, quartz, kunzite and pink tourmaline. Massive, fine-grained material is found that is sufficiently compact to yield attractive cabochons or polished slabs for ornamental purposes.

Refractive Indices	1.53–1.556
Birefringence	0.026
Optic Char./Sign	Biaxial/–
Hardness	2.5–3.0
Specific Gravity	2.8–3.3
Crystal System	Monoclinic
Habit	Tabular massive
Lustre	Vitreous–pearly
Colour Range	Colourless, rose-red, violet, yellow
Pleochroism	Nil
Cleavage	Perfect
Fracture	Uneven
Dispersion	Nil
Sources	Brazil, Madagascar, Mozambique, Namibia, Russia, USA, Zimbabwe
Transparency	Translucent, semi-transparent
Class	Silicates

SERPENTINE

$(Mg,Fe)_3Si_2O_5(OH)_4$,

Refractive Indices	1.55
Birefringence	Weak
Optic Char./Sign	Nil
Hardness	2.5–5
Specific Gravity	2.20–2.65
Crystal System	Monoclinic
Habit	Massive
Lustre	Greasy
Colour Range	Bluish, black, brown, golden, greenish, yellowish
Pleochroism	Nil
Cleavage	Nil
Fracture	Splintery
Dispersion	Nil
Sources	Canada, England, Italy, Russia, South Africa, Switzerland, USA, Zimbabwe
Transparency	Semi-transparent–opaque
Class	Silicates

■ Carvings in translucent bowenite serpentine are sold as 'new jade' in China.

LEFT: *A serpentine carving of a paradise flycatcher, from China*
BELOW: *A carved bowenite serpentine incense burner*

Serpentine (*SIR-pen-tine*), hydrated silicate of magnesium, is a major rock-forming mineral and a constituent of many metamorphic and altered igneous rocks. Typically associated minerals include biotite, calcite, chromite, garnet, olivine and talc. Serpentine is a catch-all name for a group of minerals with a similar chemistry but slightly variant structures. The most important of these are the more translucent and harder antigorite serpentines. They include bowenite, which is usually yellowish or light to dark green in hue, and williamsite, a bright green variety that carries a trace of chrome. These so-called 'precious serpentines' are widely employed as jade simulants. Bowenite figurines exported from China are sold under the misnomer 'new jade'. There are numerous deposits of serpentine marble, a mixture of serpentine, calcite, dolomite and magnesite. Among the better-known varieties are the Connemara, Iona, Irish Green and Mona Marbles.

PHOSPHOPHYLLITE

$Zn_2(FeMn)(PO_4)_2.4H_2O$

Refractive Indices	1.595–1.616
Birefringence	0.021
Optic Char./Sign	Biaxial/–
Hardness	3–3.5
Specific Gravity	3.1
Crystal System	Monoclinic
Habit	Prismatic
Lustre	Vitreous
Colour Range	Black, blue-green, colourless, grey
Pleochroism	Nil
Cleavage	1 perfect, 1 distinct
Fracture	Conchoidal
Dispersion	Very weak
Sources	Australia, Bolivia, Canada, Czech Republic, Germany, Sweden, USA
Transparency	Transparent–translucent
Class	Phosphates

Phosphophyllite (*FOS-fof-fee-lite*). Literally translated as 'phosphate leaf', the name is an allusion to both the chemistry and the cleavage of this rare zinc and manganese mineral. Twinning is common and may produce interesting specimens such as fishtail contact twins. Bolivian deposits produce gem-quality material that is compact and of a good blue-green colour. In this locality the phosphophyllite has formed as a primary precipitate in the hydrothermal veins of the tin mines. Minerals associated with phosphophyllite include cassiterite, mica and triphylite.

ABOVE LEFT AND RIGHT: *Phosphophyllite crystals*

CROCOITE

$PbCrO_4$

Crocoite (*CROC-ow-ite*) is seldom cut because it is brittle, cleavable and has a high sensitivity to heat. It can be richly rewarding for the adventurous facetier, however, and transparent crystals have been faceted into magnificent collectors' items. The vivid colour usually masks strong dispersion.

ABOVE LEFT AND ABOVE: *Crocoite crystals*

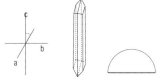

Refractive Indices	2.31–2.66
Birefringence	0.35
Optic Char./Sign	Biaxial/+
Hardness	2.5–3
Specific Gravity	5.9–6.1
Crystal System	Monoclinic
Habit	Long prisms
Lustre	Vitreous–adamantine
Colour Range	Orange, orange-red, hyacinth red, yellow
Pleochroism	Distinctly trichroic
Cleavage	Distinct (x 3)
Fracture	Conchoidal
Dispersion	Nil
Sources	Brazil, Romania, Russia, Tasmania, USA
Transparency	Transparent–opaque
Class	Chromate

■ Crocoite occurs in lead mines as oxidation product of galena.

KINOITE

$Ca_2Cu_2Si_3O_{10}-2H_2O$

Kinoite (*KI-noh-ite*) is a copper mineral but it exhibits a delicate bright blue hue totally unlike the intense colours that are typical of copper ores. A scarce mineral, it occurs in very few localities. Sought after by collectors, it can make a fine cabinet specimen especially in combination with small glittering crystals of apophyllite. In its massive form it yields pure blue cabochons with none of the greenish tones that are generally present in chrysocolla specimens.

Refractive Indices	1.638–1.676
Birefringence	0.038
Optic Char./Sign	Biaxial/–
Hardness	2.5
Specific Gravity	3.13–3.19
Crystal System	Monoclinic
Habit	Acicular radial
Lustre	Vitreous
Colour Range	Light to deep blue
Pleochroism	Nil
Cleavage	Distinct
Fracture	Conchoidal
Dispersion	Nil
Sources	Japan, USA
Transparency	Transparent–translucent
Class	Silicates

GYPSUM

$CaSO_4-2(H_2O)$

Refractive Indices	1.52–1.53
Birefringence	0.01
Optic Char./Sign	Biaxial/+
Hardness	2
Specific Gravity	2.3+
Crystal System	Monoclinic
Habit	Tabular
Lustre	Vitreous–pearly
Colour Range	Colourless, grey or white. Less often: brown, red, yellow
Pleochroism	Nil
Cleavage	Good
Fracture	Uneven
Dispersion	Nil
Sources	Italy (Sicily), Mexico, USA
Transparency	Transparent–translucent
Class	Sulphates

Gypsum (*JIP-sum*) is one of the more common minerals in sedimentary environments. Associated minerals include calcite and halite. This major rock-forming mineral produces massive beds, usually from precipitation out of highly saline waters. Since it forms easily from aqueous solutions, gypsum frequently has inclusions of other minerals. Selenite is a transparent, colourless variety of gypsum with a pearly lustre. Its name, derived from the Greek word for the Moon, alludes to this lustre. Another gypsum variety is the compact fibrous aggregate 'satin spar' that can be cut into very striking chatoyant cabochons. **Alabaster** is a fine-grained massive form of gypsum with a long history of use as an ornamental stone.

■ Vases found in Tutankamen's tomb were of alabaster, a massive form of gypsum.

ABOVE LEFT: *Gypsum crystals*
LEFT: *A carved alabaster elephant*

STEATITE (SOAPSTONE)

$Mg_3Si_4O_{10}(OH)_2$

Refractive Indices	1.54
Birefringence	Nil
Optic Char./Sign	Nil
Hardness	1+
Specific Gravity	2.2–2.8
Crystal System	Monoclinic
Habit	Massive
Lustre	Greasy
Colour Range	Brown, green, greyish, reddish, white, yellow
Pleochroism	Nil
Cleavage	Nil
Fracture	Nil
Dispersion	Nil
Sources	Worldwide: Important deposits – Canada, India, Malawi, Zimbabwe
Transparency	Translucent–opaque
Class	Meta-silicates

Steatite (*STEE-at-ite*) is a massive and usually somewhat impure variety of the mineral talc often found in association with serpentine and chlorite schists. It is very soft and easily carved with metal tools. The Eskimo people of northern Canada carve artefacts from a grey-green steatite and material of a richer green colour is used to carve souvenir ornaments in Zimbabwe. These craftsmen believe that the material is at its softest when freshly mined and that it hardens when heated.

AXINITE

$HMg_2Ca_2BAl_2(SiO_4)_4$

Axinite (AXE-in-ite) occurs in basic igneous and contact metamorphic rocks. It was named axinite because of the wedge-shaped sharp-edged habit of its crystals. This axe-like habit is sufficiently distinctive to be considered a positive identification feature. Most crystals exhibit some inclusions, usually in the form of delicate veils. Large clean axinite specimens are rare, although deposits in Baja California, Mexico have produced a few flawless crystals

Refractive Indices	1.672–1.704
Birefringence	0.009–0.011
Optic Char./Sign	Biaxial/–
Hardness	6.5–7
Specific Gravity	3.27–3.29
Crystal System	Triclinic
Habit	Axe like crystals
Lustre	Vitreous
Colour Range	Blue, brown, violet
Pleochroism	Strong: olive-green, red-brown, yellow-brown
Cleavage	Distinct, one plane
Fracture	Conchoidal
Dispersion	Strong
Sources	Australia (Tasmania), England, Canada, France, Mexico, USA
Transparency	Transparent–translucent
Class	Boro-silicates

weighing as much as 50 carats. Some of the finest crystal specimens have originated from a deposit at St Cristophe near Bourg d'Oisans, France.

Facetiers working with axinite have reported encountering marked variations in hardness in the brittle material. Axinite displays a piezo-electric effect. It has absorption spectra of Å5120, 4920, 4660, 4150, and it seldom exhibits fluorescence.

The general name axinite incorporates several sub-varieties. Most gem quality material belongs to the clove-brown iron rich sub-variety ferro-axinite. The rare violet-coloured axinite from Tasmania is classed as magnesio-axinite. As indicated by its name, mangan-axinite has a preponderance of manganese in its composition.

■ Axinite is famed for the distinctive axe-like shape of its crystals.

PREVIOUS PAGE: *Faceted axinite*
LEFT: *Rough axinite crystal*

SERENDIBITE

$(CaNa)_2(MgFe^{2+})_3[O_2(SiAlB)_6O_{18}]$

Serendibite (*ser-END-dih-bite*) carries the ancient Arab name for Sri Lanka, Serendib. It is a very rare boro-silicate that is found in a few small deposits in Sri Lanka and the United States. A typical American deposit is located in an unremarkable, coarse-grained calcite marble outcrop of the Franklin Marble in Orange County, California. The serendibite is associated with green amphibole, apatite, calcite, phlogopite, scapolite and sinhalite. The material exhibits polysynthetic twinning and comprises small anhedral to sub-hedral crystals in a matrix of phlogopite and white marble. Cut stones are rare and tend to be very small.

Refractive Indices	1.701–1.706
Birefringence	0.005
Optic Char./Sign	Biaxial/+
Hardness	6–7
Specific Gravity	3.4
Crystal System	Triclinic
Habit	Granular
Lustre	Vitreous
Colour Range	Blue, blue-green, blue-grey, yellow
Pleochroism	Marked
Cleavage	Nil
Fracture	Uneven
Dispersion	Strong
Sources	Sri Lanka, USA
Transparency	Transparent–translucent
Class	Silicates

NAMBULITE

$(Li,Na)Mn_{++}4[Si_5O_{14}(OH)]$

Refractive Indices	1.707–1.730
Birefringence	0.023
Optic Char./Sign	Biaxial/+
Hardness	6.5
Specific Gravity	3.51
Crystal System	Triclinic
Habit	Primatic
Lustre	Vitreous–adamantine
Colour Range	Orange-brown, reddish
Pleochroism	Nil
Cleavage	Perfect (1) Distinct (x2)
Fracture	Conchoidal
Dispersion	Weak
Sources	Japan, Namibia, Slovak Republic, Sweden
Transparency	Transparent–translucent
Class	Silicates

Nambulite (*NAM-bew-lite*) is a very rare mineral that has been cut into collectable orange-red specimen stones. It occurs in association with rhodonite and other manganese minerals. Gem rough originates from the Gozaisho mine, Iwaki, Fukushima, Japan. Nambulite was named for its discoverer, Japanese mineralogist Matsuo Nambu.

FELDSPAR, MICROCLINE

$KAlSi_3O_8$

Microcline (*MY-crow-cline*) has the same chemical composition as orthoclase but is classified in the triclinic crystal system because of the very slight inclination of its third axis alluded to in its name. The blue-green feldspar amazonite is the only gem variety of microcline. The material is inert under short-wave light but usually reveals distinct spring green fluorescence under long-wave ultraviolet light. Its use as an ornamental stone is somewhat limited as a result of its easy cleavage. However, it makes attractive cabochons, beads and 'chunky' ornamental artefacts.

Refractive Indices	1.522–1.530
Birefringence	0.008
Optic Char./Sign	Biaxial/–
Hardness	6–6.5
Specific Gravity	2.54–2.59
Crystal System	Triclinic
Habit	Prismatic
Lustre	Vitreous
Colour Range	Colourless, blue-green, green, red
Pleochroism	Nil
Cleavage	Easy (x2)
Fracture	Uneven
Dispersion	Weak
Sources	Brazil, Canada, India, Madagascar, Russia, Tanzania, USA, Zimbabwe
Transparency	Transparent–opaque
Class	Silicates

Perthite, named for the town of Perth, Canada, is an attractive ornamental stone formed by the intergrowth of several varieties of feldspar including microcline, oligioclase and orthoclase. Its body colour is generally reddish-brown or off-white with a predominantly orange-gold play of labradorescence.

PREVIOUS PAGE
ABOVE: *Amazonite cabochon*
BELOW: *Rough amazonite feldspar*
THIS PAGE
LEFT: *Perthite feldspar*

There are several Canadian deposits. Feldspar of a very similar nature occurs in southern Zimbabwe, and this material was found to exhibit patchy bluish and greenish fluorescence under both long- and short- wave ultraviolet light.

FELDSPAR, PLAGIOCLASE SERIES

$(NaCa)(SiAl)Si_3O_8$

The plagioclase feldspars form an isomorphous series that ranges from the sodium aluminium silicate albite to the calcium aluminium silicate anorthite. Several members of this series are important gem materials.

Albite

Plagioclase consisting of 90 percent or more of the sodium-rich molecule is termed albite feldspar. Peristerite, a sub-variety of albite, is popular as cabochon material or in beads. It shows a sky-blue labradorescence against a white or beige body colour. Canada is reputed to produce the finest peristerite, with deposits in both Ontario and Quebec.

Stones have been faceted from a transparent very light blue albite originating in Kenya. They were found to have refractive indices of 1.540–1.545, a specific gravity of 2.63 and to fluoresce a faint chalky white when viewed under long-wave ultraviolet light.

Refractive Indices	1.525–1.588
Birefringence	0.008
Optic Char./Sign	Varies with composition
Hardness	6
Specific Gravity	2.605–2.765
Crystal System	Triclinic
Habit	Crystalline masses
Lustre	Vitreous
Colour Range	Blue, brown, colourless, green, red, yellow
Pleochroism	Nil
Cleavage	Easy (x2)
Fracture	Uneven
Dispersion	Nil
Sources	Australia, Brazil, Canada, India, Madagascar, Mexico, USA, Zimbabwe
Transparency	Transparent–opaque
Class	Silicates

■ In Zimbabwe transparent blue-green albite/oligoclase feldspar is often mixed with rough aquamarine.

Oligioclase

FAR LEFT: *Sunstone from Norway*
LEFT: *Sunstones from Tanzania*

A plagioclase series feldspar comprising 70–90 per cent albite is classed as oligioclase. Sunstone or aventurine feldspar is the principal oligioclase gem variety. Filled with innumerable tiny oriented platelets of red-gold goethite or hematite, sunstone cabochons display a warm, constantly shifting reflected light. Canada, India, Russia and the USA all have deposits of sunstone but the finest material is said to originate from deposits on the south coast of Norway.

Andesine

Andesine feldspar is composed of 50–70 per cent albite and 30–50 per cent anorthite. The first discovery of andesine feldspar with gem potential was made in 1967 when a US laboratory identified a massive green jade-like cabochon grade specimen as andesine feldspar. In 2002 an exciting transparent red gem material was discovered in the Democratic Republic of Congo (formerly Zaire). It was found to be a new form of andesine feldspar. Several fine stones were cut from this pocket; the largest exceeded 30 carats in weight. Another red andesine deposit was later discovered in Tibet, China.

ABOVE: *An andesine sunstone from the Democratic Republic of Congo*

Labradorite

BELOW: *Labradorite cabochons*

Labradorite feldspar is 30–50 per cent albite and 50–70 per cent anorthite feldspar. The body colour is usually dull grey, but the fine lamellar twinning that is a feature of this material interferes with light rays and produces a play of spectacular iridescence.

Bytownite

A rare form of feldspar, bytownite comprises 10–30 per cent albite and 70–90 per cent anorthite feldspar. Stones are faceted in red, russet and green hues. Some of the specimens bear a distinct resemblance to andalusite.

Anorthite

Specimens of this end member of the plagioclase series are sometimes cut for collectors.

AMBLYGONITE

LiAl(F,OH)PO$_4$

The name amblygonite (*am-BLIG-onite*) is derived from Greek and alludes to the mineral's triclinic crystals. Amblygonite is a fluorophosphate of lithium and aluminium that usually occurs in a massive form. It shows a faint green or orange fluorescence under long-wave ultraviolet light, has a moderate heat sensitivity and is brittle. The relatively rare specimen- or facet-grade crystals are found associated with apatite, lepidolite, quartz, spodumene and tourmaline in lithium-rich pegmatites. Amblygonite is difficult to facet since it has four different cleavage directions that intersect at varied angles and exhibit different degrees of ease in cleavability.

Both Brazil and Myanmar produce fine crystal specimens of yellow amblygonite in addition to facet-grade gem rough.

Refractive Indices	1.611–1.637
Birefringence	0.024
Optic Char./Sign	Biaxial/+
Hardness	6
Specific Gravity	3.015–3.033
Crystal System	Triclinic
Habit	Usually massive
Lustre	Vitreous to pearly
Colour Range	Brown, colourless, pale green, yellow, rarely bluish or pale pink
Pleochroism	Weak
Cleavage	Perfect (x1)
Fracture	Sub-conchoidal
Dispersion	0.018
Sources	Brazil, Germany, Myanmar, Namibia, Norway, USA, Zimbabwe
Transparency	Transparent–translucent
Class	Phosphates

RHODONITE

$(Mn,Fe,Mg,Ca)_5(SiO_5)_5$

Refractive Indices	1.711–1.751
Birefringence	0.014
Optic Char./Sign	Biaxial/+/–
Hardness	5.5–6.5
Specific Gravity	3.4–3.7
Crystal System	Triclinic
Habit	Prismatic massive
Lustre	Dull–vitreous
Colour Range	Black, brown, orange, pink, red
Pleochroism	Distinct
Cleavage	Perfect (x2)
Fracture	Conchoidal
Dispersion	–
Sources	Australia, Brazil, Japan, Mexico, Russia, South Africa, Sweden, USA
Transparency	Transparent–opaque
Class	Silicates

Rhodonite (*ROE-don-ite*) occurs in various manganese ore bodies, often in association with rhodochrosite, calcite, pyrite, pyroxmangite and spessartine. It is an attractive pink mineral that is best known as an ornamental stone in its massive form. Its name is derived from the Greek word for 'rose', *rhodon*. Transparent facet rough is rare and the pieces seldom exceed 1g in weight but they can be cut as excellent gems. Fowlerite is a sub-variety that occurs in Franklin Furnace, New Jersey, USA in which zinc replaces some of the manganese.

■ Rhodonite is rarely faceted and best known as an ornamental stone.

TOP: *Rhodonite from Zambia*
BOTTOM: *A rhodonite cabochon*

BUSTAMITE

CaMn(SiO$_3$)$_2$

Bustamite (*BUST-ah-mite*) is formed by the metamorphism of manganese-rich sediments. Associated minerals include calcite, diopside, garnet, rhodonite, vesuvianite and willemite. At first thought to be a variety of rhodonite, bustamite is now recognized as a distinct species. Specimens from the type deposit at Franklin Furnace, New Jersey, USA, consist of pink prismatic crystals up to 1cm (⅖in) in size associated with blue vesuvianite, garnet and mica. Bustamite displays orange phosphorescence, and bright pink material shows a moderate to dull red fluorescence under long-wave ultraviolet light. Massive material yields attractive pink cabochons or it can be carved into objets d'art.

Refractive Indices	1.640–1.710
Birefringence	0.013–0.015
Optic Char./Sign	Biaxial/–
Hardness	5.5–6.5
Specific Gravity	3.32–3.43
Crystal System	Triclinic
Habit	Prismatic, massive
Lustre	Vitreous
Colour Range	Brownish-red, flesh pink, pinkish-orange
Pleochroism	–
Cleavage	Perfect (x1) Good (x2)
Fracture	Conchoidal
Dispersion	Strong
Sources	Australia, England, Mexico, South Africa, USA
Transparency	Transparent–translucent
Class	Silicates

PYROXMANGITE

Mn SiO$_3$

The name Pyroxmangite (*PY-rox-man-gite*) is derived from pyroxene and manganese and alludes to the composition and structure of the mineral. It occurs in regionally metamorphosed manganiferous rocks in association with alabandite, hausmannite, quartz, rhodochrosite, rhodonite, spessartine and tephroite. Pyroxmangite forms a series with pyroxferroite. Sources in Australia, Japan and the USA produce gem rough. A small proportion of this material is of facet grade but it is usually more suitable for cabochons.

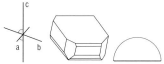

Refractive Indices	1.726–1.764
Birefringence	0.018
Optic Char./Sign	Biaxial/+
Hardness	5.5–6
Specific Gravity	3.61–3.80
Crystal System	Triclinic
Habit	Tabular, massive
Lustre	Vitreous to pearly on fresh surfaces
Colour Range	Pink, purplish, yellowish, red-brown, dark-brown
Pleochroism	–
Cleavage	Perfect (x2)
Fracture	Uneven
Dispersion	Moderate
Sources	Austria, Australia, Brazil, Czech Republic, Finland, France, Germany, Italy, Japan, Russia, Slovak Republic, Sweden, UK, USA
Transparency	Transparent–translucent
Class	Silicates

KYANITE

Al_2SiO_5

Kyanite (*KYE-an-ite*) is a polymorph with two other minerals, andalusite and sillimanite. Kyanite occurs in association with andalusite, biotite, garnet, quartz, sillimanite and staurolite. It is a colourful mineral and fine specimens may be virtually sapphire-blue with violet pleochroism. One of its unique characteristics is the fact that it exhibits a wide variation of hardness in the same crystal depending on direction: it registers 5 on the Mohs Scale when scratched parallel to the long axis of the crystal, and 7 when scratched perpendicular to it. Faceted stones seldom exceed five carats in size but a colour range can make an interesting collection.

Refractive Indices	1.715–1.732
Birefringence	0.017
Optic Char./Sign	Biaxial/–
Hardness	5–7
Specific Gravity	3.65–3.69
Crystal System	Triclinic
Habit	Prismatic
Lustre	Vitreous–pearly
Colour Range	Colourless, blue, green, grey, violet
Pleochroism	Trichroic
Cleavage	Marked
Fracture	Splintery
Dispersion	0.020
Sources	Brazil, India, Kashmir, Kenya, Myanmar, Switzerland, USA, Zimbabwe
Transparency	Transparent–translucent
Class	Silicates

■ An alternative name for Kyanite is Disthene, meaning 'double-strength'.

TURQUOISE

$CuAl_6(PO_4)_4(OH)_8*5(H_2O)$,

Turquoise (*TUR-kwoiz*) is a secondary mineral formed under the influence of evaporating surface waters in typically arid regions.

Refractive Indices	1.610–1.650
Birefringence	0.040
Optic Char./Sign	Biaxial/+
Hardness	5–6
Specific Gravity	2.6–2.90
Crystal System	Triclinic
Habit	Massive
Lustre	Dull, waxy
Colour Range	Sky-blue, greenish-blue, blue-green, green
Pleochroism	N/a
Cleavage	Perfect
Fracture	Conchoidal
Dispersion	N/a
Sources	Afghanistan, Australia, Chile, Egypt, Iran, Russia, USA
Transparency	Translucent–opaque
Class	Phosphates

Found in botryoidal masses, encrustations, nodules, veins, seams and brecciated zones in igneous or meta-sedimentary rocks, its associated minerals include clay minerals, limonite, pyrite and quartz.

Turquoise was one of the earliest gems to be used for personal adornment. Its use by the rulers of Ancient Egypt can be dated to around 5500BC. The name is generally attributed to the fact that, no matter where the mineral originated, it entered Western Europe through Asia Minor (*turquois* is French for 'Turkish'). The old French name for the mineral was *pierre tourques*, meaning 'Turkey stone'. The finest turquoise is mined from the slopes of Ali-mersai, a peak in the Nishapur district of Iran. This material, fine-grained and very compact, has a specific gravity of 2.85, which is distinctly higher than that of the more porous American material with an average SG of 2.65. In the western world the most prized colour of turquoise is 'robin's egg blue'. In Tibet, where turquoise is treasured as the national stone, it is the green material that is most highly valued.

In South and Central America, the Aztecs, Incas and Mayas wore turquoise in ceremonies as a symbol of authority. Further to the north, the Zunis people believed that the sky took on its blue colour when light from their 'spirit bird' was reflected from the top of a mountain of turquoise. In Arizona and New Mexico, the Hopi, Navajo and Zuni silversmiths create a wide range of turquoise and silver 'Indian' jewellery for the tourist market.

Crystals of turquoise are very rare, but a few small specimens have been found in Virginia, USA. Turquoise frequently occurs in a limonite matrix. Where the turquoise is disseminated throughout a network of limonite, the material is cut as a piece and sold as spider-web turquoise. When fragments of brecciated turquoise are cemented together by natural bonding in a beige sandstone base, cabochons cut from the material are sold as turquoise matrix. Turquoise is widely used for cabochons, beads, inlays and small objets d'art.

Faustite (ZnCu) $Al_6[(OH)_4(PO_4)_2]_2 4H_2O$ is a massive, bright green, zinc-rich member of the turquoise group with a hardness of 4.5 and a specific gravity of 2.9 that is mined near Neynschabour, Iran. It has the same structure as turquoise but the copper element has been replaced by zinc. It is cut as cabochons, worked as beads and carved into ornamental objects.

■ Turquoise has been prized as a gem for over 7,000 years.

LEFT: *Carved green turquoise*
BELOW: *A faustite cabochon*

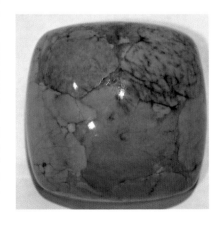

PECTOLITE

$HNaCa_2(SiO_3)3+(H_2O)$

Pectolite (*PECK–toh-lite*)'s name is derived from the Greek *pektos* meaning 'compact' and refers to its massive form. It occurs as fibrous tufts, radiating acicular crystal clusters and compact or botryoidal masses that make interesting specimens for mineral collectors. When a light-blue to sky-blue sub-variety was discovered

in the Bahamas and the Dominican Republic, the mineral also achieved popularity in the gemstone market. The compact blue material yields attractive cabochons and beads and it is marketed under the trade name Lorimar. Associated minerals are calcite, datolite, prehnite, serpentine and various zeolites.

■ Pectolite, from Alaska, has been used as a jade substitute.

Refractive Indices	1.594–1.642
Birefringence	0.038
Optic Char./Sign	Biaxial/+
Hardness	5
Specific Gravity	2.74–2.88
Crystal System	Triclinic
Habit	Acicular, botryoidal
Lustre	Vitreous–silky
Colour Range	Colourless, light blue, grey, white
Pleochroism	Nil
Cleavage	Perfect (x2)
Fracture	Splintery, brittle
Dispersion	Very weak
Sources	Bahamas, Dominican Republic, England, Italy, USA
Transparency	Translucent–opaque
Class	Silicates

CHABAZITE (ACADIALITE)

$CaAl_2Si_4O_{12}–6H_2O$

Chabazite (*CAB-ah-zite*), also known as acadialite, is a zeolite that forms in gas cavities in extrusive volcanic rocks and also as a precipitate in and around hot springs. The finest specimens to date have been found associated with apophyllite, calcite, heulandite, natrolite, scolecite and stilbite in vesicles in the basalt quarries of Poona, India. Typically the angular vitreous crystals of chabazite are rhombohedral and tend to resemble slightly squashed cubes. Aggregates form crusts

and granular masses. Twinning is frequently encountered with the penetration twin rotated around the 'C' axis. Exhibits bright green fluorescence under short-wave ultraviolet. Infrequently seen as a cut stone because clean facet rough is scarce.

Refractive Indices	1.478–1.490
Birefringence	0.002–0.005
Optic Char./Sign	Biaxial +/-
Hardness	4–5
Specific Gravity	2.04–2.17
Crystal System	Triclinic
Habit	Rhombohedral, pseudo-cubic
Lustre	Vitreous
Colour Range	Brown, colourless, orange, pink, reddish, white, yellowish
Pleochroism	Nil
Cleavage	Indistinct
Fracture	Uneven
Dispersion	Nil
Sources	Australia, Belgium, Canada, Colombia, Czech Republic, Denmark, France, Germany, Iceland, India, Italy, Kazakhstan, New Zealand, Switzerland, UK, USA
Transparency	Transparent–translucent
Class	Silicates

RHYOLITE

Refractive Indices	N/a
Birefringence	N/a
Optic Char./Sign	N/a
Hardness	6–7
Specific Gravity	2.53
Crystal System	N/a
Habit	N/a
Lustre	Earthy
Colour Range	Brown, red, white
Pleochroism	N/a
Cleavage	N/a
Fracture	Sub-conchoidal
Dispersion	N/a
Sources	Namibia, USA
Transparency	Opaque
Class	Rocks

Rhyolite (*RYE-oh-lite*) is a type of lava. A light-coloured, fine-grained igneous rock, it is largely comprised of alkaline feldspars and quartz. The name rhyolite comes from the Greek word *rhyax*, meaning 'stream', a reference to the flowing banded patterns that are typical of this material. It is an excellent ornamental stone and the attractive colours, patterns and 'picture' effects have inspired a range of varietal names including 'wonderstone', 'rainbow rock', and 'hickoryite'. The 'picture jaspers' best known from Biggs Junction in Oregon or the Namib Desert of southern Africa are probably examples of jasperized rhyolite.

■ Rhyolite is sometimes marketed as 'wonder rock'.

PSILOMELANE

MnO_2

Psilomelane (*Sill-OH-mel-ane*) is a colloidal manganese oxide that contains water and the oxides of barium, pottasium, and sodium in varying amounts. It often combines with grey pyrolusite to make an attractive stone with alternating metallic grey and sub-metallic black bands. Agate impregnated with particles of psilomelane may have a very similar appearance.

Refractive Indices	N/a
Birefringence	N/a
Optic Char./Sign	N/a
Hardness	5–7
Specific Gravity	3.3–4.7
Crystal System	Amorphous
Habit	Botryoidal, massive
Lustre	Sub-metallic
Colour Range	Steel grey, bluish-black, iron-black
Pleochroism	N/a
Cleavage	N/a
Fracture	Conchoidal
Dispersion	N/a
Sources	Brazil, England, Germany, USA
Transparency	Opaque
Class	Oxides

OPAL

SiO_2-nH_2O

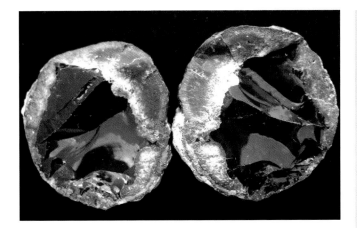

Refractive Indices	1.39–1.47
Birefringence	N/a
Optic Char./Sign	Isotropic
Hardness	5.0–6.0
Specific Gravity	1.95–2.20
Crystal System	Amorphous
Habit	Massive
Lustre	Vitreous
Colour Range	Blue, black, colourless, green, grey, orange, red, white
Pleochroism	N/a
Cleavage	N/a
Fracture	Conchoidal
Dispersion	N/a
Sources	Australia, Brazil, Ethiopia, Honduras, Mexico, Somalia, Tanzania, USA
Transparency	Transparent–opaque
Class	Mineraloids

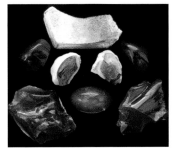

Opal (*OH-pal*): the name is probably derived from *upala*, the Sanskrit for precious stone. 'Hungarian opal' was mined for centuries, at least since Roman times, from areas that are now within the Czech Republic. The Aztecs made use of the Mexican deposits, and so did the Spaniards after the conquest, exporting the material to Europe. Today the majority of precious opal comes from Australian sources with additional significant amounts originating from Mexico and more recently from the Horn of Africa. A very wide range of material is reaching the market from Ethiopia and Somalia but some of it is very unstable. Indonesia has some production of fine black opal. Brazil, Honduras and the USA are small producers of opal of questionable stability. Opal is not a crystalline material; it is a hydrous silicate that is probably best described as a solidified silica gel. The water content in common opal may amount to more than 20 percent by weight but in precious opal the figure seldom exceeds eight percent. Early opal mining activities tended to be confined to removing any opal fillings that were discovered in the gas vesicles of extrusive igneous rocks. Opals formed in this environment tend to be small and are very difficult to remove without damaging them. The discovery of sedimentary opal in Queensland, Australia in 1872 was a revelation. This opal occurred in an amazing diversity of forms: as veins, as a filling in fractures, as a bonding agent in granular masses, completely replacing various fossils, and in some instances attaining truly remarkable sizes.

■ In 1889, 1,100km west of Sydney, Australia, prospectors who were following a wounded kangaroo discovered the White Cliffs Opal Field.

TOP: *Split opal in rhyolite nodule, Ethiopia*

ABOVE LEFT: *A variety of opals*

ABOVE: *An elephant carved from opal*

OPAL *(continued)*

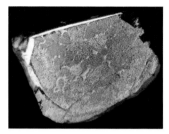

Most opals fluoresce white or pale green, some phosphoresce and all specimens can be very sensitive to impacts and low temperatures. Opaque opal is of little value and is known as potch. Some precious opal types are listed below:

Black opal: an intense play of fire on a black to near-black body colour. **Semi-black**: opal with an intense play of fire against a very dark body colour. **Red Base**: opal that reveals a red body colour in transmitted light. **Milky Opal**: pinfire play of colour against a semi-opaque milky white body colour. **Contra-luz**: play of colour revealed in transmitted light. **Yowaha nut**: a hollow ironstone concretion filled with precious opal. **Opal in matrix**: masses of tiny cracks filled with precious opal in dark brown ironstone. **Pipe opal**: solid precious opal in a natural cylindrical form. **Boulder opal**: opal-bearing ironstone boulders in sandstone or mudstone sediments. **Volcanic opal**: yellow-orange or transparent water opals that infill vesicles and cracks in igneous rocks.

FAR LEFT: *Flagstone opal*
LEFT: *Fire opal from Ethiopia*
ABOVE: *Ethiopian opal*

LEFT: *Crazed opal cabochon, Brazil*
ABOVE: *Semi-black opal cabochon, Australia*

OBSIDIAN

Obsidian (*OB-sid-ee-un*) is a natural glass that occurs if volcanic lava is subjected to rapid heat loss. For example, lava that flows into a lake or ocean will cool quickly, causing the resulting rock to have a glassy texture. Stone Age people discovered that it was relatively easy to produce a serrated cutting edge on obsidian. The material was widely used for tools or weapons and eventually for ornamentation. Basically dark brown or black in body colour, some obsidian may reveal a golden, green or blue-purple sheen. Rainbow obsidian owes its intriguing sheen of spectral hues to interference of light caused by included layers of minute bubbles. A type of black obsidian that contains numerous small radiating inclusions of cristobalite is sometimes called 'snowflake obsidian'. 'Apache tears' is a fanciful name given to small rounded pebbles of black obsidian that are found in the American Southwest.

Refractive Indices	1.48–1.57
Birefringence	N/a
Optic Char./Sign	Isotropic
Hardness	5–5.5
Specific Gravity	2.3–2.6
Crystal System	Amorphous
Habit	Massive
Lustre	Vitreous
Colour Range	Black, brown, dark green, grey, red
Pleochroism	N/a
Cleavage	N/a
Fracture	Conchoidal
Dispersion	N/a
Sources	Italy, Mexico, Scotland, USA
Transparency	Transparent–opaque
Class	Mineraloids

■ In ancient Mexico, polished obsidian was used as a divining mirror.

ABOVE LEFT: *Obsidian nodule*
LEFT: *Snowflake obsidian*

Natural glass may also be formed either along the fringes of basalt intrusions or as a filling in cavities in the basalt. This basaltic glass, or tachylyte, is brown or black in colour and tends to splinter on impact in contrast to the marked conchoidal fracture of obsidian. Its physical properties are also distinctly higher, with a hardness of about 6, density averaging 2.85 and refractive index of around 1.62. Attractively coloured and patterned material from Queensland, Australia is cut into cabochons.

Tektites are transparent glassy nodules that exhibit intriguing surface features. First discovered in 1787 near the Moldau River in western Moravia (part of the modern Czech Republic), they are widely believed to be the result of large meteorite strikes. Stones from the original source were named Moldavite after the locality. They are usually brown to green in colour and gems that are faceted from this material tend to be rather bottle-green in hue. There have been many subsequent tektite finds with the material being named after the particular source: australite, billitonite, etc. While the physical constants of tektites do show some slight variation between sources, they all fall within the parameters given for obsidian in the table above.

Crater Glass is a natural glass of very widespread occurrence. It is simply the product of the fusion of silica that takes place when a meteorite strikes sandy terrain. Generally black, green, white or yellow in colour, it contains numerous cavities and is relatively light, with a density of 2.1–2.3. Glass from Meteor Crater, Arizona, is traded under the name lechatelierite.

Fulgurites are yet another form of natural glass. They are the thin glassy tubes of fused silica that are formed when bolts of lightning strike the sands of the desert.

CHRYSOCOLLA

$CuSiO_3 + H_2O$

Refractive Indices	1.46–1.57
Birefringence	N/a
Optic Char./Sign	N/a
Hardness	2–4
Specific Gravity	2.0–2.24
Crystal System	Amorphous
Habit	Botryoidal, Massive
Lustre	Vitreous–waxy
Colour Range	Blue, green, turquoise
Pleochroism	Weak
Cleavage	N/a
Fracture	Conchoidal
Dispersion	N/a
Sources	Chile, Israel, Namibia, Russia, USA, Zambia, Zaire
Transparency	Translucent–opaque
Class	Silicates

Chrysocolla (*CRY-so-colla*) forms in the oxidation zones of copper-rich ore bodies. Pure chrysocolla is a soft and fragile material that is unsuitable for use in jewellery. Drusy chrysocolla is composed of agatized chrysocolla with a crust of small sparkling quartz crystals in small cavities (*see* chalcedony). Associated minerals are quartz, limonite, azurite, malachite and cuprite.

■ Eilat Stone is an intergrowth of chrysocolla, turquoise and pseudomalachite.

METEORITE (Metallic)

Refractive Indices	N/a
Birefringence	N/a
Optic Char./Sign	N/a
Hardness	4–5
Specific Gravity	7–8
Crystal System	N/a
Habit	Irregular nodules
Lustre	Metallic
Colour Range	Black, rust-red, silvery
Pleochroism	N/a
Cleavage	N/a
Fracture	Splintery
Dispersion	N/a
Sources	Argentina, Australia, Brazil, Namibia, etc
Transparency	Opaque
Class	N/a

Meteorite (*ME-tee-or-ite*). Metallic nickel and iron meteorites are cut as cabochons or spheres then etched with nitric acid to reveal the presence of unique crystal patterns (known as Widmanstatten figures). The material makes interesting jewellery items, especially when mounted in cuff-links.

ABOVE LEFT: *Meteorite sphere*
ABOVE: *Meteorite 'Lucy'*

■ Gibeon meteorites are composed of malleable nickel and iron in varying proportions.

AGALMATOLITE

Refractive Indices	N/a
Birefringence	N/a
Optic Char./Sign	N/a
Hardness	Hardens when fired
Specific Gravity	2.785–2.815
Crystal System	N/a
Habit	Massive
Lustre	Earthy to vitreous
Colour Range	Brown, grey, greenish, red, yellowish
Pleochroism	N/a
Cleavage	Nil
Fracture	Uneven
Dispersion	N/a
Sources	China
Transparency	Opaque

Agalmatolite (*ag-al-MAT-oh-lite*), a compact clay-like material resembling muscovite mica in composition, is of widespread occurrence. It can be readily sculpted with metal tools or turned on a lathe to form bowls, vases etc. In China, where it is known as 'pagoda stone', it is widely used to carve miniature pagodas and other religious images. (*See also* pyrophyllite and steatite.)

■ Agalmatolite is generally composed of pinite, pyrophyllite and steatite in varying proportions.

KAKORTOKITE

Kakortokite (*KA-caw-TOK-ite*) is an attractive ornamental rock that is also known as 'Lopar's Blood'. It occurs in the Julianhab District of southern Greenland and is fashioned into cabochons that are mounted in silver jewellery for the tourist trade. It can also be carved and various souvenirs and objets d'art are created from it. The material is composed of nepheline syenite generously spotted with red crystals of eudialite (a rare zirconium mineral) and black needles of arfvedsonite.

Refractive Indices	N/a
Birefringence	N/a
Optic Char./Sign	N/a
Hardness	N/a
Specific Gravity	2.7–2.8
Crystal System	N/a
Habit	N/a
Lustre	N/a
Colour Range	Black, red and white
Pleochroism	N/a
Cleavage	N/a
Fracture	N/a
Dispersion	N/a
Sources	Greenland
Transparency	Opaque
Class	Rocks

■ Kakortokite is fashioned into small bowls as souvenirs.

NAUJAITE

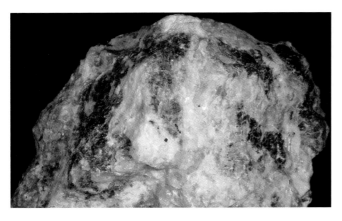

Refractive Indices	N/a
Birefringence	N/a
Optic Char./Sign	N/a
Hardness	N/a
Specific Gravity	N/a
Crystal System	N/a
Habit	N/a
Lustre	N/a
Colour Range	Black, red, white
Pleochroism	N/a
Cleavage	N/a
Fracture	N/a
Dispersion	N/a
Sources	Greenland
Transparency	Opaque
Class	Rocks

Naujaite (*NA-oo-JA-ite*), from a term meaning 'seagull' in the Inuit language, is an igneous sodalite-nepheline syenite. An attractive and colourful ornamental rock, it is composed of sodalite, alkali feldspar, aegirine, arfvedsonite and eudialite. Since the naujaite is lighter both in colour and in density than the bulk of the magma flows, it forms a whitish capping that is referred to by geologists as 'roof cumulate' and by the Inuit people as 'seagull droppings'.

NUMMITE

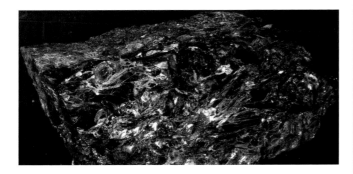

Refractive Indices	N/a
Birefringence	N/a
Optic Char./Sign	N/a
Hardness	5–5.6
Specific Gravity	N/a
Crystal System	N/a
Habit	N/a
Lustre	N/a
Colour Range	Dark brown, black
Pleochroism	N/a
Cleavage	N/a
Fracture	N/a
Dispersion	N/a
Sources	Greenland
Transparency	Opaque
Class	Rocks

Nummite (*NUM-ite*) is an attractive ornamental rock that combines two amphibole minerals, anthophyllite and gedrite, in sheaf-like groups. A striking iridescence is produced by the interference of light between these crystals. Cabochons or tumbled stones exhibit red, green and blue swathes of colour that flicker, like flames in a fire, against the dark brown to black body colour.

ORGANIC GEMS

Early man made use of primitive tools that were roughly shaped from agate or jasper, but the first gem materials to be employed for purely decorative purposes were probably of an organic nature. These may have been nacreous shells with their attractive iridescent linings or lustrous pearls accidentally discovered in the flesh of edible shellfish. Ivory, bone and horn were dual-purpose materials since they were used for tools or weapons as well as being shaped as ornaments. The unique appearance and feel of organic gems still has the ability to carry our thoughts back to a distant past. Amber, for example, provides a golden window that often encapsulates tantalizing glimpses of pre-historic life forms. Leaves, seeds, insects and small vertebrates, trapped in an instant of time by viscous resin, have been preserved.

AMBER

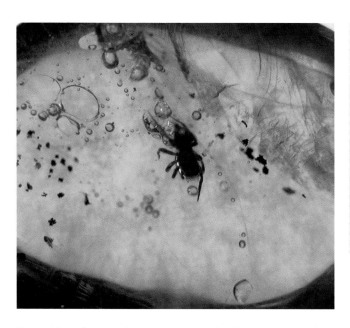

Refractive Indices	1.54
Hardness	2–2.5
Specific Gravity	1.03–1.10
Lustre	Resinous
Colour Range	Brown, golden, red, yellow
Fracture	Conchoidal
Sources	Dominican Republic, Germany, Mexico, Myanmar, Rumania, Sicily
Transparency	Transparent–translucent
Fluorescence	Chalky white under long-wave and dull green under short-wave ultraviolet
Sectility	Most simulants are noticeably more sectile and heavier than amber.

■ In Homer's *Odyssey* he describes 'a golden necklace richly wrought, and set with amber beads, that glowed as if with sunshine'.

The oldest forms of amber are probably those found in Myanmar. They are the fossilized resin of tropical angiosperms that were abundant in that area during the Eocene period about 50 million years ago. Baltic amber is considerably younger, having formed from the resin of *Pinus succinifera*, a pine tree that flourished during the Oligocene Epoch of 34–23 million

LEFT: *Golden spider captured in Dominican amber*

years ago. Amber mined in the Dominican Republic is of a similar age. Historically, the most important source of amber was the Baltic Sea. Collections of amber fragments, beads and carvings of material from this source have been found in early cave dwellings throughout Europe. An ancient name applied to amber was *electrum**, a word that in this context is believed to have meant 'I protect', referring to a widely held belief in the curative powers of amber amulets. However, the Greeks also knew amber as *electron,* a name that relates to the powers of attraction seen in amber that has been rubbed and built up a charge of static electricity. The German name *bernstein* was inspired by the sweet smell of burning amber.

* Electrum is also the name of an alloy of silver and gold that was widely used in ancient times.

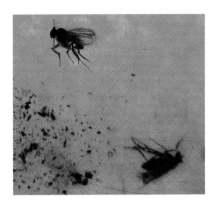

ABOVE: *Fossilized flies in amber from the Baltic*

CORAL

$CaCO_3$

Refractive Indices	1.49–1.65
Hardness	3.5
Specific Gravity	2.6–2.7
Lustre	Waxy
Colour Range	Black, orange, pink, red, white
Fracture	Hackly
Sources	Atlantic, Indian Ocean, Malay waters, Mediterranean, Red Sea, Ryukuan Islands
Transparency	Opaque
Fluorescence	Distinctly chalky under long-wave and faintly chalky under short-wave ultraviolet
Sectility	Both black and gold coral are sectile.

Coral (*KOR-al*). Gem coral, *Corallium nobile* or *Corallium rubrum*, is not the material that coral reefs are made of. Unlike the reef-building corals that are usually most active a few metres below the surface, these coral polyps build their 'trees' at considerable depths. Japanese fishing vessels dredge red, pink and white coral 'trees' from the sea-bed between Okinawa and Miyako at depths of 275–365m. Taiwan also has a coral fishing fleet working in the Midway and an important crafting industry. Noble coral occurs in Atlantic waters to the south of Ireland, through the Bay of Biscay and off the African coastline as far south as the Cape Verde Islands. The Mediterranean is the most important historical source of coral with the best ox-blood red coral being fished off the coastline of Algeria and Tunisia. On the European side, the waters off Sicily and Corsica produce some good material. The fishing boats are Italian and the coral is taken to Torre del Greco, a coastal town in the Bay of Naples, where it is cleaned and sorted into various grades from *Bianco*

■ The Romans believed that wearing coral protected children from harm and that it had the power to relieve snake bites or the sting of scorpions.

(pure white) and *Pelle d'angelo* (angel's skin) to *Rosa vivo* (bright red) and *Arciscuro* (ox blood). Then, graded and weighed, the material is given to the workers, mostly women, who fashion it into beads, cameos and small ornaments. A porous coral, *Corallium allaporosa*, was fished off the east coast of South Africa near Port Elizabeth during the 1970s and 80s. The material was mainly magenta, pink and white in colour. It was resin bonded and fashioned into bead necklaces and bracelets. Use has been made of *Allopara subirolcea*, a blue coral named Akori coral that occurs off the Cameroon coast. Black coral, *Antipathes subpinnata*, is composed of a protein-based organic material similar to conchiolin. It was first discovered in the Hawaiian Islands, then off the coast of Mexico and the Queensland coast of Australia. A slightly different form, *Antipathes spiralis*, was discovered off the coast of Cameroon. The golden corals that occur off Hawaii have a very similar character. The unusual and attractive bamboo corals from New Zealand and Alaska share something of each type, since their calcerous white nodes alternate with dark organic internodes.

ABOVE: *A laughing Buddha carved out of coral*

IVORY

Ivory (*I-vor-ee*), found in the teeth of all mammals, was one of the earliest materials to be worked and used by man. A head carved from mammoth ivory, which was discovered at Vestonie in France, is estimated to be 30,000 years old. Pieces of ivory with crudely scratched designs found in the caves of the Dordogne are thought to be much older. Elephant tusks are the ultimate medium for the ivory carver. They grow throughout the life of the elephant, with a pair of tusks on record as weighing 209kg. Close examination of a polished transverse section of elephant ivory reveals a uniform delicate pattern that has the appearance of 'engine-turning'. This effect, created by the 'lines of Retzius' (referred to in USA as 'Schreger lines'), is only seen in elephant ivory. The lines of Retzius are very fine canals called dentinal tubules that are filled with a gelatinous substance that in life serves to carry the nerve fibrils. The typical grain lines that run parallel to the length of the tusk are not definitive and may even be simulated in plastic imitations of ivory. Elephant ivory ranges in density from 1.70 to 1.90.

Hippopotamus ivory is close-grained with a finer undulating pattern and at 1.90+ it is also slightly denser than elephant ivory. Both the incisor and canine teeth are used for ivory. When cross-sectioned the incisor teeth have a radiating structure with distinct concentric bands in the dentine.

Refractive Indices	1.54
Hardness	2.25–2.75
Specific Gravity	1.7–1.9
Lustre	Waxy
Colour Range	Cream, white
Fracture	N/a
Sources	Elephant, hippopotamus, narwhal, walrus, warthog, whale
Transparency	Opaque
Fluorescence	Chalky blue under long-wave and faintly chalky under short-wave ultraviolet
Sectility	Ivory is sectile to a varying degree

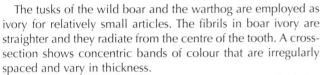

The tusks of the wild boar and the warthog are employed as ivory for relatively small articles. The fibrils in boar ivory are straighter and they radiate from the centre of the tooth. A cross-section shows concentric bands of colour that are irregularly spaced and vary in thickness.

The fibrils in the teeth of sperm whales and the smaller killer whales follow a similar pattern to that of the boar. Seen in transverse section, they reveal distinct concentric dentine rings. The ivory of these teeth was frequently decorated with scrimshaw designs by whaling crews both as a pastime and as a source of income.

The narwhal is a rare and very unusual arctic whale. The male of this species has a modified left upper incisor that forms a spirally twisted tusk that can measure up to 7m in length. The tusk is usually twisted counter-clockwise and the pulp cavity extends for most of its length giving it a hollow cross-section.

The upper canines of the Pacific walrus may reach a length of 1m, the other walrus teeth are also used as ivory but they are relatively small averaging 5cm in length. Walrus ivory has a fine texture and grain but the central core of the canine teeth resembles bone in appearance and properties.

The so-called 'Fossil Ivory' is ivory obtained from the frozen remains of the numerous woolly mammoths *Elephas primigenius* that remain trapped in ice in the frozen wastes of Siberia. Their long spirally curved tusks are often perfectly preserved and the ivory handles in exactly the same way as elephant ivory. In fact, these ivories are so alike that it requires accurate measurement of the angles in the lines of Retzius to distinguish between them.

Hornbill Ivory is the polished casque from the upper mandible of the endangered Helmeted Hornbill of Borneo. It has a distinctive bright red peripheral colour and it may attain a size of 8 x 5 x 2.5cm.

Bone is sometimes carved as a simulant of ivory, especially bone from the mandibles of large whales or long ox bones. It is heavier than ivory with an average density of 2.0 and it has a very different structure.

LEFT: *Whaling scene, executed in scrimshaw work, on the tooth of a sperm whale*

ABOVE TOP: *Carving, lower incisor of a hippopotamus*

ABOVE: *Carving, warthog tusk*

Stag-horn has also been widely used, especially as an inlay on firearms in Germany and for netsuke and other small carvings in Japan. It bears a general similarity to bone in structure but it tends towards a darker brownish hue.

VEGETABLE IVORY

Refractive Indices	1.54
Hardness	2.25–2.5
Specific Gravity	1.38–1.43
Lustre	N/a
Colour Range	Creamy–white
Fracture	N/a
Sources	North and Central Africa, Colombia, Peru
Transparency	Opaque
Fluorescence	Chalky blue under long-wave and faintly chalky blue under short-wave ultraviolet
Sectility	Moderately sectile

Vegetable Ivory is used for small carvings, beads etc. It is obtained from the fruit of the ivory palm of Colombia and Peru. The fruit is roughly the size of an American football and it contains about eight nuts, each the size of a hen's egg. The vegetable ivory they contain is almost pure cellulose, white in colour, 2.5 in hardness and with an average density of 1.41. A section of the material will reveal a series of torpedo-shaped cells in parallel lines unlike anything in animal ivory or bone.

Doum Palm nuts are obtained from the fruit of the Doum Palm or gingerbread tree of Central Africa. The fruit has one nut that is about the size and shape of a fig. The nut has a translucent white kernel with thick walls and a central cavity. It has a hardness of 2.25 and density of 1.38–1.40. A thin peeling will reveal a similar structure to that in vegetable ivory from the ivory palm.

JET

Jet (*JET*) is a form of fossilized wood. It is 'jet black' and hence its inevitable association with mourning. The use of jet in items of jewellery reached its zenith during the Victorian era when to be in mourning seems to have been the height of fashion. The

Refractive Indices	1.66
Hardness	2.5–4
Specific Gravity	1.33
Lustre	Waxy
Colour Range	Black
Fracture	Conchoidal
Sources	England, France, Scotland, Spain, USA
Transparency	Opaque
Fluorescence	N/A
Sectility	N/A

LEFT: *A jet necklace*

centre of the British jet industry was Whitby on the Yorkshire coast. The mines there have been worked for approximately 3,000 years and quantities of British jet were sent to Rome during the Roman occupation.

PEARLS

Usually termed oysters, the bivalve molluscs that produce gem pearls actually belong to the genus *Pinctada*, popularly known as 'wing shells'. This name refers to the fact that, unlike oysters, they build attachments from the hinge and are able to open and close both shells. They are widespread and occur in many sizes and shapes ranging from the 6cm *Pinctada radiata* of the Persian Gulf and the Gulf of Manaar to the 30cm *Pinctada maxima* of the South Seas. To understand something of pearl formation it is necessary to review the basic nature of these molluscs.

The mantle is a very important organ for this animal since it not only builds the shell that protects it but it also provides storage space for nutrients that will carry it through lean times. The outer surface of the mantle is bounded by highly specialized epithelial cells capable of secreting the shell-building substances. This shell is composed of three layers that must grow with the mollusc. The growth process begins with the dark outer layer or periostracum that is composed of a complex protein called conchiolin. This fibrous matting is then given some strength and rigidity by layers of prismatic calcium carbonate that are bonded with conchiolin. Logically enough, this second layer is termed the prismatic layer. The third and final layer, the

■ Many cultures share a belief in the curative power of powdered pearls. The English philosopher Francis Bacon (1561– 1626) suggested that the powder of a pearl should be taken mixed with the juice of a lemon (providing calcium, mineral salts, amino acids and vitamin C).

nacre, which comprises minute overlapping platelets of aragonite, is then deposited on the whole outer surface of the mantle. This layer will continue to grow and thicken throughout the life of the mollusc. The same specialized cells that build the shell play an essential part in the growth of a pearl. If an irritant lodges itself between the mantle and the shell, the cells will build layer upon layer of nacre over it eventually creating a blister pearl. If an irritant that lodges in the body of the mollusc has brushed against the mantle and carried a few of these cells with it then they will multiply, enclose the irritant and constantly build layer upon layer of nacre around it creating a whole or 'cyst' pearl.

MARINE PEARLS

Pearl oysters of the genus *Pinctada* are widely distributed, occurring in several seas of the tropical belt as well as in the sub-tropical region. There are many species but only three are of commercial importance in the culture of pearls:

Pinctada fucata is distributed in the Red Sea, Persian Gulf, India, China, Korea, Japan, Venezuela and Western Pacific Ocean. This is the mollusc most widely used in the culture of marine pearls.

Pinctada margaritifera, the black-lipped pearl oyster, is widely distributed in the Persian Gulf, Red Sea, Sudan, Papua New Guinea, Australia, French Polynesia, Indonesia, Andaman and Nicobar Islands, the southwestern Indian Ocean, Japan, Pacific Ocean and India (sporadic). This is the oyster used in the Tuamotu Atolls to produce South Sea black pearls.

Pinctada maxima, the gold or silver-lipped pearl oyster, occurs along the north coast of Australia, Burma, Thailand, Indonesia, Philippines and Papua New Guinea at depths ranging from low tide level to 80m. This huge oyster attains diameters of 30cm and may weigh up to 5.5kg. The silver lipped oyster is used in Australia to produce large South Sea pearls and mabés. The gold-lipped oyster lives in the waters of Indonesia, Thailand and Myanmar.

Pteria penguin, the black-winged oyster, is used in the production of fine mabé or half pearls. A shaped section of the shell is often cut out around the mabé with a view to creating jewellery pieces that make more of a statement.

The strength of the cultured pearl market is such that the demand for natural pearls has shrunk and become highly specialized. Many of the traditional pearl fisheries are now focusing on the production of shell and handling the rarely encountered natural pearls as a by-product.

Refractive Indices	N/a
Hardness	2.5–3.5
Specific Gravity	2.68–2.74 *pinctada fucata* 2.67–2.78 *p. margaritifera* 2.67–2.78 *p. maxima*
Lustre	Ranges from dull to brilliant
Colour Range	Black, bluish, bronze, creamy, greenish, grey, pink, lilac, silvery, white.
Fracture	N/a
Sources	Australia, Mexico, Persian Gulf, Philippines, Red Sea, Sri Lanka, Venezuela
Transparency	Translucent
Fluorescence	Strong chalky blue under long-wave and moderate blue under short-wave ultraviolet
Sectility	N/a

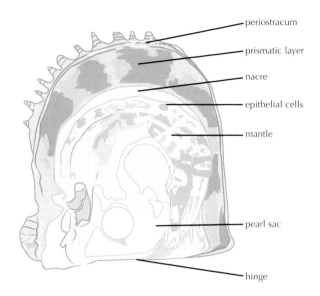

periostracum

prismatic layer

nacre

epithelial cells

mantle

pearl sac

hinge

Marine Cultured Pearls

The culture of a fully round marine pearl was first accomplished using the Japanese pearl oyster, *Pinctada fucata* or *martensi*. The process most commonly employed for this form of culture is called the Mise/Nishikawa method after its inventors. It involves taking a healthy three-year-old oyster, wedging it open with a wooden peg and securing it in a clamp. An incision is then made into the animal's gonad and a spherical mother-of-pearl nucleus is introduced together with a tiny square section of outer mantle. It is important to ensure that the outer surface of the mantle section with its specialized growth cells is in contact with the bead. Provided the implant is not rejected, these cells will multiply and completely encompass the bead, constantly coating it with nacre. The operation often produces separate small areas of irritation that the animal coats with nacre creating tiny pearls which the Japanese call *Keshi* or 'poppy seed' pearls.

Marine cultured pearls have a fairly consistent specific gravity because the mother-of-pearl bead nucleus constitutes a very significant part of their mass.

Refractive Indices	N/a
Hardness	2.5–3.5
Specific Gravity	2.72–2.78 *pinctada fucata* 2.72–2.78 *p. martinesi.*
Lustre	Ranges from fair to brilliant
Colour Range	Black, blue, bronze, cream, green, grey, lilac, pink, purple, silver, white, yellow
Fracture	N/a
Sources	Australia, Japan, Thailand
Transparency	Translucent
Fluorescence	Strong chalky blue under long-wave and moderate blue under short-wave ultraviolet
Sectility	N/a

FRESHWATER PEARLS

Roman officers on duty in the misty Cassiterides (British Isles) were not very complimentary about the weather they experienced. However, they were highly impressed with the bright lustrous pearls that could be recovered from a species of large mussel that abounded in the clear streams. British pearls have not lost their beauty, but the freshwater mussels (*Unio*) are no longer plentiful and it is illegal to fish for them. The rivers of Europe and of Russia, once productive sources of mussel pearls, appear to be depleted.

The early explorers of America found the rivers of the Mississippi valley to be a prolific source of freshwater pearls. The Indians of the region attached great importance to their pearls, which were worn by both men and women. Pearls were also frequently given as a tribute between tribes and they were buried with their owners. In the 19th century, the rivers were overfished as a result of the fashion for mother-of-pearl. Pearls were an added bonus to the vast tonnages of shell that were removed from the river system. At its peak, 10,000 people were said to have subsisted on pearling in Arkansas alone.

ABOVE: *Freshwater pearls from China*

Freshwater Cultured Pearls

Some 3,000 years ago, the Chinese were employing a species of freshwater mussel *Cristaria plicata* to coat objects with nacre. They still use the same technique to produce religious images. The mantle is eased away from the shell with a bamboo spatula then small lead images of Buddha are introduced that, given time, become coated with nacre.

In 1924, the pearl farmers of Lake Biwa, Japan, began experimenting with the use of the large mussel *Hyriopsis schlegeli* in the production of cultured freshwater pearls. Small pieces of mantle tissue were inserted into the mantle of the host mussel so effectively the pearls were non-nucleated and composed entirely of nacre the same as natural pearls. The production enjoyed a marked degree of success and for decades the name Biwa was synonymous with the finest of freshwater cultured pearls.

When China attempted to follow suit, the production was of a very low grade, wrinkled and poorly dyed in a limited range of garish hues. The pearls of this early production were often compared to Rice Krispies™.

Chinese pearl culture has subsequently shown steady improvement and a large proportion of their current production is rounded, lustrous, white or subtly coloured and overall of a very fine grade.

Refractive Indices	N/a
Hardness	3 +/-
Specific Gravity	2.67–2.70
Lustre	Ranges from medium to brilliant
Colour Range	Brown, bluish,greenish grey, lilac, purple, pink, white, yellowish
Fracture	Conchoidal
Sources	China, Europe, Japan, Russia, USA
Transparency	N/a
Fluorescence	Very strong chalky blue under long-wave and moderate blue under short-wave ultraviolet
Sectility	N/a

SHELL

The principal shells that are used for carving cameos include the Helmet shell *Cassis madagascarensis*, the Cornelian shell *Cypraeacassis rufa*, the Queen conch, *Strombus gigas* and the Tiger cowry, *Cyprea tigris*.

Mother-of-pearl is still quite widely used for decorative purposes and many species of shell are fished for their mother-of-pearl including the large *Pinctada* varieties *maxima* and *margaritifera*. Shells of the *Haliotis* group that are fished for their colourful blue, green and purple nacre include the *paua* shells of New Zealand, the American abalones and the South African *perlemoen*.

TOP LEFT: *Paua shell*
TOP RIGHT: *Abalone*
ABOVE: *Red helmet shell*

TORTOISESHELL

Tortoiseshell was not taken from the shell of a tortoise but from the carapace of the Hawks-bill turtle *Chelone imbricata*. The hawk's bill is a medium sized sea turtle with a carapace length of slightly less than 1m. It has been hunted close to extinction for the 13 plates of attractively coloured protein that make up the top of its shell. Once they had been softened in hot water and pressed flat the ridges were filed away. Fine saws were used to saw the plates to shape and the surface was smoothed with a paste of charcoal dust. Once the shell had been inlaid into the back of a brush or mirror, it was given a final polish with oil and a leather buff. The material from the belly shield or plastron was originally discarded but with shortage of shell caused by the decreasing numbers of turtles, it was eventually marketed as blond shell and achieved a degree of popularity. The hawk's bill turtle is now on the endangered species list.

Refractive Indices	1.55
Hardness	2.5
Specific Gravity	1.29
Lustre	N/a
Colour Range	Brown, yellow
Fracture	N/a
Sources	Tropical reefs of the Atlantic, Indian and Pacific Oceans
Transparency	Translucent
Fluorescence	–
Sectility	Tortoiseshell is readily sectile

■ Tortoiseshell has a long history of use as an inlay in furniture. Known from Roman times, this practice reached a peak during the reign of King Louis XIV of France. The king's cabinet maker Boule made extensive use of dark tortoiseshell and brass in his signature range of 'Buhl' furniture.

Chapter 7
Simulants, Synthetics and Schlenters

The superficial resemblance of simulants to the gemstones they imitate often amounts to little more than a degree of similarity in colour. Synthetic gemstones on the other hand must, by definition, have essentially the same chemical composition, physical and optical properties as their natural counterparts. They may exhibit some slight variation in the presence or absence of trace elements but then this is frequently the case between natural stones of differing origin. In some instances, however, traces of elements not associated with the natural mineral may be detected, providing the researcher with useful clues regarding the nature and origin of the stone. 'Schlenter' is a term used in the jewellery trade to describe a fake gemstone, rough or cut, that has been created for fraudulent purposes.

SIMULANTS
Faience

The practice of gem simulation has a long and colourful history that dates back to pre-dynastic Egypt. Lapis lazuli, malachite and turquoise were rare and highly favoured in ancient Egypt. Craftsmen simulated them with carved steatite coated with appropriately coloured paste and fired it to give it a glaze. As their knowledge of fluxes developed, they were able to create 'faience', a simulant that had the fine siliceous glaze of true glass.

Glass

The more frequently encountered glasses can be split into two groups by composition: crown glasses consist of silica, lime, soda and potassium and are used in the manufacture of the cheap moulded gems used in costume jewellery; lead or flint glasses contain silica, lead oxide, potassium and traces of thallium, boron or arsenic. These are the highly dispersive glasses sometimes referred to as strass, used in better quality imitation jewels.

Glass opal These simulants usually contain flecks and slivers of metallic foils embedded in the glass that give them a superficial resemblance to opal.

ABOVE: *Simulated opals containing metallic foils*

Goldstone is a colourless glass filled with tiny precipitated crystals of copper, which give it an aventurescent appearance. It is also made in green and deep blue.

Amber simulants

Copal, a relatively recent fossil resin, is frequently used as an amber imitation. Kauri gum is a variety of copal that originates from the kauri pines of New Zealand. Copal frequently holds plant and insect inclusions. Unusual amber simulants have included bull's horn (cherry amber) and rhinoceros hide (golden amber).

Porcelain

Porcelain is sometimes used to simulate opaque or semi-opaque gems such as lapis lazuli or turquoise. It has a vitreous lustre and a specific gravity of around 2.3.

Plastics

Numerous plastics have been employed to simulate amber, ivory and tortoiseshell. These include bakelite, celluloid, casein, Perspex™ and polystyrene. Bernat and Polybern are amber imitations of German origin; they often have insects, seeds and fragments of real amber embedded in them.

Imitation Pearls

Beads created from glass, plastics and shell are used in the creation of pearl simulants. These beads acquire their pearly lustre when repeatedly dipped in vats containing guanin ('essence d'orient') a substance recovered from herring scales.

Hemitine

A general term for hematite simulants. Unlike hematite, the majority of these simulants will respond to a magnet.

Stainless steel

Stainless steel is often used as a simulant for marcasite.

Composite stones

Garnet-topped doublets usually simulate ruby, sapphire and emerald. They are cut from glass of an appropriated colour, capped with a sliver of garnet.

Corundum doublets can be very deceptive especially when they are mounted in a closed setting. They have a crown of natural sapphire bonded to a synthetic corundum pavilion.

LEFT: *A corundum doublet*

'Emerald' doublets frequently consist of a moderately included aquamarine crown bonded to an emerald green glass pavilion.

Opal doublets and triplets are among the most frequently encountered of composite stones. An opal doublet comprises a very thin sliver of precious opal backed by dark potch opal, onyx or even clear glass, bonded to the opal with a black adhesive. If the doublet is then capped with a highly polished protective dome of glass or clear quartz it is referred to as a triplet.

LEFT: *A range of opal triplets*

Quartz stars Rose quartz from Madagascar frequently has the potential to cut very fine six-rayed stars. These cabochons have been given a coloured backing and used to simulate fine star ruby and sapphire.

Composite diamond simulants range from stones that have a diamond crown backed by a synthetic pavilion to those that are total simulants. One example of the latter is the good looking but soft strontium titanate, which may be capped with a synthetic white sapphire crown.

Foil backs have a mirror-like backing that may be a metallic foil or paint to enhance the brilliance of a paste or rock crystal.

ABOVE: *A blue-black quartz star*

SYNTHETICS

There were numerous attempts to synthesize precious stones during the 19th century, especially in France and Germany. Experiments were focused on the flux melt process either using small fragments of the actual gems or salts that contained the basic elements of their composition.

In 1888, P. Hautefeuille and A. Perrey succeeded in growing small emerald crystals in a flux that combined lithium molybdate and lithium niobate. However, the first gem to be synthesized commercially, ruby, was created by a totally different process.

Flame fusion process

French chemist, August Verneuil, perfected what came to be known as the flame fusion process and lodged details of his apparatus and method with the French Academy of Science in 1891. The early, almost spherical, products were termed *boules*. However, improvements to the process yielded larger and more cylindrical shapes

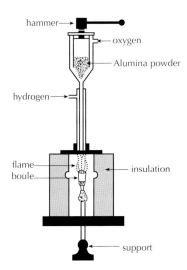

LEFT: *Verneuil furnace*

Method

The Verneuil furnace employs a vertical torch in which finely powdered alumina doped with a trace of chrome is carried in a stream of oxygen until it joins the hydrogen input at the point of combustion. The tiny molten droplets of aluminium fall onto a rotating ceramic pedestal where they cool too rapidly for the molecules to orient themselves correctly. As the boule grows, the pedestal is gradually lowered, maintaining the position of the growth point. The stress caused by the lack of molecular alignment builds up in the boule. The completed boule is nipped off its stem and given a light tap that splits it lengthwise, relieving the stress. In larger stones cut from these half boules the colour is a give-away to the experienced eye. This is because the table is always parallel to the 'C' axis and not perpendicular to it as is most frequently the case with natural stones.

Turning his attention to the production of blue corundum, Verneuil established that a combination of iron and titanium oxides were required to create the hue of natural sapphire. Producing a uniform colour in sapphire boules proved to be a problem. The blue boules revealed srongly coloured, curved growth lines, spots and cracks.

Today, flame fusion corundum is produced in many colours including purple, red, pink, orange and yellow hues, as well as colourless and colour-change varieties.

Asteriated synthetic corundum

In 1947, the Linde Division of the Union Carbide Corporation of America succeeded in producing a flame fusion corundum containing a dense mat of fine oriented rutile silk. Polished as a cabochon, this material exhibits a dramatic six-rayed star. Linde enjoyed a monopoly of this product during the early years but the technology was eventually acquired by producers in Germany, Israel, Japan, Switzerland and the USSR.

TOP: *Synthetic spinel boule*
ABOVE: *Colours produced by the flame fusion process*

Flame fusion synthetic spinel

L. Paris, a student of Verneuil, experimented with the effect of using various elements as dopants, in the hope of overcoming the problem with blue synthetic corundum. He found that adding a quantity of magnesium produced boules of a magnificent even blue. However, it was evident that these new boules were not corundum since they were singly refractive with a squarish cross-section. He had stumbled on a new material! While it had no exact natural counterpart, it was closely aligned to spinel. Hard and bright, the uniform cornflower blue of this synthetic makes it an attractive sapphire simulant. The light blues achieved considerable popularity as a substitute for aquamarine. Attempts to produce a good red in this material have met with little success. The few boules that have survived have been badly distorted and highly stressed. In the 1930s, a colourless form was introduced to the market under the trade name Jourado diamonds. Synthetic spinel is also produced as a blue-green tourmaline simulant and in a yellow-green intended to simulate peridot.

ABOVE: *A synthetic spinel created by the flame fusion process*

The Czochralski process

Jan Czochralski perfected the process of pulling synthetic gem crystals directly from the melt in 1918. This technique is capable of producing much larger, cleaner crystals than the flame fusion process but it does have the disadvantage of being significantly more expensive.

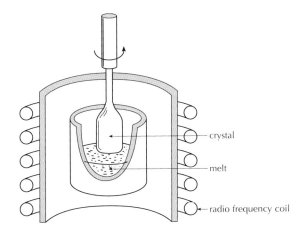

crystal

melt

radio frequency coil

ABOVE: *Synthetic Czochralski forsterite oval*
LEFT: *Czochralski apparatus*

Method
A mixture comprising the constituents of the target material plus a suitable flux is placed in an iridium crucible and brought to a temperature slightly higher than its melting point. A precisely oriented seed crystal is then lowered into the crucible until it just makes contact with the melt. The rod holding the seed is set to rotate slowly and pull up from the melt at a steady rate as the crystal forms. Fluctuations in the temperature of the melt serve to increase the diameter of the crystal. In the case of commercial Yttrium Aluminium Garnet (YAG), this is normally stabilized at about 3.75cm and the pull proceeds until the crystal is about 30cm in length.

This technique is often used in the production of single crystals of ruby, scheelite, Gadolinium Gallium Garnet (GGG) and YAG. A Russian laboratory uses a variation of this process to create synthetic alexandrite chrysoberyl.

LEFT: *Gadolinium Gallium Garnet*

Flux-melt process

Experiments with the flux-melt process had been ongoing for almost a century when, shortly after World War II, Carroll Chatham of San Francisco began his commercial production of synthetic emerald. Today the Chatham laboratory also grows flux-melt ruby and sapphire in blue, pink and padparadschah hues.

Pierre Gilson has been the major European producer of synthetic emerald since the early 1960s. Both Chatham and Gilson emeralds tend to have slightly lower properties than natural stones. Their refractive indices are in the range 1.562–1.559, birefringence is 0.003 and their specific gravity is 2.65.

Method

Beryllium oxide, aluminium oxide and a trace of chromic oxide are placed in a platinum crucible and dissolved in a flux of lithium molybdate. The third major component, silica, is light and floats on the surface when added. The silica gradually diffuses into the flux where it encounters and interacts with the beryllium and alumina to form beryl crystals. The hint of chromic oxide in the flux gives the crystals an intense emerald green hue.

FAR LEFT: *Flux-melt synthetic Chatham sapphire*
MIDDLE: *Flux-melt synthetic red spinel*
LEFT: *Flux-melt synthetic Chatham emerald*

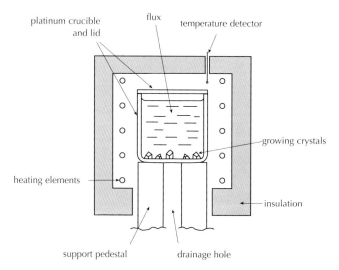

platinum crucible and lid

flux

temperature detector

growing crystals

heating elements

insulation

support pedestal

drainage hole

LEFT: *Flux-melt apparatus*

Hydrothermal process

Method

Hydrothermal quartz and beryl gems are grown in reinforced steel autoclaves at pressures in the order of 10,000 to 20,000 psi and temperatures between 400°C and 600°C. The base of the autoclave is heated to dissolve the nutrients and the upper region, with its racks of seed crystals, is cooled to speed up deposition. The pH of the water that fills the autoclave may be anything from strongly alkaline to highly acidic, depending on the nature of the crystals that are being synthesized. The autoclave is often lined with a noble metal such as platinum or gold in order to render it resistant to corrosion.

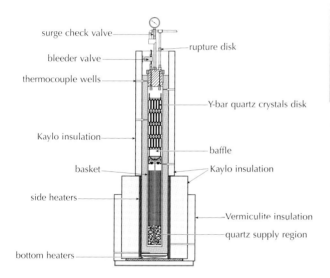

ABOVE: *Synthetic hydrothermal quartz*
LEFT: *Autoclave*

Diamond synthesis

Small industrial diamonds have been manufactured in quantity since the 1950s. However, it was only in 1970 that the General Electric Company of America announced the successful synthesis of gem diamond. The soft hexagonal mineral graphite is the stable form of carbon at normal temperatures and pressures. Diamond on the other hand is a modified high-temperature cubic form of carbon that occurs in an environment where pressures are in the region of 100,000 atmospheres and the temperatures are in excess of 2,000°C. The synthetic conversion of graphite or a similar carbon source to diamond also requires the presence of a catalyst in the form of molten iron and/or nickel.

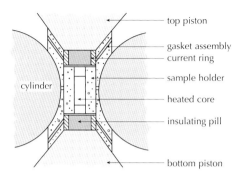

ABOVE: *Gemesis synthetic diamond*
LEFT: *General Electric belt apparatus*

Method

Employing high pressure and high temperature (HPHT) technology, the Gemesis Corporation of Florida USA creates synthetic gem-quality diamonds, the crystals attaining a size of 3–4cts. Cut in the USA or South Africa, the intense fancy yellow stones are already featured in jewellery ranges.

Chemical vapour deposition (CVD) is used by Boston-based Apollo Diamond Inc. Small cut stones are said to exhibit similar characteristics to natural Type IIb diamonds. They carry a brownish or greyish hue but are nearly colourless with HPHT treatment.

Skull-melt process

Method

This process enables the synthesis of materials that crystallize at very high temperatures; Zirconia for example has a melting point of 2,750°C. Referred to as the 'cold crucible' or 'skull method', radio frequency energy is used to melt the component materials within a crust that is formed from their own powder.

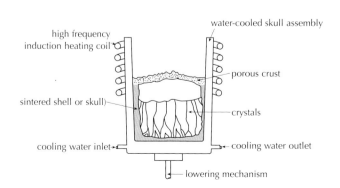

ABOVE: *Skull-melt cubic zirconia*
LEFT: *The skull-melt process*

Synthetic and simulant gems

H = hardness; RI = refractive indices; D = dispersion;
SG = specific gravity

Diamond simulants that lack a natural counterpart:

Cubic Zirconia, ZrO_2, is grown in a wide range of colours using the skull-melt process. It is not a true synthetic since it has no natural counterpart. The constants for calcium stabilized cubic are H: 8.5, RI: 2.18, D: 0.066, SG: 5.7.

Gadolinium Gallium Garnet, $Gd_3Ga_5O_{12}$, is grown using the Czochralski technique. It is colourless to light beige, but also blue, green, red, and yellow. The unstable colourless material gradually assumes a brownish hue. H: 6.5, RI: 2.02, D: 0.038, SG: 7.05.

Lithium Niobate, $LiNbO_3$, is grown using the Czochralski technique in several colours. H: 6, RI: 2.21–2.30, D: 0.120, SG: 4.64.

Strontium titanate, $SrTiO_3$, is grown by flame fusion in a range of colours but usually seen in its colourless form. H: 6, RI: 2.409, D: 0.190, SG: 5.13.

Yttrium Aluminium Garnet, $Y_3Al_5O_{12}$, grown using Czochralski and flux-melt techniques. Generally colourless, but also produced in green, blue, pink, red, yellow, lilac and pale green. H: 8, RI: 1.83, D: 0.028, SG: 4.55.

Moissanite, SiC. This diamond simulant is classed as a synthetic since tiny natural crystals were found in the Canyon Diablo Meteorite, Arizona, USA. The closely guarded method of synthesis is probably a modified form of the flux-melt process. Moissanite has a faint metallic greenish hue, marked thermal and electro-conductivity. H: 9.25, RI: 2.6–2.7, SG: 3.1–3.2.

'Recco' gems These are claimed to consist of fragments derived from the relevant natural mineral bonded in a cement or resin. They are marketed as reconstructed lapis lazuli, sugilite etc.

TOP: *A range of cubic zirconia*

BELOW: *Recco slabs*
BOTTOM: *Quartz schlenter*

Schlenters

Crackle-dyed quartz frequently provides a basis for the type of fraudulent gem materials known in the trade as schlenters. When heated quartz crystals are dropped into icy cold dye, they crack and the dye fills the fractures. Adhesive is applied to the crystals, leaving a strategically placed 'window', and they are rolled in flakes of mica. In more sophisticated schlenters, the artificial 'matrix' is applied to synthetic emerald crystals. These fakes may also simulate ruby, sapphire and tanzanite rough.

The Art of the Gem

Chapter 8
Diamanteering

The art that is involved in transforming a rough diamond into a scintillating gem has undergone dramatic changes in recent times. A glimpse beneath the cloak of mystery that traditionally surrounds this craft will reveal an intriguing mixture of ancient skills and cutting-edge technology.

Marking

When parcels of rough are received at a diamond cutting works the stones are checked, weighed and entered in the diamond register. The goods must then pass through the marking room for analysis and marking.

Diamond is an isotropic mineral. This means that light moves at a constant speed within the stone regardless of the direction in which it is travelling. However, in sharp contrast, the physical properties of a diamond are of a distinctly directional nature. Diamonds can only be cleaved parallel to octahedral planes, sawn in directions that lie in cubic planes or point to point of the dodecahedron and polished in directions that are governed by the relationship of a facet to dodecahedral planes.

The diamond markers/designers must be fully aware of these and many other factors as they carefully examine each stone to establish its potential. Depending on its crystal shape and nature a stone might be made as a single stone or sectioned by cleaving, sawing or lasering to produce two or more stones. A marker must have the ability to visualize the gem encapsulated in a piece of rough before sealing its fate with a drop of Indian ink.

The ink markings placed on each stone serve to indicate the route they must follow through the factory.

Many factories have invested in imaging technology and this has had a profound effect on the systems employed for handling rough and on the percentage recoveries achieved.

One after another, the stones are centred on the end of a cylindrical rod and filmed as the rod rotates. The operator/marker can view a stone from any angle once the video has been captured in the computer memory. The programme outlines potential gems within the image of the rough on screen and enables the marker to rotate these combined images checking the fit from every angle. When the marker wishes to determine the total recovery from a sawable stone the image of a second stone can be created in a contrasting colour (see right).

Imperfections will inevitably be present in a fairly high proportion of the rough. The marker must devise and punch in alternative ways of handling the stone then use the computer to create new images and calculate revised recovery figures.

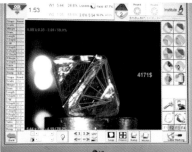

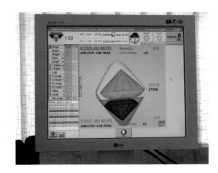

TOP: *Diamond marker*
MIDDLE: *Plotting stones in rough data*
BOTTOM: *Proposed stones*

Recently, more advanced units have been developed that are equipped with laser *feelers* enabling them to detect and make provision for irregularities in the surface of the rough. Laser marking systems have also been developed that can quickly produce accurate indelible lines on diamond surfaces.

Makeables

The marker will usually use a dot or cross to indicate that a stone is to be treated as a makeable and to establish the position of the table. A decade or so ago approximately 10 per cent of the goods selected for South African manufacturers by the DTC would have been treated as makeables. Today this figure has risen to something between 25 and 30 per cent due to shortages of good-sized rough and a greater demand for fancy shapes.

Sawables

These are usually simple or slightly modified octahedra that are sawn in the cube plane to yield two pieces of rough suitable for cutting round brilliants. If the marker notes an inclusion in a stone he will often try to remove the defect by having the cut pass through it. The saw blade is a phosphor-bronze disc about 7.5 to 10cm in diameter and 0.06 to 0.12mm thick, charged with diamond powder. The blade is mounted between two thick flanges that reach to within about 10mm of the edge of the blade. A small *kerf* or notch is often made to start the saw in a cut. With larger stones a laser may be used to cut this starting kerf. Once the spindle is moving, the high speeds involved in sawing, often in excess of 6,000rpm, serve to impart further rigidity to the blade. Sawing is a slow process and it can take anything from a few hours to a full day to saw through a carat stone.

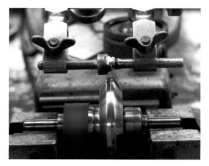

Cleavables

The disadvantage of cleaving is that it yields poor shapes and the technique has not enjoyed extensive use since the advent of the laser. Cleaving might still be used to divide large cleavage fragments or stones with heavy marks in a specific area that can be most economically removed by this method.

TOP: *Diamond sawyer*
BOTTOM: *Diamond saw*

Lasering

The laser may be employed to:

- divide stones that cannot be sawn because of cross graining or knot;
- divide stones in a direction other than the cubic, dodecahedral or octahedral planes;
- outline stones of fancy shape such as butterflies, flowers etc.;
- cut a small kerf that will act as an aid to starting the saw in sawable goods;
- cut a kerf to facilitate the use of the cleaver's blade.

ABOVE: *Diamonds on a sorting pad*

Bruting

The workman who is responsible for shaping up all the rough in preparation for polishing is known as the cutter or bruter. The process involves securing the stone on a *dop* (metal rod) and keying the dop into the chuck of a lathe. He uses a second diamond, mounted on a short rod and known as a sharp, as a lathe tool to shape the stone that is rotating on the lathe.

Hand bruting is on the wane and many of the more modern factories have installed electronically controlled, automatic bruting machines. Factories that specialize in calibrated smalls use automatic bruting machines to produce the type of uniformly rounded goods best suited for processing by automated polishing units. Automated blocking units have also been developed that save many man hours and can efficiently prepare larger stones for the brillianteer.

BELOW: *Polishing a diamond*
BOTTOM: *The polishing room*

The Polishing Process

Diamanteers use a special lap, referred to in the trade as a scaife, to grind and polish the facets on a diamond. The scaife is a heavy cast iron disc approximately 30cm in diameter and 25mm thick with a surface that has been lathe turned and lapped to ensure that it is as flat as possible. The surface has then been scored with a coarse silicon carbide stick in order to create grooves that will help to retain diamond paste. The paste comprising diamond powder and olive oil is now applied to the scaife and rubbed in to ensure that the diamond fragments are firmly bedded in its surface. The vertical built-in spindle that runs through the centre of the scaife is housed in bearings

top and bottom to ensure that the disc will run smoothly free of any vibration when it reaches its basic operating speed of approximately 2,500rpm. The craftsmen use a hand tool known as a tang to position and rotate the small clamp called a dop that is used to hold the diamond.

The Cross Worker

The polishing process begins with the cross worker or blocker. Before securing a stone in the dop and placing the first facet this craftsman must visualize how the stone is oriented in relation to invisible but very real directional properties. He will examine it carefully for inclusions, imperfections and any grain lines left by the bruter that may give him a clue as to how well the stone will *run* in a given direction. Once he has oriented himself within the stone he may lightly block out the corner facets to create windows that will let in more light. This will make it easier for him to detect any fine inclusions in the table that he may be able to remove while working the stone. Now he must place and polish the corner and bezel facets on the crown, the corner and pavilion facets on the base, the table and if required a culet.

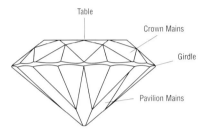

ABOVE: *Cross working facets*

At this stage the top quality stones are often examined under the microscope. If any small defects are detected their location is marked so that the brillianteer can try to remove them while working the stone.

The Brillianteer

If he is polishing a classic round brilliant the brillianteer will place and polish a further 40 facets on the stone. These comprise the eight star facets around the table, 16 halves running up to meet them from the girdle and 16 girdle halves on the pavilion. If required the brillianteer may also facet the girdle. Alternatively the stone may go back to the cutter to have the girdle polished in the round. In many factories a specialist craftsman who works on larger stones or fancy cuts will place and polish all the facets on the stones that he makes.

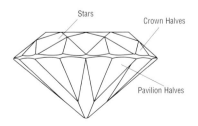

ABOVE: *Brillianteering facets*

Chapter 9
Lapidary Craft

Many of the tools used by primitive hominids would have been created from such readily available materials as bone, horn or wood. Organic materials decompose relatively quickly when exposed to the elements so very few examples have survived. However, stone is a far more durable medium and early man has left us a lasting legacy in the form of skilfully crafted flint and chalcedony artefacts. These range from basic hammer stones, hand-axes and scrapers to finely pressure-flaked cutting edges, spear- and arrow-heads. Quite often late Stone-Age tools exhibit attractive colours and patterns. Examining and handling these pieces gives you a feeling that the craftsman must have appreciated something more than the utilitarian aspect of his work. There must have come a point during his constant search for food when primitive man made a conscious decision to carry with him attractive shells or stones that he had discovered. Probably the next major step was to drill holes through these objects so that he could string them and wear them around his neck. This arrangement was probably prompted by the necessity to keep his hands free. The origins of personal decorations of this nature are certainly very ancient as evidenced by drilled snail shell beads discovered in South Africa that are estimated to date back 75,000 years.

ABOVE: *A collection of stone-age tools*

Tumbling

This is the most basic method of preparing stones for use in jewellery. The rough gemstone material (*see* right) is simply crushed or hammer broken to suitable sizes, off-cuts and fragments from other processes often being added to the mix. The fragments are then placed in rubber-lined drums to be rounded, smoothed and polished. When preparing a batch of rough for tumbling, it is advisable to select materials that are fairly similar in their physical properties.

The drums simulate the action of the waves that smooth and round pebbles on a beach. Large rotating drums are most effective in rounding the stones especially the hexagonal and octagonal models that are specifically designed to create a rolling action in the load. Vibratory drums will usually impart the best final polish to the stones. However, many hobbyists achieve very satisfactory results using a single drum. Plastic pellets and scraps of leather are often introduced at the polishing stage in the commonly held belief that they serve to improve the finish.

This process is particularly successful with agate, chalcedony, jasper, quartz and tigers-eye, yielding highly polished irregular baroques (tumbled stones). These may be drilled and strung as beads or linked up with mass-produced bell-caps, to form necklaces and bracelets. Small tumbled stones and twisted wire are combined to create gem trees, stands of aloes, butterflies and numerous other ornamental objects. Pictures may be created employing extremely small tumble-polished stones that are bonded in place to provide the coloured segments.

Sawing

There are three basic processes involved in converting rough rocks and minerals to brilliant polished gems: sawing, grinding and polishing. The sawing of gem materials can be divided into three categories based on scale: sectioning, slabbing and trimming.

Sectioning involves the use of saws capable of cutting through jade boulders and other large blocks of gemstone rough. There are three main types of sectioning saw: continuous-wire, straight-blade and circular-blade. Continuous-wire saws employ a twisted wire that circles around a series of pulleys and carries abrasive grit through a cut in the boulder. This is a concept that was developed by the Chinese, who have used hand-driven wire saws for many centuries (see illustration below). Straight bladed saws also employ a slurry of abrasive grit slowly to grind their way through blocks of stone, but they have a cam-driven action similar to that of the power hacksaws used in the engineering industry for cutting metal. Large circular sectioning saws are very costly but they have a much quicker action that can save a great deal of time (see illustration overleaf). They usually have segmented sintered rims that contain coarse particles of diamond.

LEFT: *Sawing*

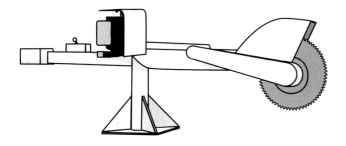

Slabbing saws (see right) are used to cut slabs of predetermined thickness from medium-sized rough or blocks that have been divided by a sectioning saw. They have diamond-charged circular blades that range from 25 to 90cm in diameter.

Trim saws range from 7.5 to 20cm in diameter. The larger sizes are used to cut and trim slabs and small units with ultra-thin blades function in the preparation of facet rough.

Polished Slabs

The sawn slices may simply be smoothed and polished either by hand on a horizontal lap or automatically on a vibratory lapping machine. Overhead oscillating units are frequently employed to grind, smooth and polish very large slabs or assembled pieces. The polished slices may be used in items of jewellery, hung as wind chimes or incorporated into 'dream-' and 'sun- catchers'. They may also be trimmed to precise shapes for use in inlay work, panels mounted in screens and lamp-shades, panes in leaded windows, intarsia or parquetry mosaics. Diamond-charged core drills are sometimes used to cut out round cabochon blanks, gemstone rings and bangles from slabs. Somewhat thicker and more substantial slabs may be employed as clock faces, decorative tiles, bookends or other ornamental objects, inlaid into table-tops or displayed as specimens.

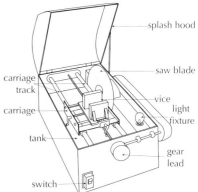

ABOVE LEFT: *Circular sectioning saw*
ABOVE RIGHT: *Slabbing saw*
BELOW: *Circular blades used in slabbing saws*

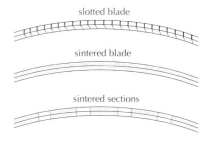

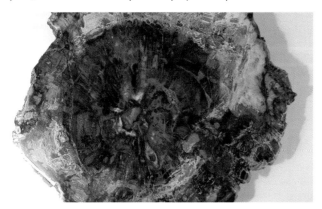

ABOVE: *Polished ammonite*
LEFT: *Polished petrified wood*

Cabochons

The term cabochon is derived from the French word *caboche* which means 'knob'. Usually fashioned from translucent to opaque materials, cabochons may be cut in free form or symmetric shapes but they are most frequently oval with a highly polished smoothly domed top, a bevelled bottom edge and a flat base. This basic shape is derived from the scarab stones carved in the shape of a dung beetle that were once worn as a symbol of immortality by the ancient Egyptians. Double cabochons have a base that is also cut with a shallow dome and they are often mounted with an open back. Dark toned material such as some almandine garnet may be cut with a hollow back to lighten the stone. This type of cabochon is termed a carbuncle. The cabochon form is also employed for those gems that display such optical phenomena as asterism, chatoyancy, schiller, play-of-fire, etc.

Wetting the sawn slabs will bring out the colour distribution and patterns when selecting material for cabochons. Templates can be used to frame particularly attractive areas and assist in selecting the best size and shape for a cabochon. The outline of the proposed gemstone can then be drawn in using a slender aluminium, brass or phosphor-bronze rod that has been ground to a fine point. Once the stone has been cut out and trimmed with a trim saw, it is ground to conform to the stencilled outline, domed on water-cooled grinding wheels and polished with a suitable oxide on a hard felt buff.

The term 'flat-topped cabochon' is distinctly contradictory but it is in general use with reference to stones cut with an open table, bevelled sides and a flat back. The girdle outline may be cushion, octagonal, oval, round or square, to name a few. This cut is frequently encountered in opaque stones including agate, black onyx, bloodstone, tiger-eye and lapis-lazuli.

TOP: *Red coral cabochon*
MIDDLE: *Unakite cabochon*
BOTTOM: *Vesuvianite cabochon*

Beads

One of earliest forms of fashioned gems, beads are currently enjoying a tremendous revival. Numerous books and a range of specialized magazines are available on the subject. In recent years the long established *Lapidary Journal*, a magazine that is widely distributed and very popular with hobbyists, has devoted its entire October issue to beads.

Spherical gem beads are made by sawing the rough material into cubes, removing the sharp corners by grinding, then rounding the stones in a bead mill and finishing them in a tumbler.

ABOVE: *Lapis lazuli and coral beads*

Whether gem beads are preformed to yield symmetrical shapes or simply random tumbled baroques, they can be drilled either lengthwise or crosswise to afford limitless variations of shape and colour. Beads that are destined for use in rings, ear-studs or pendant earrings may be half-drilled. Faceted beads are usually preformed and drilled before faceting. The drilling of a limited number of beads may be accomplished with a lapidary drill press using diamond-tipped drill bits, but production on a larger scale requires the use of modern ultra-sonic drills. The finished beads can be strung as bracelets, necklaces or dangle earrings possibly in combination with pearls, gold or silver beads to add contrast.

ABOVE: *A strand of bull horn beads*

Spheres

As with round beads, the key to the creation of fine spheres lies in the production of accurate cubes from the rough. The edges are then sawn off the cube while maintaining its symmetry to achieve a regular 18-sided polygon. The angles where the faces meet must be reduced by hand-grinding before the preform is ready to be set up in one of the two- or three-cup automatic sphere-making machines. There the piece undergoes a rather lengthy process of rounding, smoothing and polishing.

Cameo

In cameo work, material is cut away so that the design, usually embodied in a layer of contrasting colour, is raised above the level of the base. The most common subjects are beautiful ladies with masses of intricately styled hair. Historical, mythical or religious figures are also reproduced in this art form. The materials employed generally have layers of colour that can be used to create or embellish the image. The magnificent red Helmet shell (*Cassis madagascariensis*) is the most popular material for cameos. The shell of the giant conch (*Strombus gigas*) also yields beautiful cameos but its rose pink hue fades with prolonged exposure to light. Banded carnelian, onyx and sardonyx are typical cameo materials and ivory, coral, jet and lava have all enjoyed some use. Commercial manufacturers, especially those in Japan, employ computer-assisted lapidary units to create replicas of original hand-worked cameos.

ABOVE: *A sphere of copper minerals*

Curvette (USA *chevee*) This is a variation of cameo work in which the subject is raised from the centre of a bowl-shaped depression in the stone.

ABOVE: *A selection of lava cameos*

Intaglio Intaglio means the design is incised into the surface of the gem. Intaglio rings are generally worn by men and should the ring be intended for use as a signature seal, the design is engraved in reverse and cut much more deeply into the stone. A typical commonly encountered intaglio takes the form of the head of a Roman centurion cut into either hematite or tiger-eye.

Scrimshaw A traditional craft, the designs are often hunting scenes. The shallow grooves that are engraved into baleen (whalebone), hoof, horn, bone or ivory surfaces are impregnated with ink to provide colour and contrast.

Surface carving Carving designs into the surface of a cabochon is by no means a new concept; in fact it was a typical feature of Egyptian scarabs. On the other hand, reverse carving is a relatively modern innovation. Highly transparent materials are employed so that the design cut into the bottom of the stone will create a picture when it is viewed from the top. This art form calls for great skill but the resulting three-dimensional scenes can be very striking.

ABOVE: *An intaglio image of the Greek god Hermes carved out of carnelian*

Carvings

True three-dimensional carvings may be grouped into three broad classes: representational, stylized or abstract. In representational carving the lapidary attempts to reproduce the subject as realistically as possible. In stylized carving the subject is portrayed in a conventional but unrealistic form. Abstract carvings are often the result of the artist letting himself go wherever the medium and his imagination may take him.

The majority of modern gem carvers and engravers use electrically powered tools. In the West it is the dentist's hanging drill with its flexible shaft, tubular hand-piece and chuck fitting that is the most commonly used tool for carving and engraving. It can be used at variable speeds, controlled by a foot pedal. Any one of the numerous different diamond or silicon carbide charged cutting, drilling, carving, sanding and polishing tools can be driven by this unit.

Many craftsmen, especially those in the Far East, favour the reverse system. They secure the small tools in a chuck on a 'fixed arbour' and manipulate the item that is being carved between their fingers.

To an increasing extent. modern commercial production involves the use of computer-assisted automatic lapidary units to create replicas of original gem carvings.

ABOVE: *A carving of a Shona woman in verdite*

Faceting

Sourcing rough

Faceting is undoubtedly the most popular method of working transparent gem materials. Rare gem rough is obviously difficult to obtain and professional cutters generally purchase any exceptional pieces of the popular gem varieties that come on the market. However, the budding amateur facetier will find that through gem and mineral clubs, rock shops, gem shows, surfing the Internet and subscribing to one or two of the numerous hobby magazines, he or she will have access to a variety of good-quality facet rough ranging from amethyst to zoisite.

Quartz might seem to be the obvious material for a novice to begin with, since it is both cheap and readily available. However, rock crystal can frequently give the amateur problems when it comes to polishing large facets, such as the table of his or her first stone. Beryl will prove to be a better choice since it is much more responsive to polishing. It is worth paying a little more up front to acquire some inexpensive light-coloured beryl to start with. Beryl occurs in many hues and seeking out suitable rough to build up an attractive and valuable colour suite is an ideal project for the novice facetier. Suites of stones in the garnet family, quartz and tourmaline could follow.

Shape, clarity and colour are the basic factors to consider when buying facet rough. Well-rounded or chunky pieces are best suited for most cuts. Each piece should be checked carefully in good light and material that reveals fractures and inclusions should be rejected. When examining rough for colour it should not be held up to a bright light. Rather place the stones on a sheet of white paper in average lighting conditions then eliminate any that appear to be virtually black since they will prove to be too dark in tone to be cut as attractive gems.

Preforming

This involves studying the rough to determine how to achieve the best recovery in terms of orientation, shape and size of stone. Then the rough is sawn, should this be necessary, and ground to create a slightly oversized version of the proposed gem.

Dopping

The preformed gem is now ready for mounting on a dop stick. Accurate alignment is essential in faceting and facetiers who use mechanical facet heads generally employ metal dop sticks that are machined from aluminium, brass or steel. Dops that are intended for emerald cuts and baguettes have a V-cut in the head. The dops designed to take round preforms have a cone-

TOP LEFT: *A beryl crystal*
TOP RIGHT: *A tourmaline crystal*
ABOVE: *A suite of faceted beryl*

shaped cavity machined in the head. The preforms are secured in a dop by means of shellac, dopping wax or strong glue depending on the sensitivity of the material.

Once the crown is cut and polished the stone must be transferred to a second dop that will be bonded to the crown thus enabling the facetier to cut the pavilion. This task is simplified by the use of a transfer jig.

Faceting Heads

The placement of facets on a stone is based on a combination of two angles: the angle of rotation around the girdle and the angle of inclination away from the girdle. In the case of jamb-peg faceting, the height of the chosen hole determines the angle of inclination and the skill and experience of the cutter determines the angle of rotation. Most production faceting is accomplished using this method. Mechanical facet heads enable the facetier to read and set the exact angle of inclination against a quadrant and to employ a series of notched index plates to control the degree of rotation. There are various manufacturers of these precision units that are used by a number of specialized professionals as well as the vast majority of amateur facetiers.

TOP: *Dop sticks*
ABOVE: *A transfer jig*

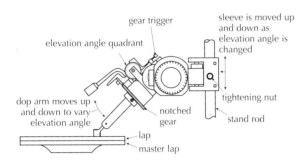

gear trigger

elevation angle quadrant

sleeve is moved up and down as elevation angle is changed

dop arm moves up and down to vary elevation angle

notched gear

tightening nut

stand rod

lap

master lap

LEFT: *Mechanical facet head*

LEFT: *Rough crystals of spessartite from the garnet family*

Laps

To produce the flat precisely matched facets that are essential for lively gems, the cutting and polishing laps must run true and in perfect alignment with the facet head assembly. To accomplish this, the master lap unit and the facet head assembly are mounted on a substantial common base. The function of the 'master' is to provide a solid backing for the interchangeable working laps.

In major cutting centres like Jaipur in India or Chantaburi in Thailand, the facets are usually cut quickly and economically using cast iron, steel or lead laps and a slurry of abrasive grit. However, the major disadvantage of this process is the extensive clean-up that it involves to prevent grit causing wear of the equipment or contamination of the polishing process.

Diamond-charged copper laps are much simpler and cleaner to work with. They have the added advantage that recharging by the user is a fairly straightforward process. Permanently charged sintered diamond laps are available. They are somewhat expensive but make a good investment since they offer very smooth cutting and a long working life. Two diamond-charged laps are necessary to prepare the surface of facets for polishing: a cutting lap that is charged with 200–400 grit and a pre-polish lap with 1,200–1,800 grit. Water is the preferred lubricant for use with all these laps.

Polishing laps may be made from various soft metals and alloys such as tin, type-metal, tinners' solder, lead and pewter. Certain plastics are also used especially vinyl and Plexiglas (the laps are sold as 'Lucite'). 'Lucite' laps and a watery paste of cerium oxide are particularly effective for polishing the quartz gems. Beryl, garnet and tourmaline respond well to a thin emulsion of ultra-fine alumina on a pure tin lap.

Facet cuts

The brilliant cut comprises triangular and kite-shaped facets and it is best suited to take full advantage of materials with a high degree of refraction and dispersion. It is frequently used on round, oval, heart-shaped, marquise, pear, pendeloque and trilliant cuts and on the crown of mixed cut stones. The step cut features tiers of rectangular or square facets that serve to intensify and bring out colour. This is the cut employed in baguette, emerald cut, keystone, lozenge, trapeze, kite and trap cut stones and on the pavilion of mixed cut stones. There are many fancy cuts including the opposed bar cut with a crown comprising rows of parallel facets, the chequerboard cut with regular squares forming a domed crown and the rose cut, one of the oldest of facet cuts, with a flat back and a pyramidal crown of triangular facets. Briolette cut stones are basically teardrops in the round covered with a myriad of triangular facets. Buff-tops (formerly known as cabochettes) have a smoothly domed cabochon cut crown and a faceted pavilion creating an interesting play of brilliance and magnification. Facetchons also embody intriguing lighting effects with a faceted crown and a cabbed or carved pavilion. Concave cuts are shaped and polished on a rotating cylinder. This technique can create spiral forms and unique reflective patterns. Fantasy cuts combine faceting and carving techniques to create flowers and abstract designs.

TOP: *Faceted yellow diamond*
ABOVE: *Faceted tanzanite*

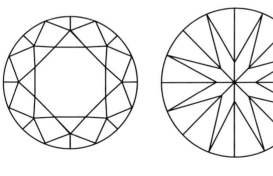

FAR LEFT: *Brilliant cut crown*
LEFT: *Brilliant cut pavilion*

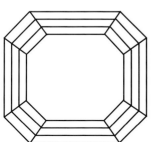

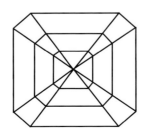

FAR LEFT: *Emerald cut crown*
LEFT: *Emerald cut pavilion*

Chapter 10
Gem Enhancement

The artificial enhancement of gem materials is a very ancient practice. Writing in the first century AD, Caius Pliny II states that he studied numerous much earlier works when compiling his data on the nature of gem treatments. The methods used to dye, heat, oil, stain and foil gemstones that he describes are not far removed from those employed today. The Emperor Diocletian (300AD) was so strongly opposed to the artificial enhancement of gems that he ordered the destruction of all books recording details of these practices. This edict appears to have been enforced with some measure of success with regard to the written material but the ingenuity of the human mind has ensured that the practices themselves have survived, multiplied and diversified.

Today, many gem treatments that are stable and do not involve the introduction of artificial elements are considered acceptable. In fact it can be safely assumed that the majority of the following gems have been subjected to some form of enhancement: carnelian, onyx, lemon quartz, tanzanite, blue topaz, Paraiba tourmaline, and white and blue zircon. Gemstones that are very likely to have been enhanced include aquamarine, citrine, emerald, lapis lazuli, morganite, marine and freshwater, natural and cultured pearls, ruby, sapphire and turquoise.

Backings

In the 16th century, it was normal and perfectly legal to use yellowish diamonds in jewellery items and then back them with purple or blue metallic foils that made the diamonds look like brilliant white stones. Sapphire, ruby and garnet cabochons were also greatly enhanced by the use of metallic foils, mirrors and such colourful substances as butterfly wings, peacock feathers and silk cloth as backings. Intersecting sets of bright parallel scratches were sometimes inscribed on the foil backings to simulate star stones. Such rouses are frowned on today and foil-backs or mirror-backed stones are seldom encountered in fine jewellery except in very deeply coloured cabochons in closed back settings, estate jewellery or antique pieces.

Bleaching

Black coral varieties may be converted to an attractive golden colour through bleaching with hydrogen peroxide. The surface of the bleached material may either be completely smooth or rather spiny, but in either case it is far removed from the dimpled surface of natural golden coral. Ivory is another material that is sometimes bleached with hydrogen peroxide or laundry bleach to lighten it. It is standard practice for the greenish tones and occasional dark patches of conchiolin present in natural and cultured pearls to be removed by bleaching with a combination of hydrogen peroxide and sunlight. Brown tiger-eye may be lightened to a honey colour by treating with a chlorine bleach or saturated oxalic acid.

Coatings

Coating gemstones with lacquer or varnish is an unacceptable form of treatment, which is sometimes encountered in coral, lapis lazuli, rhodonite, sugilite and turquoise.

Inking is another misleading practice, in which a slightly yellowish hue is disguised by the application of a trace of blue or purple ink to the girdle of a diamond or to the inside surface of the claws securing it. A hint of the bluish sputter coating used to protect optical lenses has been applied to the pavilion of yellowish diamonds to give them a whiter appearance when viewed through the crown.

A wide range of colours and special interference effects have been created through the application of thin films to quartz and topaz, both as crystal specimens and faceted stones. Coated topaz, created by the physical vapour deposition (PVD) process, is available in many colours – 'amethyst', 'emerald' and 'rubellite' being amongst the more popular shades. The various metallic coatings include specimens deriving a striking blue colour from a transparent ultra-thin film of gold that are marketed as 'Aqua Aura' and titanium-coated specimens that exhibit a veritable rainbow of hues. These coatings are very thin and the stones will soon show wear and tear if they are not packaged individually and handled with care.

TOP: *Coated 'rubellite' topaz*
ABOVE: *Coated topaz*

Diffusion

Surface diffusion

Blue sapphire owes its colour to a combination of titanium and iron. The process known as surface diffusion dramatically enhances the hue of pale to virtually colourless sapphire. The cut stones are placed in a crucible filled with alumina, titanium and iron oxides. When the crucible is heated to a high temperature, molecules of the titanium and iron oxide penetrate the crystal lattice of the corundum. This inevitably results in superficial damage and the stones must be re-polished. The enhanced colour is most evident along facet junctions and around the girdle. This is revealed in the characteristic 'spider-web' pattern that is seen when a diffusion-treated stone is examined under immersion. The re-polish may also have completely removed the colour from some facets causing the 'holes' in the colour that are a typical giveaway. These stones also reveal the normal signs of heat-treatment such as re-worked girdles, stress haloes around melted solid phase inclusions and resorbed silk.

This process is also used for colouring cabochons and if the cooling of the crucible is correctly controlled, the titanium dioxide that has diffused into the stone can be ex-solved in the form of needles to artificially create asterism.

ABOVE: *Diffusion-treated sapphires immersed in highly refractive liquid*

Bulk or lattice diffusion

Padparadschah sapphires exhibit a rare and highly valued orange-pink hue. This variety was always scarce with demand far in excess of supply until January 2002 when suddenly an inexplicable number of fine stones began to enter the market. Some form of enhancement was immediately suspected but examination of the stones did not reveal the signs typically associated with diffusion treatment. The researchers also found no evidence of irradiation. It was eventually established that the source material was pale pink sapphire from Madagascar. Processed in Thailand, the stones were undergoing a new form of diffusion treatment that involved beryllium. Being small and light, beryllium atoms are able to effect very deep penetration to the extent that they sometimes diffuse the whole stone. Tests revealed that much of the poorly coloured corundum from other sources responded well to the new treatment. Colourless rough yielded fine yellows; greenish or brownish yellow rough converted to gold; and pinkish rough converted to orange-pink.

Dyeing

Onyx by definition is a layered black and white chalcedony. In current trade usage, however, the term refers to totally black stones cut from light grey chalcedony impregnated with sugar water then boiled in sulphuric acid to carbonize the sugar. Light coloured porous Andamooka matrix opal is frequently treated with the same sugar/acid process. The product can bear a striking resemblance to good quality black 'pin-fire' opal.

ABOVE: *Dyed agate*

'Smoking' is another process that is used to blacken opal. The stones are preformed then wrapped in brown paper that has been soaked in old black engine oil. The batches of stones are laid out on racks positioned above a fire where the heat is sufficient to carbonize the paper. 'Smoked' Mexican hydrophane opal may bear a strong resemblance to Australian black opal.

Gems that are frequently dyed include coral, chalcedony, howlite, jade and pearls. It is often possible to detect dyed gems by examining them closely with a loupe. Look for accumulated dye in pores, surface fractures or drill holes in beads. Howlite is an inexpensive mineral that is widely used to simulate lapis lazuli, rhodonite and turquoise. It is white with areas of grey/black veining, porous and it does not react unfavourably with the various colours of dye. The dye does not penetrate very deeply so look for chips or scratches that will reveal the underlying white howlite.

TOP: *Howlite dyed to simulate turquoise*
ABOVE: *Dye-treated lapis lazuli beads*

Fracture Filling

Oiling and fracture filling are both processes that involve filling surface-reaching fractures or cavities with colourless substances such as oils, resins or glass. The primary aim of this form of treatment is to enhance the appearance of the stone. Filling fractures with a substance of a similar refractive index is a very effective way to reduce the visibility of flaws. Oils are commonly used to fill fractures in emerald. More modern treatments involve the use of resin filling in a vacuum. Corundum gems to be treated are usually coated with flux and exposed to a high temperature environment. This results in the fractures being filled with a combination of re-crystallised corundum and glazed flux. Fractures in diamond are filled with high lead glass-like compounds that have low- to moderate-melting temperatures. This makes them very suitable for a process requiring the filling material be drawn into breaks while it's in a liquid state. These compounds have an intrinsic yellow to red colouration and this accounts for the slightly yellowish tint of the filling material and the consequent drop in colour grade of diamonds after treatment.

Any fracture-filled gem must be properly disclosed to its purchaser with details of the nature of the filling and appropriate instructions for the care of the stone. Emeralds that have been oiled should not be steam- or ultrasonically-cleaned. Jewellery that contains fracture-filled diamonds, rubies or sapphire should not be repaired or resized unless the stones are removed from their settings.

Heat Treatment

Many established forms of treatment are almost universally accepted. Heat treatment, for example, is widely regarded as the continuation of a natural process, since it only involves the application of energy and the resulting colours are usually stable.

Amber is frequently subjected to various forms of heat treatment, intended to clarify it by removing innumerable tiny bubbles, to darken it giving it the look of antiquity or to induce the attractive rounded stress patterns called 'sun-spangles'. The combination of heat and pressure is used to bond numerous small fragments into larger more workable blocks of 'pressed amber'.

Beryl may be heated to remove yellow-brown tones. This is especially true of aquamarine, which is often heated to remove any yellow that may impart a hint of green to its colour. Heat is also used to remove the brownish element from peachy-pink morganite leaving it with a delicate lilac-pink hue.

Corundum Sapphires may be heated to intensify, lighten or darken their hues, to create or remove asterism or to change their colour. Rubies are heated to remove brown or purple tones, to remove silk or to induce sufficient silk to form a star.

Diamond Type Ia diamonds subjected to high pressure and heated to 2000°C will take on a bright yellow hue. The colour of brown type IIa diamonds subjected to HPHT (high pressure, high temperature) treatment can be improved to fine white. The colour of irradiated diamonds can be modified by heat treatment to yield brown, green, orange, pink, purple, red and yellow stones. Heat is also used to change the colour of chameleon diamonds.

Ivory is heat treated to give it a darker antique appearance.

Quartz Heating carnelian or red agates serves to intensify the orange to reddish element in their colour. Heating amethyst may yield dark citrine, greenish prasiolite or remove the colour completely. Citrine is usually lightened and brightened by heat treatment. Smoky quartz may be lightened, or changed to golden citrine, greenish-yellow or colourless. Brown tiger-eye is converted to red ox-eye.

Spodumene Heating will make pastel shades of spodumene paler or colourless. Low temperatures are used to convert bluish or purplish pink kunzite to lighter, clearer pink.

TOP AND MIDDLE: *Treated sapphires*
BOTTOM: *Treated amethyst*

Topaz Heating of brownish or orange topaz, traditionally known as pinking, is used to take the brown out of the hue leaving a good clean pink. Heating of yellow, brown or blue topaz will render it colourless but the colour can be replaced by irradiation.

Tourmaline is a complex boro-silicate with a reaction to heat treatment that is very variable. The dark blue to blue-green material from Namibia will yield a good green when heat-treated but very similar dark green material from Mozambique, Zambia or Zimbabwe shows no response to heat. Khaki-coloured tourmaline from Mkushi, Zambia will heat-treat to an attractive apple green. Salmon-pink, brownish-red and cognac colours from Mozambique and Zambia will heat to attractive pinks.

ABOVE: *Heat-treated brown tiger-eye converts to red ox-eye*

Zircon Reddish-brown Thai zircon is usually heated in the hope that it will yield more saleable colours. When heated in an oxidizing environment, the majority of the stones will become colourless, yellow or reddish. The colourless stones were very popular for use as diamond simulants prior to the development of cubic zirconia. A good proportion of the stones take on the attractive blue colour termed 'Starlite' in the USA when the rough is heated in a reducing atmosphere. Unfortunately, the distinct blue exhibited by recently treated material is not stable and it will fade on exposure to sunlight to a pale aquamarine blue.

Zoisite Natural violet-blue crystals are rare and the majority of this material occurs with an overall reddish-brown hue that will be seen under closer examination to comprise strongly pleochroic purplish-red/violet-blue/yellow-green axes. Heat treatment converts the yellow-green axis to blue.

HPHT

The HPHT (high pressure, high temperature) process can be used to enhance the colour of specific diamonds by removing any brownish element in their colour. However, the target group of diamonds is extremely small since the HPHT treatment can only be applied to rare Type IIa stones of good clarity. Stones that have been treated by GE POL in the USA should have an inscription GE POL lasered on the girdle. Failing this, there are no obvious signs that would serve to indicate that a Type IIa stone has undergone HPHT treatment and a laboratory analysis would be required.

Impregnation

Impregnation with a colourless agent such as oil, plastic, resin or wax can dramatically enhance the appearance of porous or fractured gem material. If the agent has a similar refractive index to its host it may very effectively hide cracks. The colour of porous materials often shows a very marked improvement once the agent has filled the pores and reduced light scattering. By effectively sealing the surface wax or plastic, agents can protect porous gems from the harmful effects of perfume, skin creams and body oils. Wax-filled lapis or turquoise gems frequently have a more lustrous finish than the more valuable untreated stones. Paraffin and beeswax are the substances most frequently used.

Amazonite, coral, emerald, jadeite, lapis lazuli, nephrite, opal, quartzite, rhodochrosite, ruby, sapphire, serpentine, turquoise and variscite are among the stones that are most frequently impregnated with colourless agents.

Artificially coloured oils or other agents are sometimes used, in the hope that this will have the added advantage of improving the colour of the gems. This is most commonly encountered with emerald and less frequently in ruby and sapphire.

Irradiation

Beryl If the beryl crystals contain iron as Fe^{2+} then irradiation will change colourless material to yellow, blue to green, and pink to peach. Heat treatment will reverse these changes. Irradiation of morganite from a few specific localities has been found to produce an intense blue very similar to the Maxixe beryl; the colour is just as unstable, fading when exposed to light.

Diamonds can be irradiated to green, blue-green or black (this is actually an extremely dark green). The irradiated stones can then be annealed to give blue, brown, pink, red and yellow. The irradiated and annealed stones tend to be too vivid and uniformly coloured to be mistaken for natural fancies.

Pearls

Gamma irradiation has the effect of darkening the mother-of-pearl nucleus of nucleated marine cultured pearls. The nacre is not affected and the pearls have a grey or grey-blue hue. In freshwater pearls the nacre becomes metallic black, gold, silver or multi-hued. It is interesting to note that the nuclei used in marine cultured pearls are made from the shells of freshwater mussels.

Quartz Irradiating colourless quartz will generally produce smoky quartz in a variety of shades. However, when the colourless quartz from certain deposits in Brazil is subjected to irradiation, it assumes an attractive greenish-yellow colour that is being marketed as Lemon, Neon or Oro Verde Quartz. Inexpensive and available in large clean pieces, it has been an instant hit with amateur lapidaries.

Scapolite is found naturally in light to medium shades of yellow, and also in pale lavender. The yellow material can be irradiated to a much deeper, and more brownish, shade of lavender than that which occurs naturally.

Spodumene Pink kunzite can be irradiated to give a deep green but the colour is not stable, fading rapidly when the stone is exposed to light.

Topaz Blue topaz is probably the most important irradiated gem, in terms of both value and volume. The duration, type of irradiation, and nature of the heating processes used will determine if the product is to be Sky, Swiss or London blue. Other minor colour variations include 'electric blue' and 'neon blue'.

Tourmaline The world's supply of attractively coloured pink to red tourmaline has recently been greatly increased by new discoveries. Some Brazilian tourmalines that were formerly rejected due to poor colour, and the majority of the large new deposits being found in Africa, can be treated to diminish brownish tones.

Zircon Irradiation is seldom used; it reverses the heating procedure converting colourless material to brownish or reddish.

Lasering

The 1970s saw the development of a technique that improved the appearance of dark spotted diamonds. A minute laser hole is drilled from a nearby facet and the inclusion is either vaporized with the laser or etched out with acid. In some instances, a highly refractive filling is used to close the resulting cavity.

TOP: *Irradiated topaz*
ABOVE: *Irradiated blue topaz*

Chapter 11
Gem Collecting

Contrary to general belief, it is not necessary to possess bottomless pockets in order to indulge in the pastime of gem collecting. Furthermore, involvement at any level with this fascinating hobby will expand your world, encouraging you to explore new places, meet new faces and acquire new skills. You will discover that individual gem collections can be every bit as diverse as their owners. There are the purists who believe that it is 'cheating' to buy specimens and limit their collection to gems they have found and/or cut themselves. Then there are equally serious collectors who scout gem dealers' offices, gem and mineral shows, the Internet, and antique and pawn shops, using the 'silver pick' (money) to acquire desirable specimens.

Getting started

Should you wish to 'test the water', then your first step should be to make contact with a gem and mineral society in your area. Such societies are very widespread and an Internet search will help you to locate a convenient group. Attend one of their meetings and take the opportunity to chat to some of the established collectors. Examine any specimens they may have brought along to show or sell. Look at the range of equipment on hand if there is a workshop and enquire about tuition. Most clubs offer their members the opportunity to cut a cabochon or try their hand at faceting under the guidance of experienced lapidaries. Make enquiries to find out about gem occurrences in your area and get details of any field trips

nap-free cloth   dichroscope   stone scope   chelsea filter   gem filters

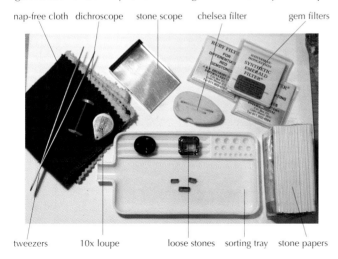

tweezers   10x loupe   loose stones   sorting tray   stone papers   LEFT: *The gem collector's kit*

that the group may have planned. You might even avail yourself of the opportunity to purchase one or two specimens. Attending gems shows will provide a more diversified oportunity to meet with 'rock-hounds' from other areas, to meet dealers and to view their ranges. It is also a good idea to subscribe to one of the popular gem and mineral magazines in order to keep abreast of things that are happening in the world of gems.

A good quality 10x loupe, a pair of medium stone tweezers, a packet of stone papers and a jeweller's nap-free cloth or square of chamois leather are the initial requirements of a budding collector. These items are readily available from gem and mineral dealers or jewellers' and goldsmiths' supply shops.

Storage, display and sizing

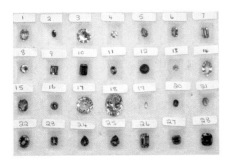

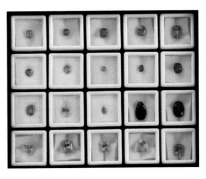

ABOVE: *Storage trays*

Stone papers holding individual stones are often transported or stored in zipped leather wallets. More permanent housing for a collection of cut stones may take the form of padded leatherette boxes fitted with individual recesses. In some of the modern units the stones are placed in plastic boxes that fit into recesses in the storage tray.

Collections of gem and mineral crystals are grouped into internationally recognized categories, based on size. Micro-mount specimens feature perfect miniature crystals that require magnification to be appreciated. These should be mounted in 2.5cm square plastic boxes that are clearly labelled with identity and locality information. The website of the French Association of Micromineralogy, available in French and English (see Appendix, page 246), is an excellent source of information on this aspect of the hobby. This site also contains an extensive international directory of micro-mounters and collectors.

LEFT: *Storage unit*

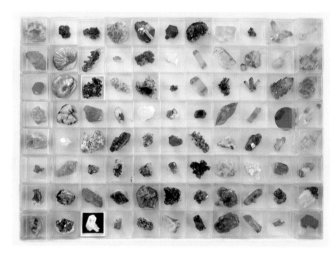

LEFT: *Thumbnail specimens*

Thumbnails usually embody crystals that are large enough to be appreciated with the naked eye. The specimens should not measure in excess of 3.1cm if the collection is to be shown in competition. A small stationary unit, such as the one illustrated above, affords inexpensive and compact housing for 1,056 micro-mounts/thumbnails.

Miniatures are specimens that measure between 3.1 and 5cm. A variation of the above stationary unit containing six-deep drawers can be used to provide storage for 72 miniatures.

Finally, important pieces that measure in excess of 5cm are referred to as cabinet specimens. Fine display items in this category can be extremely expensive.

Adding to your collection

Carved gemstone artefacts that are much sought after by collectors include Japanese *netsuke* (belt-buttons), Chinese *chops* (signature seals) and snuff bottles. Finding fine specimens is a challenge but a collection of good pieces in a small well-lit cabinet makes an intriguing display.

Gem collections do not necessarily consist of polished stones. Well-formed gem crystals, especially those still attached to matrix, are usually more difficult to obtain and can hold more interest than cut stones. Quartz crystals may be relatively common but they may play host to a wide range of fascinating inclusions. Frequently they will contain crystals of hematite, rutile, tourmaline, beryl and other gem varieties. In terms of the fascinating inclusions to be found in gems, amber must undoubtedly take the ribbon. Pre-historic arachnids, insects, small reptiles and a vast array of botanical specimens are to be found as inclusions in amber.

Buying tips

It requires vast experience to buy with confidence in this field. Be sure to develop a good relationship with a knowledgeable expert and do not make any significant purchase without consulting him or her. When buying important stones ensure that you receive the relevant certificate issued by a recognised laboratory.

Take every opportunity to familiarise yourself with current prices. *The Gemstone Forecaster*, the *Gemworld International Guide* and *Jewelers' Circular Keystone* carry price charts and information on movements in the market. Information available online is extensive and a search for 'Gemstone price guides' will yield numerous resources.

It pays to buy the best quality you can afford. Fine stones hold their value better in a down market, appreciate faster in a rising market and will always be easier to sell. Never allow yourself to be pressured into making a hurried decision and bear in mind if a deal sounds too good to be true it probably is!

TOP: *Ivory Netsuke 'Wisdom'*
MIDDLE: *Alabaster Chop*
BOTTOM: *Coral Buddha*

Chapter 12
Gemmology

The Study of Gemmology

Gemmology is a relatively new science, which involves the scientific study of gem minerals and ornamental stones, organic gems, gemstone enhancement, synthesized gem materials, gem simulants and precious metals. Initially regarded as a minor offshoot of mineralogy, it has gradually evolved to its present position as an independent science. The world's first complete diploma course in gemmology, produced and run from 1910 to 1913 at the Chelsea Polytechnic in London, was presented under the name 'Mineralogy for Jewellers'. Nowadays, the initials F.G.A. (Fellow of the Gemmological Association) after one's name indicate successful completion of the diploma course of the Gemmological Association of Great Britain (Gem-A).

Robert M. Shipley, a jeweller from Wichita, USA, who enrolled at the Chelsea Polytechnic in 1928, was profoundly influenced by the time he spent studying gemmology in London. On his return home, Shipley quickly set about the establishment of a gem education facility in the USA. Through his boundless energy and enthusiasm, the Gemological Institute of America (GIA) was successfully founded in 1931 with a base in Los Angeles, California. Today the GIA is a world leader in the field, offering a wide range of courses from numerous centres. Graduates of the Institute's diploma course use the initials G.G. (Graduate Gemologist) after their name.

In 1932, a facility for gemmological research and education was established at Idar-Oberstein in Germany, the traditional centre for the cutting, polishing and marketing of gemstones in Europe. The abbreviation DGemG is used by the holders of the gemmological diploma awarded by the

Deutsche Gemmologische Gesellschaft, of Idar-Oberstein, Germany. (*See* Appendix on p246 for details of major Gem Education facilities.)

Students of gemmology begin by studying the nature of gem materials, their chemical composition, crystal structure, and physical and optical properties. They also examine the theory and application of basic gemmological instruments, in particular the microscope, polariscope, refractometer and spectroscope. At this point they are required to pass a preliminary examination before moving on to more advanced studies.

The focus now moves to a study of the more practical aspects of gemmology. Students must gain experience at employing the various instruments to their best advantage while they identify and familiarize themselves with a wide range of rough and cut gem materials, synthetics, composite stones and simulants.

Practical Gemmology

A consultant gemmologist may be called on to fill widely divergent roles. There are certain aspects of the profession that may bear close comparison to the work of a detective. For example, practical gemmology often involves identification, elimination, evaluation, forensic analysis, the reconstruction of fraudulent crimes, the uncovering of counterfeits and fraud, the ability to see through an endless variety of disguises, the preparation and presentation of evidence and appearances in court as an expert witness.

All of the fore-mentioned situations are in marked contrast to those occasions when the knowledge and experience of a gemmological consultant may be required during the processes involved in gem exploration, prospecting and mining. Hands-on work of this nature may frequently involve coping with extreme conditions.

LEFT: *Diamond barge, Democratic Republic of Congo*
ABOVE RIGHT: *Water monitors, Guyana*
RIGHT: *Trommel, Zaire*

A gemmologist specializing in this aspect of the profession could find himself freezing amid the snow and ice of Letseng-La-Terai diamond mine in Lesotho, rubbing shoulders with big game in the dense bush of the Zambezi Valley or being roasted to a crisp among the shimmering mirages of the Namib desert.

Or he might be providing sustenance for innumerable leeches and mosquitoes while sweltering in the humid jungles of Zaire, wading waist-deep through Madagascar's crocodile infested rivers or dodging bullets in the diamond fields of Angola. Of course such delights are reserved for a fortunate few.

Most newly qualified gemmologists are destined to find more mundane employment in retail jewellery stores, laboratories or educational facilities.

The gemmologist may occasionally find himself envying the lot of mineralogists. Since they usually work with rough fragments, they can enjoy the luxury of being able to carry out destructive tests on the specimens in question. He, on the other hand, is obliged to limit himself to tests that involve no risk of inflicting any form of damage on the items he has to identify and value. Gemmologists are frequently required to work on stones that are set in pieces of jewellery. In such instances it is obviously impossible to determine specific gravity. The nature of the mounts may also impose severe restrictions on the use of instruments to apply other tests to the stones. In other words, despite the numerous gadgets that modern technology has developed to assist the gemmologist, there can be no substitute for innate ability, a wealth of experience and the power of observation.

Gem identification

Identification work usually involves gems that are set in rings or pieces of jewellery, loose cut or rough gems or carved artefacts. The gemmologist must begin by submitting the article to a careful and detailed visual examination. During this process the nature, size, shape, colour, hue, tone, intensity, lustre, transparency, brilliancy, dispersion, pleochroism, zoning, texture, heft, crystal form, cleavage, fracture, thermal conductivity, touch, smell, taste, general overall condition, signs of wear and tear, and any evidence of damage are observed and recorded. A photograph is taken and, if the stone is set, a record is made of the type of metal that has been employed together with a detailed description of the nature and design of the mount.

The 10x loupe now comes into play to enable a closer examination. In the case of faceted stones, the gemmologist will often begin by focussing on the girdle and the facet junctions since these areas frequently hold clues regarding the nature of the item. While it is possible to pick up the joining plane of a doublet when looking through the table they are usually much easier to detect when examining the stone through the girdle plane. He notes if the girdle is thick, uneven, medium, thin or knife-edge and whether its surface is bruted, faceted, moulded or polished. Then, turning the stone about on its axis, he checks the pavilion-halves immediately below the line of the girdle looking for naturals, fractures, fracture-filling, chips, cleavages, extra facets or concentrations of colour that may be indicative of coating, dyeing, staining, diffusion treatment or irradiation.

Gem identification has become a highly specialized field with the advent of so many high-tech enhancements and synthesized gem materials. The essential textbooks that a gemmologist keeps on hand would include Webster's *Gems, their Sources, Descriptions and Identification*, Anderson's *Gem Testing*, Liddicoat's *Handbook of Gem Identification* and the Gubelin/Koivula *Photo Atlas of Inclusions in Gemstones* (*See* Bibliography, p251). It is also necessary to keep up to date with new developments by subscribing to 'Gems & Gemology', the quarterly journal of the GIA, and Gem-A's 'The Journal of Gemmology', and to pay regular visits to gem information sources on the Internet.

ABOVE: *A binocular microscope with dark-field illumination, overhead lighting and an independent fibre optic light source is the instrument of choice for detailed forensic work and other more difficult cases.*

Chapter 13
Gem Grading and Certification

High technology and gems

In today's high-tech world, tasks such as gem identification, forensic investigations, the detection of gem enhancements, and certification will in some instances be beyond the ambit of the average gemmologist. If his initial examination reveals that he is dealing with stones of a complex nature, he should refer the item to a reliable, well-equipped laboratory. He is most likely to refer stones that he suspects to be HPHT- (high pressure, high temperature) and CVD- (chemical vapour deposition) created synthetic diamonds, natural stones that may have been HPHT-treated to improve their colour, fancy colour diamonds that may have been irradiated and/or annealed, and also any sapphires or rubies that may have undergone beryllium treatment.

Diamond Certification

COMPARATIVE GRADING CHARTS

COLOUR		CLARITY	
G.I.A.*	**C.I.B.J.O.*/H.R.D.***	**G.I.A.***	**C.I.B.J.O.*/H.R.D.***
D	Exceptional White Plus	FL	Loupe Clean
E	Exceptional White	IF	
F	Rare White Plus	VVS₁	Very Very Small Incl.
G	Rare White	VVS₂	Very Very Small Incl.2
H	White	VS₁	Very Small Inclusion1
I	Slightly Tinted White	VS₂	Very Small Inclusion2
J		Sl₁	Small Inclusion
K	Tinted White	Sl₂	Pique One
L		I₁	
M/O	Tinted Colour One	I₂	Pique Two
P/R	Tinted Colour Two	I₃	Pique Three
S/U	Tinted Colour Three	Reject	Rejection
V/Z	Tinted Colour Four		

***G.I.A.–** Gemological Institute of America
***C.I.B.J.O.–**International Confederation of Jewellery, Silverware, Diamonds, Pearls and Gems (Paris)
***H.R.D.–** High Diamond Council (Antwerp)

This report summarizes the observations made through Gemolite microscopes employing 10 × magnification, binocular vision and Darkfield illumination by two independant qualified graders.

LEFT: *Comparative grading chart*

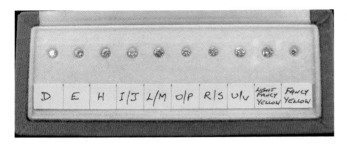

Diamond certification was introduced in 1976 and it is now so well established that an internationally recognized certificate is a prerequisite for any significant diamond sale. Certificates verify that a stone is a natural diamond and detail its colour, clarity, weight, shape and cut. Numerous specialized laboratories have been established to handle the volume of work this involves.

The DiamondSure unit

Stones submitted for certification are initially tested with the DiamondSure unit. This instrument, developed by the De Beers research laboratory, reads and analyzes the absorption spectrum of the stone and displays the results on a small screen. The stones that pass enter the certification laboratory.

Stones that fail this test are sent for gemmological evaluation. At the Johannesburg Laboratory in South Africa, the DiamondSure unit refers approximately one per cent of stones, including HPHT and CVD synthetics, the rare Type II natural stones and occasionally a Type I or a diamond simulant.

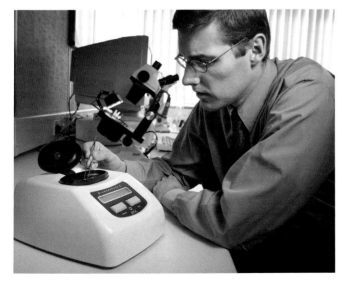

LEFT: *DiamondSure unit*

LEFT: *Mini Certificates, including the grading of the gem*

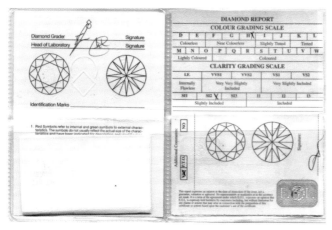

LEFT: *Inside of the Mini Certificates, including inclusion diagrams*

The DiamondView unit

In the gemmological laboratory, referred stones are examined with the DiamondView unit (also developed by the De Beers research laboratory). A stone placed in the DiamondView chamber is bathed in intense short wave ultraviolet light. A digital camera is employed to view the fluorescent pattern that this creates on the polished stone and to transmit this picture to the monitor. These patterns are diagnostic and reveal the different growth structures of natural, HPHT and CVD synthetic diamonds. The CVD synthetics tested to date have exhibited a distinctive bright orange in the DiamondView unit.

The DiamondView automatically detects and stores an image should the stone exhibit a degree of phosphorescence (afterglow) when the ultraviolet light source is switched off. While all near-colourless HPHT-created diamonds phosphoresce, this phenomenon is seldom seen in natural near-colourless diamonds.

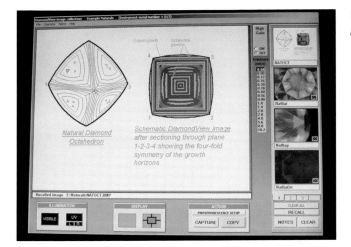

LEFT: *Natural diamond, octahedral growth pattern, DiamondView*

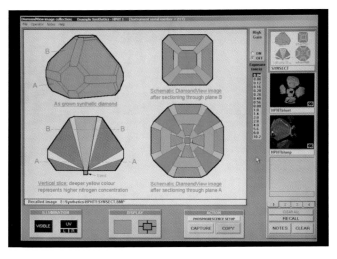

LEFT: *HPHT Diamond, complex growth, DiamondView*

The Raman Spectrograph

Significantly lowering the temperature of a gem will serve to enhance the visibility of its absorption spectrum. At the Jewellery Council of South Africa's Gem Testing Laboratory, stones are super-cooled by immersion in liquid nitrogen (nitrogen liquefies at -196°C) before they undergo analysis by the Raman Spectrograph. The spectrograph has proved to be a key instrument in the identification of coloured stones and the detection of many forms of gemstone enhancement.

These advanced instruments are wonderful reinforcements but there is no substitute for a good microscope, the right lighting and a depth of knowledge in the constant battle against misrepresentation and fraud.

Hardness of Gems
(based on Mohs' Scale)

Hardness	Gem	Hardness	Gem (*continued*)
10	Diamond		Lazurite, Melinophane, Mesolite, Microlite, Obsidian, Thomsonite, Sphene
9.25	Moissanite		
9	Corundum		
8.5	Chrysoberyl	5	Apatite, Charoite, Dioptase, Pectolite, Triplite, Wardite
8–8.5	Pezzottaite		
8	Rhodizite, Spinel, Taaffeite, Topaz	4.5–5	Apophyllite, Augelite, Childrenite, Gaspéite, Hemimorphite, Hodgkinsonite, Legrandite, Scheelite
7.5–8	Beryl, Phenakite		
7.5	Euclase, Grandidierite, Hambergite, Painite, Sapphirine, Zircon		
		4.5	Bayldonite, Colemanite, Conichalcite, Ekanite, Pseudomalachite
7.25	Pyrope, Spessartite		
7–8	Lawsonite	4–5	Chabazite, Friedelite, Lithiophilite, Meteorite
7–7.5	Almandine, Andalusite, Boracite, Iolite, Jeremejevite, Simpsonite, Staurolite, Tourmaline		
		4–4.5	Bastnasite, Purpurite, Smithsonite, Zincite
7–7.25	Danburite	4	Creedite, Fluorite, Tugtupite
7	Chalcedony, Dumortierite, Quartz, Uvarovite	3.5–5	Variscite
		3.5–4.5	Magnesite, Siderite
6.5–7	Andradite, Axinite, Gadolinite, Grossular, Jadeite, Kornerupine, Peridot, Spodumene	3.5–4	Aragonite, Azurite, Breithauptite, Cuprite, Dickinsonite, Dolomite, Kutnohorite, Ludlamite, Malachite, Mimetite, Pyromorphite, Rhodochrosite, Scorodite, Shattuckite, Sphalerite, Wavellite
6.5	Baddeleyite, Idocrase, Nambulite, Nephrite, Pollucite, Sinhalite		
6–7	Cassiterite, Epidote, Fibrolite, Hydro-Grossular, Narsarsukite, Rhyolite, Serendibite, Zoisite	3.5	Adamite, Anhydrite, Coral
		3–4	Tennantite
		3–3.75	Witherite
6–6.5	Benitoite, Chondrodite, Marcasite, Microcline, Petalite, Prehnite, Pyrite, Rutile, Sugilite, Tantalite	3–3.5	Barite, Boléite, Celestite, Cerussite, Domeykite, Millerite, Phosphophyllite
6	Amblygonite, Clinohumite, Orthoclase, Plagioclase	3	Bornite, Calcite, Shortite
5.5–6.5	Bustamite, Hematite, Rhodonite	2.75–3	Anglesite
5.5–6	Actinolite, Afghanite, Anatase, Beryllonite, Brookite, Haüyne, Lazulite, Leucite, Milarite, Natrolite, Nepheline, Pyroxmangite, Sodalite	2.5–5	Serpentine
		2.5–4	Jet
		2.5–3.5	Howlite, Pearl
		2.5–3	Crocoite, Lepidolite, Phosgenite
5.5	Brazilianite, Cobaltite, Enstatite, Plancheite, Willemite	2.5	Kinoite, Tortoise-shell
5–7	Kyanite (hardness varies with direction in crystal), Psilomelane	2–4	Chrysocolla
		2.5	Pyrargyrite
		2.25–2.75	Ivory
5–6	Cancrinite, Chlorastrolite, Diopside, Opal, Periclase, Richterite, Samarskite, Scapolite, Tremolite, Turquoise	2.25–2.5	Vegetable Ivory
		2–2.5	Amber, Cinnabar, Proustite
		2	Gypsum
5–5.6	Nummite	1.5–2.5	Stichtite
5–5.5	Analcime, Datolite, Durangite, Eudialyte, Goethite, Herderite,	1.5–2	Covellite, Pyrophyllite
		1	Steatite (talc)

Appendix B
Birthstones

The following table shows which gem has been considered as the birthstone for a particular month throughout history. It is broadly based on notes prepared by the Gemological Institute of America.

Month	Culture					
	Jewish	Roman	Arab	Russian	Western world: 15–20th centuries	Western world: current
January	Garnet	Garnet	Garnet	Garnet Hyacinth	Garnet	Garnet
February	Amethyst	Amethyst	Amethyst	Amethyst	Amethyst Hyacinth Pearl	Amethyst
March	Jasper	Bloodstone	Bloodstone	Bloodstone	Jasper Bloodstone	Aquamarine
April	Sapphire	Sapphire	Sapphire	Sapphire	Diamond Sapphire	Diamond
May	Chalcedony Carnelian Agate	Agate	Emerald	Emerald	Emerald Agate	Emerald
June	Emerald	Emerald	Agate Chalcedony Pearl	Agate	Cat's eye Turquoise Agate	Pearl Alexandrite
July	Onyx	Onyx	Carnelian	Ruby Sardonyx	Turquoise Onyx	Ruby
August	Carnelian	Carnelian	Sardonyx	Alexandrite	Sardonyx Carnelian Moonstone Topaz	Peridot
September	Chrysolite	Sardonyx	Chrysolite	Chrysolite	Chrysolite	Sapphire
October	Aquamarine	Aquamarine	Aquamarine	Beryl	Beryl Opal	Opal Tourmaline
November	Topaz	Topaz	Topaz	Topaz	Topaz Pearl	Topaz Citrine
December	Ruby	Ruby	Ruby	Turquoise	Ruby	Turquoise Zircon Tanzanite

Appendix C
Worldwide Gem and Mineral Associations and Federations

American Gem Society
www.americangemsociety.org

American Society of Gemcutters
P. O. Box 826, Beavercreek, OR 97004-0826, USA

Asian Institute of Gemological Sciences
www.aigsthailand.com

Australian Federation of Lapidary and Allied Crafts Association
5 50/266 High Street, Kangaroo Flat, Victoria 3555, Australia

Canadian Gemmological Association
1767 Avenue Road, Toronto, Ontario M5M 3Y8, Canada
www.canadiangemmological.com

Federation of Southern African Gem and Mineralogical Societies
www.fosagams.co.za

French Association of Micromineralogy
www.micromineral.org

Gem and Mineral Federation of Canada
www.gmfc.ca

Gemmological Association and Gem Testing Laboratory of
Great Britain
www.gem-a.info

Gemmological Association of All Japan
www.gaaj-zenhokyo.co.jp

Gemmological Association of Australia
www.gem.org.au

Gemmological Association of China
7F Jin Mao Tower, 88 Century Boulevard, Shanghai, China
www.gac@dac.gov.cn

Gemological Institute of America
The Robert Mouawad Campus, 5345 Armada Drive,
Carlsbad, CA 92008, USA
www.gia.edu

German Gemmological Association
www.dgemg.com

National Association for New Zealand Rock and Mineral Clubs
219 Maidstone Road, Avonhead, Christchurch, New Zealand

Glossary

Aberration	In optical terms the failure of a lens to bring all the light rays from a single point into focus.
Absorption spectrum	The distribution of dark lines or bands seen when light that has been transmitted through or reflected from a gemstone is examined with a spectroscope.
Acicular	Needle-like.
Adamantine	Very high lustre, typical of diamond.
Adularescence	Mobile sub-surface sheen as seen in moonstone. Reflective points not seen.
Allochromatic	Term for minerals that are colourless when in purest state.
Allotropic	May assume different forms, e.g. diamond and graphite are both carbon.
Amorphous	Lacking form, no definite internal structure.
Analyser	Upper Polaroid disc in polariscope or Nicol prism in polarizing microscope.
Angstrom Unit	Used in the electro-magnetic spectrum, it is one ten millionth of a millimetre.
Anhedral crystal	Crystal that fails to show good outward form.
Anisotropic	Exhibiting double refraction.
Anomalous D.R.	Double refraction found in isotropic material due to internal strain.
Arborescent	Resembling the branches of a tree.
Asteria	Cabochon-cut gem exhibiting a four, six or twelve-rayed star of light.
Asterism	The star effect produced in a cabochon by the reflection of light from oriented sets of parallel fibres.
Autoclave	Massive steel cylinder used in the production of hydrothermal synthetics.
Aventurescence	Bright reflections from visible platelet inclusions.
Basal pinacoid	Face at right angles to the vertical axis of a crystal.
Bezel facets	See 'Mains'; this is an alternative name used by those in the diamond trade.
Biaxial	Anisotropic crystals that have two optic axes.
Birefringence	The difference between the minimum and maximum refractive indices of an anisotropic gem.
Boart	Industrial diamond.
Botryoidal	Spherical protuberances resembling bunches of grapes.
Boule	Cylindrical or pear-shaped body of flame-fusion corundum or spinel.
Breccia	Coarse-grained sedimentary rock made of large angular pieces set in a finer matrix.
Bubbles	Rounded gas inclusions encountered in most glasses and some synthetic stones.
Cabochon	Cut gemstone with a flat base and a domed top.
Carat	Standard unit of weight employed for gems, equal to 0.2 gram.
Cat's-eye	Cabochon-cut stone with a shifting band of light running over the dome.
Chameleon diamonds	Olive-green diamonds that change colour to yellow when stored in the dark or gently heated. They will revert to olive on exposure to light.
Chatoyancy	The cat's eye effect produced by the reflection of light from numerous fine parallel fibres or fibrous cavities within a stone. The shifting line of light runs at right angles to the direction of the fibres.
Chemical composition	Formula detailing the nature and proportions of the elements present in the make-up of a molecule of a mineral.
Chromophore	Element that acts as a colouring agent, e.g. chromium, cobalt, copper, iron, manganese, nickel, and vanadium.
Chromatic aberration	Dispersion of light by the lens glass results in coloured fringes to the image. A common fault with inexpensive loupes.
Cohesion	Term for the forces of attraction that exist within a mineral and their resistance to separation (toughness).

Colour filters	Film or glass that can be used to filter out certain wavelengths of light.
Composite stones	Simulant stones that are constructed of two or more components.
Conglomerate	Sedimentary rock largely composed of rounded pebbles bedded in matrix.
Crown	The portion of a faceted stone above the girdle.
Crown glass	A basic glass that has lower properties than 'flint' or 'lead' glass.
Crypto-crystalline	Composed of sub-microscopic crystals.
Crystal axes	Imaginary reference lines running through an ideal crystal.
Culet	Tiny facet that can be used to remove the sharp point of the pavillion of a diamond or other gem.
Dendritic	Tree-like. From the Greek for tree, *dendron*.
Dichroism	Differential selective absorption of light seen in some anisotropic minerals.
Dichroscope	Simply a short tube housing a rhomb of calcite and a lens system this instrument is used to view the effects of dichroism.
Diffraction	The breaking up of white light into the colours of the spectrum when it passes through a grid of narrow apertures.
Dispersion	Breaking up of white light into the colours of the spectrum when a ray passes through two inclined prism faces.
Dop	A device used to hold a gemstone while it is being worked.
Dopants	Trace elements employed to give colour to synthetic gems.
Double refraction	The splitting of a ray of light into two rays with differing wavelengths. This effect takes place in all crystals except those belonging to the cubic system. It accounts for the double image seen when an object is viewed through a rhomb of calcite.
Drusy	Covered with small crystals
Durability	The degree of resistance a stone possesses to chemical and physical forces that may destroy its finish.
Euhedral crystal	Well-formed crystal with good faces.
Extraordinary ray	A ray of light that varies in its velocity when passing through a uniaxial crystal, dependent upon its direction of travel.
Feathers	Liquid or liquid and gas inclusions with a feather-like appearance.
Fire marks	Also known as chatter marks, these small parallel cracks often found at facet junctions are the result of overheating in polishing. They are most prevalent in synthetic corundum but their presence is only indicative and not conclusive of synthetic origin.
Flame fusion	Method used to grow synthetic boules.
Flint glass	Bright heavy glass containing lead oxide, which gives it high dispersion but a low degree of hardness. Used to simulate gemstones.
Fluorescence	Emission of visible light when illuminated by ultraviolet, cathode, gamma or x-rays.
Flux-melt	Method used to grow synthetic crystals in a metallic flux.
Foliated	Resembling the pages of a book.
Fossicking	Searching for specimens or gem rough in mineral rich areas.
Frictional electricity	An electrical charge developed by certain substances. When rubbed briskly with a cloth, diamond, topaz and tourmaline acquire a positive charge, whereas amber becomes negatively charged.
Geode	Roughly spherical mass of mineral/rock with a hollow centre that is often lined with crystals.

Girdle	The outer circumference of a cut stone.
Globular	Rounded, spherical.
Habit	The shape or crystal form that is most characteristic of a mineral.
Halves	Series of triangular facets above and below the girdle of a brilliant cut gem.
Inclusions	A general name covering solids and liquid- and/or gas-filled cavities trapped within a stone. Frequently characteristic of a specific gem variety or even of a source, they are the surest way to distinguish natural from synthetic stones.
Intaglio	Designs carved into a concave depression in a stone.
Intarsia	Pattern of suitably coloured and shaped slices of stone. Also Florentine mosaic.
Iridescence	Spectral colours resulting from interference of light. Usually caused by thin films, a typical example being oil on water.
Isomorphous	Having the same crystal structure but differing in chemical composition.
Isotropic	A term that denotes materials within which light travels as a single ray of constant velocity and character regardless of direction. Cubic crystals and amorphous materials are isotropic.
Kerf	Groove to facilitate cleaving or sawing a diamond created by a diamond or laser.
Knife edge	Stone that either lacks or has an extremely thin girdle.
Knot	If a tiny diamond crystal is included in the diamond that is being cut, it is referred to as a knot when it is on a different orientation to its host.
Labradorescence	Broad play of colour seen in Labradorite.
Lamellar	Consisting of thin sheets like leaves of a book.
Lap	The disc on which gems are cut and polished.
Loupe	Hand lens, a basic magnifying aid; 10x magnification is most practical.
Mabé	(Also called half or blister pearl.) Mabé pearls are dome-shaped cultured pearls created by slipping a mother-of-pearl hemisphere between the shell and the mantle of the mollusc.
Macle	A flat, triangular, twinned diamond exhibiting 180-degree rotation.
Mafic	Dark-coloured igneous rocks rich in ferromagnesian minerals.
Mains	Kite-shaped facets on crown and pavilion of brilliant cut stones.
Make	A term used to describe the proportion and finish of a stone.
Mammilliary	Breast-shaped.
Matrix	Host rock in which mineral occurs.
Monochromatic light	Light of a single wavelength seen as a single pure colour (e.g. sodium light – pure yellow).
Natural	A portion of the surface of the original rough diamond, usually just below the girdle.
Nicol prism	Calcite filter used to produce polarized light.
Nodule	Small spherical mass of a mineral/rock with no opening or central void.
Noodling	Sorting through mine waste dumps to find specimens and rough.
Optic axis	A direction of single refraction in a doubly refractive stone.
Optic character	Defines an important aspect of the optical nature of a mineral – whether it is isotropic, uniaxial or biaxial.
Optic sign	Minerals in which the extraordinary refractive index is of a higher value than the ordinary are stated to have a positive sign. If the value of the ordinary refractive index is the greater then the mineral is said to have a negative sign.

Ordinary ray	A ray of light that passes through a uniaxial stone at a constant velocity.
Painted Lady	Quartzite boulder split to reveal a slick of precious opal.
Pavé setting	A style in which very closely set small stones cover an element of the jewel.
Pavilion	The portion of a faceted stone below the girdle.
Phosphorescence	Persistence of light emission after illumination by ultraviolet or x-rays.
Piezo-electricity	Electrical charge acquired by certain crystals (e.g. quartz and tourmaline) when subjected to pressure in specific directions.
Pinacoid	A crystal face that lies parallel to two or more crystal axes.
Pique	Widely used French term for imperfect.
Pleochroic	Mineral showing different colours depending on the direction in crystal.
Point	One-hundredth of a carat.
Polarized light	Light vibrating in a single plane perpendicular to its direction of movement.
Plumose	Feathery.
Prismatic	Crystal form in which faces meet at parallel edges.
Pyro-electricity	Electrical charge acquired by certain crystals when heated (e.g. tourmaline).
Quartzite	Sand bonded so completely that fractures pass through the individual grains.
Radiated	Fanning out from a central point (see Sunburst).
Refraction	The bending of a ray of light that takes place as it moves between media of varying optical density (e.g. pencil in glass of water).
Reticulated	Slender crystals forming a lattice.
Reversible photochromism	See tenebrescence.
Sandstone	Compacted sand; fractures will affect the cementing agent but not the individual grains of sand.
Scaife	A cast iron lap used for polishing diamonds.
Sheen	Bright reflections from numerous minute points beneath the surface.
Silk	Numerous oriented fine needles of rutile.
Solid solution series	A solid solution series is present if two or more elements can substitute for one another within a crystal structure, thus changing the chemical balance without significantly altering that structure.
Spherulitic	More or less spherical.
Star	The triangular facets radiating from the table of a brilliant cut gem.
Stalactitic	Resembling stalactites.
Stellate	Forming a star.
Step cut	Cut with parallel rows of rectangular facets.
Sunburst	Radiating from a central point.
Table	The large central facet in the crown of a faceted stone.
Tang	A device used to clamp and position the dop in diamond cutting.
Tenebrescence	The ability of minerals to change colour when kept in the dark then exposed to sunlight. Also known as *reversible photochromism*.
Thermoluminescence	A light that emanates from certain substances when exposed to infra-red rays.
Triboluminescence	A luminosity exhibited by certain minerals when they are rubbed.
Uniaxial	Describes an anisotropic mineral with a single optic axis.
Vesicle	Gas cavity in volcanic rock.
Vitreous	Having the lustre of glass.
Vug	A cavity in rock usually lined with small crystals.
Wave-length	The distance between the crests of two successive waves in the electro-magnetic spectrum.

Bibliography

Anderson, Basil W., *Gem Testing* 9th edition (Butterworths, 1980)

Balfour, Ian, *Famous Diamonds* (Collins, 1987)

Bank, Herman, *From the World of Gemstones* (Pinguin Verlag, 1973)

Barnes and Townsend, *Opal: South Australia's Gemstone* (Geological Survey S. A., 1982)

Bauer, Max, *Precious Stones* (Tauchnitz, 1909)

Becker, Vivienne, *Fabulous Fakes* (Grafton Books, 1988)

Bernard, J. and Hyrsl, J., *Minerals and Their Localities* (Granit, 2004)

Blakey, George, *The Diamond* (Paddington Press, 1977)

Bruton, Eric, *Diamonds* 2nd edition (N.A.G. Press, 1978)

Cairncross, Bruce, *Rocks and Minerals of Southern Africa* (Struik Publishers, 2004)

Copeland, L., *Diamonds: Famous Notable and Unique* (G.I.A., 1966)

Dana, Edward S., *Textbook of Mineralogy* 4th edition (John Wiley and Sons, 1932)

Desautels, Paul, *The Gem Kingdom* (Random House, 1971)

Dietrich, R.V., *The Tourmaline Group* (Van Nostrand, 1985)

Downing, Paul B., *Opal Identification and Valuation* (Majestic Press, 1992)

Eyles, Wilfred C., *The Book of Opals* (Charles E. Tuttle, 1964)

Farn, Alexander E., *Pearls: Natural, Cultured and Imitation* (Butterworths, 1986)

Federman, D., *Colored Gemstones: Consumer Guide* (Van Nostrand, 1990)

Fraquet, Helen, *Amber* (Butterworths, 1987)

G.I.A., *Diamond Dictionary* (G. I. A., 1960)

Graf, Bernhard, *Gems: The World's Greatest Treasures* (Prestel, 2001)

Gübelin, Eduard, *Internal World of Gemstones* (ABC Edition, 1974)

Gübelin, E., and Koivula, J., *Photoatlas of Inclusions in Gemstones* (ABC Edition, 1986)

Hemrich, Gerald, *Jade: The Handbook* (Gembooks, 1966)

Hughes, Richard W., *Corundum* (Butterworth-Heinemann, 1990)

Hughes, Richard W., *Ruby and Sapphire* (R.W.H. Publishing, 1997)

Hyrsl and Niedermayr, *Quartz: The Magic World of Inclusions* (Rainer Bode, 2003)

Kazmi, A. and Snee, W. (Eds), *Emeralds of Pakistan* (Van Nostrand, 1989)

Keller, Peter, *Gemstones of East Africa* (Geoscience Press, 1992)

Korbel, P. and Novak, M., *Encyclopedia of Minerals* 3rd edition (Rebo Publishers, 2005)

Kunz, George F., *The Curious Lore of Precious Stones* (Dover, 1971)

Kunz, George F., *Gems and Precious Stones of North America* 2nd edition (Dover, 1968)

Laufer, Berthold, *Jade* (Dover Books, 1974)

Liddicoat, Richard T., *Gem Identification Handbook* 12th edition (G. I. A., 1988)

MacInnes, Daniel, *Synthetic Gem and Crystal Manufacture* (Noyes Data Corp., 1973)

Matlins, Antoinette, *Colored Gemstones* (Gemstone Press, 2001)

Matlins, Antoinette, *Gem Identification Made Easy* 3rd edition (Gemstone Press, 2003)

McIver, John R., *Gems Minerals and Rocks of Southern Africa* (Purnell and Sons, 1966)

Muller, Helen, *Jet* (Butterworths, 1987)

Mumme, Ivan, *The Emerald* (Mumme Publications, 1982)

Nassau, Kurt, *The Physics and Chemistry of Color* (John Wiley and Sons, 1983)

Nassau, Kurt, *Gemstone Enhancement* (Butterworths, 1984)

Nassau, Kurt, *Gems Made by Man* (Chilton, 1980)

National Palace Museum, *Chinese Masterworks of Jade* (N. P. M. Taipei, 1969)

Ng, John and Root, Edmond, *Jade for You* (Jade N Gem Corp., 1984)

O'Donaghue, Michael, *Identifying Manmade Gemstones* (N. A. G., 1983)

O'Donoghue, Michael, *Artificial Gemstones* (N. A. G. Press, 2005)

O'Leary, Barrie, *Australian Opals: Field Guide* 2nd edition (Gemcraft, 1984)

O'Neil, Paul, *Gemstones (Planet Earth)* (Time Life Books, 1984)

Orlov, Yu L.,*Mineralogy of the Diamond* (John Wiley and Sons, 1977)

Pagel-Theisen, Verena, *Diamond Grading Handbook* 4th edition (Pagel-Theisen, 1973)

Pearl, Richard M., *Rocks and Minerals* (Barnes and Noble, 1956)

Pough, Frederick H., *A Field Guide to Rocks and Minerals* (Compton Printing, 1970)

Quick, Lelande, *Book of Agates* (Chilton Books, 1963)

Read, Peter G., *Gemmological Instruments* (Newnes-Butterworths, 1978)

Rouse, John D., *Garnet* (Butterworths, 1986)

Sauer, Jules R., *Emeralds around the World* (J. R. Sauer, 1992)

Schumann, Walter, *Gemstones of the World* 3rd edition (Sterling, 2006)

Schoon, Theo, *Jade Country* (Jade Arts, 1973)

Shirai, Shohei, *Pearls* (Marine Planning Co., 1981)

Sinkankas, John, *Gemstones and Minerals* (Van Nostrand, 1961)

Sinkankas, John, *Gem Cutting: Lapidary Manual* (Van Nostrand, 1955)

Sinkankas, John, *Mineralogy for Amateurs* (Van Nostrand, 1964)

Sinkankas, John, *Gemstone and Mineral Data Book* (Winchester Press, 1972)

Sinkankas, John, *Standard Catalog of Gems* (Van Nostrand, 1968)

Sinkankas, John, *Emerald and Other Beryls* (Chilton Book Co., 1981)

Sorrell, Charles A., *Minerals of the World* (Golden Press, 1973)

Speckels, Milton L., *Complete Guide to Micromounts* (Gembooks, 1965)

Taburiaux, Jan, *Pearls: Origin, Treatment and Identification* (N. A. G., 1985)

Vargas, Glen and Martha, *Faceting for Amateurs* (Vargas, 1969)

Vargas, Glen and Martha, *Descriptions of Gem Materials* (Vargas, 1972)

Watermeyer, Basil, *Diamond Cutting* 4th edition (Basil Watermeyer, 1991)

Willis, Geoffrey, *Jade* (Mayflower, 1970)

Wilson, Arthur N.,*Diamonds from Birth to Eternity* (G. I. A., 1982)

Zancanella, Valerio, *Tanzanite: the True Story* (V. Zancanella, 2004)

Index

Major page references are in
bold
Illustrations placed separately
are in *italics*

Acknowledgments

My sincere and heartfelt thanks go to the following people for the time and effort they have devoted to assisting me in this project: Howard Bell (ZDCW), Ian Campbell (ICSL), Mike Elliot (Abstral Diamonds), Costa Exarchos (WRDCW), Anthony Kampf (Natural History Museum LA), Roger Lappeman (LDCW), Shimon Lusky (Stone Age), Les Milner (JCSA), MinDat.org – a great website, Jason Selby (Diamond Exploration), Rob Smith (African Gem and Mineral), Karl Sprich (Gem Dealer), Horst Windisch (Chairman, FOSAGAMS).

A special vote of thanks to the following who generously permitted the use of their images to illustrate this book. (All images not credited are by Arthur Thomas. Number refers to page reference: t = top, b = bottom, l = left, c = centre, r = right.)

Photographs courtesy of Charles Greig Jewellers, South Africa: 47b diamond rings, 118b/208tr peridot jewellery, 122b tanzanite rings, 208tl 'Isabella' range of earrings.
Fotalia: 50t/208br garnet brooch, 67b/209c rutilized quartz bracelet, 76cr/208c aquamarine necklace, 89tr/208b sapphire ring, 93b/209bl amethyst and aquamarine ring
Tom Loomis from Dakota Matrix: 51b spessartite, 54b uvarovite, 58t lazurite, 58b microlite, 63t domeykite, 68b anatase, 82t milarite, 108b pyrargyrite, 109t proustite, 112t lawsonite, 121 tantalite, 129t conichalcite, 134t adamite, 152t lazulite, 154b childrenite, 156b mesolite, 157b legrandite, 158b friedelite, 161b shattuckite, 163tl azurite, 167br crocoite, 168t kinoite, 168bl gypsum
Rob Lavinsky from i-Rocks.com (photo and specimen): 55t pollucite, 57b cobaltite, 62b tennantite, 66b narsarsukite, 70b wardite, 72tl scheelite, 74 phosgenite, 75b pezzottaite, 79t painite, 84t bastnasite, 85b mimetite, 86t pyromorphite, 90b simpsonite, 117b hambergite, 126b samarskite, 127bl goethite, 128b hemimorphite, 131 scorodite, 134b witherite, 137t shortite, 146b clinohumite, 153b triplite, 155b durangite, 159t bayldonite, 167tl phosphophyllite, 170b serendibite, 176b pyroxmangite, 179t pectolite.
Herb Yeates: 57tl sodalite, 68c tugtupite
Stephan Wolfried: 72b ekanite
Chris and Helen Pellant: 82b nepheline, 141b gadolinite, 149t tremolite
Dave Wellbrock from ChroLithix: 81b afghanite, 84b zincite, 85t breithauptite, 157t hodgkinsonite, 179b chabazite
Richard Bell: 107t millerite.
Prof B. Cairncross, University of Johannesburg: 141t chondrodite
MinerShop.com: 186b kakortokite, 187t naujaite, 187b nummite
Susan Kirkland: 193/208tr jet